THE PROBLEM WITH SECULARISM

THE PROBLEM WITH SECULARISM

KOENRAAD ELST

VOICE OF INDIA
New Delhi

First Published 2007
Reprint 2015
Third Reprint 2020
Fourth Reprint, 2022

ISBN 13: 978-93-85485-02-2

Published by Voice of India, 2/18, Ansari Road, New Delhi – 110 002.
Printed at Replika Press Pvt. Ltd.

This book is dedicated to
Harish Chandra, that quiet rock
you can build on.

Contents

Foreword to the 2015 edition

In the eight years since this book was first published, a few things ought to have changed. In this new foreword I will explore these.

Feedback

Though I would like to report their answers to my critiques of their works, I have seen no reply by any of the people addressed here, such as Robert Hathaway, Richard Eaton, Mira Kamdar or Thomas Hansen. This is typical of secularist behaviour: while the record shows that I consider it normal to answer my critics, the other side occasionally lambasts me but doesn't bother refuting me. Either they are just too smug, comfortably established in their own academic positions, or they have decided not to draw attention to the weakness of their positions.

No paper in this book, nor really any other book, has had any noticeable effect on organized Hindu activism. They give me the same silent treatment as the enemy side. Individual Hindus, by contrast, have informed me of their appreciation.

Failed predictions

Two trends mentioned in this book have not persisted. In Europe, the cleansing of Hindus has remained extremely marginal, limited to a few cases in former Soviet territories, now fiercely Christian. In the Anglosphere, there have been cases of Hindus, especially Sikhs, being confused with Muslims and therefore scolded. But Hinduism as such has not been the target of anymore friction than can be expected between any two communities, at least in the West. Likewise in South Africa, Black majority rule has not, as I had feared, led to a repeat of the expulsion of "Asians" as in Uganda and Tanzania. Hindus had made themselves more acceptable by siding with the anti-Apartheid struggle, and this seems to have prevailed over basic ethnic hatreds.

In Muslim countries, by contrast, harassment of Hindus has continued. No government in Delhi has taken any steps against this phenomenon. The related Yezidis of northern Iraq even suffered mass rape, enslavement and killing at the hands of the Islamic State. Here at least, Hindu activists have shown solidarity and provided the only serious platform worldwide to Yezidi representatives. In advocacy for the Hindu refugees from Pakistan too, their effort has made a difference.

A needed correction concerns the title of chapter 7: "What if Rajiv Gandhi hadn't unlocked the Babri Masjid in 1986?" The title was given me by the magazine, *Outlook India*, but on second thought, that doesn't preclude a measure of responsibility for it. So, as a matter of correction, let me clarify that it was not Rajiv Gandhi who threw open the temple (still with mosque architecture) for general Hindu worship, though it took place while he was in power. The temple was thrown open by Court order. It was not a political move in itself, but only a step in the very long-winded judicial process. Rajiv Gandhi was ready to make proper use of it, even being tipped for the stone-laying ceremony of the projected Hindu building. This was only one of several instances where the Congress Party favoured the Hindu demands concerning Ayodhya. Only after 1989 did it become identified with the BJP, opposed by all others.

Wahi, the prophetic trance

The part about Mohammed's mental affliction, "Wahi", follows a growing trend of medical diagnosis across the centuries. A good recent example is Delhi biotechnologist Ramakrishnan Sitaraman's paper: "Medical evidence as a decisive determinant of historicity in ancient texts: trimethylaminuria in the Mahabharata", (*History Today*, vol.13, 2012, pp.1-6), about Matsyagandha ("having a fish-smell") Satyavati's disease described in the Mahabharata. The text faithfully describes, without understanding it, a case of the condition known as *trimethylaminuria*, or fish malodor syndrome, caused by a liver enzyme deficiency, in which a woman has a fish smell but can lose it due to hormonal changes, esp. in pregnancy.

Religion in the sense of "belief", while no doubt tougher than Lenin or Atatürk thought, is being battered by scientific findings. In India, the media are controlled by secularists who shield their readers and viewers from international developments not to their liking. That is why people tend to be insufficiently aware that an increasing number of publications confirm something amiss in Mohammed's psyche. Ibn Warraq, Ali Sina , Radheshyam Brahmachari, all represent this swelling recognition that Islam was spawned by a man's mental condition, a mere delusion. Islam is fundamentally a *folie à deux* (the phenomenon that someone close to a delusional person also starts to interiorize this delusion) on a billionfold scale. All those Muslims who only utter the name of Mohammed by wishing him peace, all claim to share his own belief that he was extraordinary. While Islam insists that Mohammed had no divine status, it treats him as an absolute precedent. In that sense, the obsolete European name *Mohammedanism* was correct.

In my book *Psychology of Prophetism*, I had already reported on the case against Jesus as made by a number of 20th-century psychiatrists. Sigmund Freud, who only knew about Judaism and Christianity, which strongly believe in a sovereign Creator-God and in "revelation", wrote about *Religion, the Future of an Illusion*. A very recent publication, by the American psychiatrists Evan D. Murray,

Miles D. Cunningham and Bruce H. Price, viz. "The Role of Psychotic Disorders in Religious History Considered" (*The Journal of Neuropsychiatry and Clinical Neurosciences*, 24:4, Fall 2012, pp. 410-426), confirms the impression that the Jesus described in the Gospels suffered of a psychotic disorder. A lone Hindu sequel to this line of research is contained in *What Every Hindu Should Know about Christianity* by a Californian Hindu, Kalavai Venkat (2014).

After publishing my paper on *Wahi*, I did not receive any death threats nor even ordinary hate mail. This would not have been the case if I had lampooned the Prophet (cartoons) or attacked him in a cruder manner, particularly involving sex, as in Salman Rushdie's *The Satanic Verses*, of which most Muslims only knew that it "depicts the Prophet's wives as prostitutes". It seems Islamic radicals who not only threaten but actually commit violence, don't read abstruse academic papers. However, the Tamil translation, circulated as a booklet in its own right, did trigger death threats to the translator. Fortunately he had used a pseudonym. The secular establishment won't protect candid writers against fanatics, so they have to resort to their own devices.

Hindu precedent for Islamic iconoclasm?

Prof. Richard Eaton's theory that Islamic iconoclasm, which he tries to minimize but nonetheless admits, is simply due to Hindu precedent, has gained ground among secularists. I have refuted it here as well as in my earlier book *Ayodhya: the Case against the Temple*, but to no avail. However, regardless of my own contribution to the debate, the secularists have at least decided that it is wiser not to deny Islamic iconoclasm completely anymore, as they did during the Ayodhya debate. So they have retreated to a next line of defence (of the Islamic record): admitting Islamic iconoclasm but blaming the Hindus for it.

I can only point to the argumentation I have developed in the past, and which remains completely unrefuted. There is simply no instance of a Muslim iconoclast citing Hindu precedent as his justification. On the contrary, wherever they feel a need to justify themselves, they refer to Islamic precedent, particularly to the Prophet's very own destruction of the 360 statues in the Kaaba of Mecca. Unlike the secularists, who pretend that the world ends at India's borders, Muslim war leaders were not so narrow-minded as to draw their inspiration exclusively from the history of India, with which they did not identify with anyway. Their behaviour pattern was quite like that of their Islamic colleagues in other parts of the world, and quite unlike that of Hindu kings.

Secularist book-banning

At several places in this book, I have discussed matters of book-banning and freedom of expression. About Christianity such demythologizing theories as mentioned in the Wahi section can now be openly talked and written about. It is only in India that this discourse is muzzled by the still-preponderant secularist hold on the public debate. (Western readers will be surprised that a pressure-group in favour of opinion control regarding religion can be called "secularist", but in India this term is used for anything anti-Hindu ergo including pro-Christian.)

Article 295A of the Indian Penal Code punishes writers in case they, through their publications, have offended the tender feelings of a religious community. The influence of this law extends much farther than its literal application. Authors, publishers and editors practise self-censorship in order to be on the safe side of this penal provision. The law was enacted to protect Islam from critical scrutiny by a Hindu (Arya Samaj) author, but the Churches have also taken umbrage behind it, such as to proscribe Dan Brown's fictional thriller *The Da Vinci Code.*

However, it is only when Hindus started using it to get UR Ananthamurthy's book *300 Ramayanas* and Wendy Doniger's *Alternative History of the Hindus* banned, that Western Indologists started demanding that this Article be scrapped, mercifully not realizing its pro-Islamic origins. Me too, I signed two petitions against this banning, one of them circulated by Laurie Patton and led by Romila Thapar. Admittedly these books are flawed in their assumptions, factually riddled with errors, and simply anti-Hindu. But that counts for numerous books and can be no valid excuse for banning them: the only right answer to a flawed book is another book. In the case of Wendy Doniger, a counter-book detailing its errors was indeed provided by Vishal Agarwal (digitally 2009, in print 2014).

Secularism and the BJP government

In the realm of facts, the biggest event since the first print-run of this book has been the election of a BJP government in May 2014. Given the abysmally bad performance of the preceding Congress government, it had been expected that the BJP would win; more than likely, it was going to be a relative majority necessitating a coalition. The coalition partners were then expected to veto the choice of Narendra Modi, so that Rajnath Singh would become Prime Minister. That was the scenario preferred by the time-servers and opportunists in the BJP. However, the campaigning by Modi and his team of whiz kids generated such enthusiasm at the mass level that the otherwise apathetic Hindu voters turned out in record numbers and gave the BJP a solid majority. Countless people, from Baba Ramdev on down, testified that they had voted for Modi, not for the BJP.

At any rate, after giving the throne to Modi, it was the BJP that profited. All manner of people who had never done anything for the Hindu cause came to man the ministerships, chairs of committees and other plum posts that the BJP was now in a position to dole out. Many well-known faces of the secularist camp suddenly discovered the BJP activist in themselves and acceded to the Modi camp. In there, they have gone on promoting secularism and treating Hindu concerns as backward and outdated. The bygone antagonism between the "Hindu fanatical" BJP and so-called "pseudo-seculars" has been replaced by an antagonism between the secularist and Hindu wings within the BJP. Hindu society as such remains under represented.

Foreword

This book is a collection of articles about secularism and its relationship with religious communalism, mainly the Islamic variety. In India and now also in Europe, liberal secularism and militant Islam make for strange bedfellows. In Christian Europe, secularism used to be a way of curtailing the intrusive power of the Churches. In that sense, I am a secularist myself. I believe that human society should be governed by human decisions, not by imaginary decrees from above. In India, however, "secularism" has acquired a wholly different meaning. Ever since the term was propagated by Jawaharlal Nehru, being an Indian secularist did not require you to reject theocracy and the intrusion of religion into politics. On the contrary every Islamic obscurantist in India swears by "secularism". The word's effective meaning has shifted to a concern quite unknown to its European coiners, viz. the struggle against Hinduism.

In political practice, as also in the editorial policies of the dominant media, secularists patronize all enemies of Hinduism: Islam the Christian Churches, the Communists and Naxalites, the anti-Hindu voices among Sikhs, Jains and neo-Buddhists. Historically, however, it is only Islam that triggered the genesis of "secularism" During the struggle for freedom, Hindus tried in vain to win the Muslims over to the national cause, only to find them ready and determined to partition the motherland over a million dead bodies. In desperation, they started constructing and ideology that would lay the blame for Muslim "grievances" with the Hindu side, thus hoping to win the Muslims over at last, though no longer to the national cause nor to a polity recognizable as "secular" but to an arrangement that usurps this self-description all while humiliating the Hindus.

The secularist-Islamist alliance is one of the wonders of the world and requires ever new exercises in hypocrisy on the part of the former, sometimes descending into grotesque buffoonery. It is a different matter that the hollow and crassly superficial ideology of Nehruvian secularism is secure in its power position because of the absence of credible challengers. With a political opposition claiming to be "positive secularists" and "genuine secularists", India's official "pseudo-secularism" has no one to fear.

In public discourse, Nehruvian secularism today is mainly a form of snobbery that confers a cheap moral superiority on self-hating Hindus to mark them off as enlightened sophisticates against the cramped and backward Hindu "fundamentalists". It relieves them, in the comfort of their positions of privilege, of the duty to look into the cause of Hindu discontent. I hope nonetheless that once in a while a sincere attempt to discuss matters can penetrate their wall of self-righteousness, and that this book will promote dialogue between the Nehruvian secularists and rest of us.

Mortsel (Belgium), April 2007 KE

1. US thinker gives unthinking support to anti-India demands: a reply to Robert Hathaway

[This article was originally published on 30 August and 3 September 2002, *Rediff on the Net*; and was also included in Ramesh Rao & Koenraad Elst: *Gujarat after Godhra: Real Violence, Selective Outrage*, Har-Anand, Delhi 2003.]

The American South Asia scholar Robert M. Hathaway has used the opinion page of the Chennai-based daily *The Hindu* (8-8-02) as a forum for tendering advice to his own Government. Dr. Hathaway is the director of the Asia Program at the Woodrow Wilson International Center for Scholars, a famous think-tank in Washington D.C. The beautiful think-tank network in Washington D.C. should, to judge from the generous amounts of money oiling it, provide the American policy-makers with the fullest information and analysis base available to any government in world history. And yet, American foreign policy is by no means the most intelligent even in the contemporary world scene.

Hathaway's article illustrates what the problem is. Instead of laying down general principles or specific American national interests, his advice concerning Washington's South Asia policy focuses on sectional demands whispered into his ear by a foreign lobby whose nature and motives he fails to comprehend. In particular, he wants his own employer to investigate and eventually to block fund-raising in the U.S. by "groups implicated in the Gujarat violence". This is a demand recently pushed by US-based Indian Communists such as

FOIL (formerly "Forum of Indian Leftists", now "Forum of *Inqilābī* [= Revolutionary] Leftists") as their latest weapon in the struggle against the nationalistic compatriots.

Hathaway correctly reminds us that "terrorism comes in many guises": armed assaults, suicide bombings, assassinations and "yes, hate-consumed mobs butchering innocent women and children". The latter expression presumably refers to the Muslim attack on Hindu pilgrims, a majority of them women and children, in a train in Godhra, Gujarat? Well, no, unfortunately Hathaway is blind in one eye and exclusively refers to those phases in the conflagration when Muslims were the victims. I will charitably assume that this bias is not a matter of considered opinion on Hathaway's part, merely an unreflected borrowing from his Indian sources.

1.1. Terror in Kashmir

Apart from poetry about a "sore" to be "healed", Hathaway takes no interest whatsoever in India's main terrorist problem, Islamic armed separatism in Kashmir. He merely warns Hindus not to use Kashmir as an excuse for Gujarat, and denies that Hindu exasperation at Muslim violence in Kashmir has anything to do with the Hindu reaction in Gujarat, as if he had investigated the matter. Yet, it is precisely on the Kashmiri frontline that America is most directly concerned, for it has provided indirect support to the terrorists for more than a decade. Many Hindus have been killed with American-made weapons and bombs.

The only act of terrorism in Kashmir which has registered in his consciousness is "the assassination earlier this year of Abdul Gani Lone, who opposed Indian rule in Kashmir but who in his final years had come to the realization that violence and extremism offer Kashmiris no way out in their struggle with New Delhi", a struggle which Hathaway refuses to take distance from.

Outrageously, he insinuates that this murder is the handiwork of the Indian Government or its much-maligned Hindutva allies. That indeed is the unmistakable implication of his statement: "The Gujarat violence, Lone's assassination, and most recently, the designation of L.K. Advani as Deputy Prime Minister and most likely successor to Mr. Vajpayee have all raised new concerns about India's future among India's friends in the U.S."

Misinformed by Indian "secularists", whose Communist background seems unknown to him, Hathaway assumes that the soft-spoken Advani is some kind of extremist, and he blames the Indian Government for Advani's promotion as this is obviously a governmental decision. (It is of course none of America's business whom the democratic Indian Government nominates; for months after his election, George W. Bush rightly gave the cold shoulder to European politicians who had overstepped diplomatic decorum by openly supporting Bill Clinton and deploring Bush's victory.) Again leaning on secularist sources, Hathaway blames the Gujarat violence at least partly on the Indian Government; why else should it "raise concerns" as potentially damaging the inter-state relations between India and the US? Finally, in the same breath, in his list of blameworthy moves tainting the Indian Government, Hathaway claims that Lone's murder is a cause for worry about the course India is taking. This is simply despicable.

Lone was murdered by Islamic separatists more extreme than himself, by the very terrorists whom India has been fighting for over a decade. The murder was one more anti-Indian blow struck by the international Islamic terrorists against whom America claims to be waging a war. How should it be a cause for worry among pro-Indian Americans that India was targeted once more, now in the person of the relatively loyalist opposition leader Lone, by the terrorists? Isn't the merciless hostility of the terrorists rather proving that India is doing something right?

1.2. Sovereignty

Hathaway probably doesn't understand why the vast majority of the human race is fed up with American arrogance. And by this, I don't just mean the anti-American fanaticism and conspiracy theories in the Muslim world, but also the healthy skepticism about the boundless American self-centredness which you may encounter in India, China or Europe. He might do well to reread this statement of his: "Some Indians, of course, say that the tragic events in Gujarat are a domestic Indian affair, and that the United States and the rest of the world have no business intruding into a purely internal Indian matter. This is a self-serving falsehood."

No, this is purely a matter of national sovereignty. India wants no foreign interference, a principle which America not only endorses but takes to inordinate lengths. Just recently, President Bush has declared that he will not tolerate the arrest and sentencing of American intervention personnel by a non-American court, not even the UN-sponsored international tribunal in The Hague. He even reserved the right to invade the Netherlands to free American citizens brought before that Court. India's insistence on managing its own communal problems is far more modest than the bullying American conception of national sovereignty.

1.3. America and the Muslim world

While not providing any reason whatsoever why India should have an interest in conceding to America a right to intervene, Hathaway focuses on America's own self-interest in supporting the Muslim *pogromchik* side in the Gujarat carnage: "Important American interests, including the global war against terrorism, can be directly impacted by what the U.S. says — and fails to say — about Gujarat. At this particular moment in history, the U.S. cannot allow the impression to take hold that Americans somehow value a Muslim life less than the life of a person of another religion."

In the Indian subcontinent, there is no danger whatsoever that anyone will get this impression, for the reality is too obviously the opposite. American meddlers, Hathaway among them, consistently turn a blind eye towards Hindu victims of Muslim violence, in India as well as in Pakistan and Bangladesh. America has consistently given material and diplomatic support to the very forces that have been butchering Hindus.

Hathaway insists strongly on this point, that America is not at all anti-Muslim: "Sadly, there are those in the Islamic world who assert that the present conflict is a war directed not against terrorism, but against Islam. That the U.S. does not care about Muslims. That Washington seeks to hijack the tragedies of 9/11 to carry out long-held plans to repress the Islamic world. These are detestable lies, but many in the Muslim world are prepared to believe them."

If Muslims believe these "detestable lies", it must be because of America's anti-Palestinian position in the Middle East, or because of its tacit support to Russia's campaign in Chechnya. It seems that Muslims just want to have it all and are ungrateful for the American support to the Muslim side in many other conflicts: against the Greeks in Turkish northern Cyprus, against the Soviets in Afghanistan, against the Serbs in Bosnia and Kosovo, against India in Kashmir. No further pro-Muslim gesture is going to convince those who attribute anti-Muslim motives to an American government which has already so consistently supported Muslim interests on many fronts.

What anti-American Muslims also fail to understand, is the structural economic reason for America's preferring the Muslim world over the fledgling infidel superpower India. The Muslim world is not very dynamic and has a lot of purchasing power, so it is the perfect market for American hi-tech (and low-tech, e.g. agricultural) products. India, by contrast, has only limited purchasing power but is a very dynamic competitor in all advanced industrial sectors. For this reason, and also to compensate the Muslim world for the permanent grievance over American support to "the Zionist entity", America is bound to take the Muslim side in purportedly peripheral conflicts, especially against India. The pep talk about India and the US being "natural allies" as "the biggest and the oldest democracy" has little impact on real-life policies. In practical terms, Bush and Hathaway are the running-dogs (or rather, to borrow another Leninist term, the "useful idiots") of Pakistani jihadism.

1.4. War against terrorism

Hathaway's concept of a "war against terrorism" is flawed: terrorism is a strategy, not an enemy. As Daniel Pipes has remarked, "war against terrorism" makes as much sense as "war against trenches" or "war against carpet-bombing". If American policy-makers cannot define their enemy more properly, their mindless muscle-flexing dooms them to misdirected aggression and ultimately to humiliation and defeat. You can bomb only so many Afghan wedding parties by mistake without paying a price.

But at least Hathaway is aware of India's consistent stand against terrorism: "Following the trauma Americans experienced on September 11, India was one of the first countries in the world to step forward with a pledge of unconditional and unambivalent support for the U.S. in its quest to bring to justice those responsible for the terror attacks in New York and Washington. The administration of George W. Bush, already keen to upgrade relations with Delhi, took notice."

Unfortunately, it is unclear to what this "notice" has amounted in practice. True, the US has lifted the sanctions imposed against India for conducting nuclear tests in May 1998. But this gesture of goodwill toward an anti-terrorist frontline state was counterbalanced by the same gesture towards Pakistan, the prime sponsor and organizer of terrorism, eventhough Pakistani links have been proven in a number of terrorist attacks against not only Indian but also

American targets. Just recently, the US has resumed the delivery of advanced weaponry to the Pakistani Army, whose prime target is not terrorism but India.

1.5. Impact of Gujarat riots

We may quote here without comment the following secularist platitude by Hathaway: "So leaving aside the moral issue, it is essential that India's friends in the U.S. speak out to condemn the injustice and hatred so prominently displayed in Gujarat, and to lend support to those Indians, of all religious beliefs, who are working to strengthen the forces of secularism, tolerance and multiculturalism."

Hathaway has two opinions about the consequences of the Gujarat riots for Indo-American relations. The first one belongs to *Realpolitik*: "Some have asked what impact the recent events in Gujarat will have — should have — on the new and healthier relationship that the U.S. is developing with India. (...) Prior to the February 27 Godhra attack that touched off the bloodshed in Gujarat, this new and more sanguine relationship between the U.S. and India was widely viewed by Americans as in the national interest. It remains so today; Gujarat has not changed this calculation."

In Pakistan, terrorists with links to the CIA-trained secret service ISI have recently killed Americans and allied French citizens posted there for purposes of the "war against terrorism", as well as a few dozen Pakistani Christians, deemed a pro-American fifth column. Yet, this has not led to any American reprisals against Pakistan. It would be odd if internal Indian troubles which have not hurt any American citizens or direct allies would jeopardize Indo-American relations.

And yet: "And yet, it is neither possible nor practical simply to pretend that Gujarat did not happen. The violence in Gujarat, and the steps the Indian Government might take in coming months in response to those events, could have a significant impact on American views of India, and hence, on political and public support in the U.S. for a close and collaborative U.S.-India partnership."

Here, Hathaway is clearly abandoning *Realpolitik* and seeking a moralistic scapegoat, a pretext for keeping Indo-American relations in lower key than they ought to be if America meant business with its "war on terrorism". Why should America bring a moral hypersensitivity to bear on its relations with India when it has always turned a blind eye to Pakistani human rights violations, open and proxy aggression against India, open interference in Afghanistan, and unmistakable covert involvement in international terror? Clearly, morality or concern for communal harmony in a distant country is not what moves American policy-makers. Hathaway is cynically playing this up in order to justify the American refusal to take the side of the Indian victim against the Pakistani aggressor in the "war on terrorism".

At the recent meeting of the Indo-American Friendship Council (Washington DC, 16 July 2002), which I attended, two spokespersons for the US National Security Council likewise refused to take the side of India against Pakistan. They picked up the quarrel in the middle, as if there could be a moral equivalence between democratic India and dictatorial-theocratic Pakistan, one of the world's prime sponsors of terrorism. Not that India is in such terrible need of American support, but America itself is in need of reliable allies, and at present American policy-makers are fooling themselves by assuming that General Perwez Musharraf is their friend and will deliver the goods in the struggle against the Taliban, Al-Qaeda and his own Islamist militias terrorizing Indians in Kashmir.

1.6. Cut the money supply

The practical bottom-line of Hathaway's paper turns out to be a plea for cutting off the flow of donations to Hindu charities such as the *Ekal Vidyālaya* scheme of village schools. US-based Indian Communists have recently opened a campaign against Hindu charities, and Hathaway offers to serve as their loudspeaker in Washington: "Credible reports have recently suggested that substantial sums of money are sent from Indians resident in the U.S., and from American citizens of Indian origin, to groups and organizations in Gujarat and elsewhere in India that are directly linked to the violence in Gujarat. I do not know if these accounts are true. But respected Indian journalists have uncovered disturbing linkages. If these reports prove accurate, then it is possible that such financial transactions violate U.S. anti-terrorism statutes."

How does Dr. Hathaway know that the reports which have reached his eye are "credible"? How does he know his sources are "respected" except in the purely conventional sense of enjoying prestige within the existing establishment? It is, at any rate, not hard to find out that these sources are extremely partisan, for they themselves aren't exactly keeping it secret.

At any rate: "It is probably advisable for the American Government to hold an official inquiry into fund-raising in the U.S. by groups implicated in the Gujarat violence, to ensure that U.S. laws are not being violated. (...) Nor would such an inquiry be new or unusual. The U.S. has acted in the past to regulate or even to ban fund-raising activities by groups advocating violence and ethnic or religious intolerance in other countries, as well as activities where fraud may be an issue."

Hathaway's concern goes beyond terrorism. Even non-violent religious bigotry should be curbed by American governmental action: "Responsible sources report that some U.S. residents make financial contributions to overseas religious groups in the belief that these funds are to be used for religious or humanitarian purposes, when in fact the monies so raised are used to promote religious bigotry."

If Hathaway wants to thwart religious "charities" promoting both "religious bigotry" and "violence and religious and ethnic intolerance", he can start much closer to home. American Baptist and Evangelical groups are financing the propagation of Christian religious bigotry of the most obscurantist kind in India's Northeast and tribal belts. Much of this bigotry has resulted in armed separatism, terrorism and ethnic cleansing of tribes refusing to become Christians.

Hathaway's patronizing conclusion adopts a false formula of even-handedness:

"An official U.S. investigation into Gujarat-related fund-raising, voluntarily facilitated by the Government of India, would go far towards easing those concerns and further strengthening the new partnership between our two peoples."

The Indian people is not financing movements violently disrupting American society. By contrast, American citizens are financing Church activities in India which often shade over into armed separatism, social disruption of tribal societies and ethnic cleansing. The American state is arming Pakistan, and even if it were to fully stop arms deliveries to Pakistan, it still carries a legacy of having armed the Pakistani Army and trained the Pakistani secret service, agents of terror against Indian citizens and the Indian state. The guilt for keeping Indo-American relations unfriendly is entirely on the American side. If Dr. Hathaway believes in a "new partnership between our two peoples", he had better advise his Government to investigate American private support to missionary-cum-terrorist subversion and to halt every form of American state support to Pakistani jihadism.

2. "Indian secularism is systematically dishonest"

[This is the text of an interview with Koenraad Elst, by Ramesh Rao, *Sulekha*, 19 August 2002. The numbered questions have retained their number but have been regrouped by topic. Ch.2.8 is my reply to a comment on the interview.]

2.1. WAVES

1. You just attended the WAVES (World Association for Vedic Studies) conference in Dartmouth MA. On the "Religion in South Asia" e-list, some have accused the organizers of ignoring Muslim, Christian, Sikh and other contributions to Indian civilization. What is your take on it?

My paper was about the historical relation between Zoroastrianism, Buddhism and Christianity. Is that non-Hindu enough? The critics may also keep in mind that the central concern of WAVES is Vedic studies, and the Vedic corpus was complete even before Christianity, Islam and Sikhism came into being. They don't discuss the Vedas at Biblical Studies conferences, do they? So why gate-crash non-Vedic traditions into a Vedic conference? It makes sense to study the influence of the Vedas on younger religions, not vice versa. I agree that we should devote some attention to the veneration for the Vedas attested in the writings of the Sikh Gurus. Unfortunately, that still wouldn't satisfy the critics because it would confirm the Hindu essence of Sikhism, which they prefer to construe quite unhistorically as an anti-Hindu rebellion. As for Islam, we might discuss the fate of the Vedic insight *"Aham Brahmāsmi"* (I am Brahma) in Islam.

In Arabic, Mansur al-Hallaj rendered it as *"Ana'l Haqq"* (I am the Truth), and he was beheaded for it. I suppose that's not what the critics would want to see highlighted either. It's always the same story: Hindus are damned if they do, damned if they don't.

2. WAVES had initially gained the attention by giving a forum to critics of the Aryan Invasion Theory (AIT). What has happened on that front?

The debate has moved into somewhat quieter waters. The WAVES conference contained two important papers in this field, apart from Kalyanaraman's continuing reconstruction of the history of the Saraswati river. Narahari Achar has shown how over a dozen astronomical data in the Mahabharata converge on the classical chronology for the epic's core events, viz. ca. 3100 BC. This is moreover coherent with the chronology implied in the stray astronomical information in the Vedic corpus but quite incompatible with the conventional AIT timeline. The second paper was David Frawley's defence of his argument that the Vedas are rich in references to seafaring and the ocean, *samudra*.

3. Frawley's theory has indeed been challenged. It is said that this term was only used in a figurative sense, as the "heavenly ocean", meaning simply the heavens.

Which would imply that all the Vedic references to seafaring actually pertain to space travel... I've always disliked Sri Aurobindo's symbolic interpretation of the Vedas, and he was an AIT critic, but now the same stratospheric approach is taken by the AIT defenders. At any rate, people can only think up a metaphorical ocean after they have seen the real thing, so either way, the Vedic people were not cowherds belonging to a landlocked Central-Asian habitat. In my reading, the Vedas contain plenty of down-to-earth historical information, and it includes familiarity with seafaring as well as a movement from India to Afghanistan, not the reverse.

That information obviously argues against the AIT, but not definitively: it could still be compatible with an Aryan invasion at an earlier date, or perhaps another as yet unsuspected scenario. From the beginning, I have been puzzled by the immense certainty on both sides of the debate. To me, it's an open-ended search.

2.2. The Gujarat riots

4. The communal conflagration in Gujarat has been claiming the attention throughout the past months. Was the attack on Hindu pilgrims in Godhra pre-planned? What kind of consequences did the planners expect?

Let me say first of all that I am winding up my work as an observer of Indian communalism. I think the patterns are clear, and filling in more details may be an interesting job for other people, but I want to move to more fundamental issues. Dealing with communal confrontations at face value has never solved the problem. Most secularist writings on the Gujarat riots manage to leave *madrassa* education unmentioned. How serious are you about weeding out Hindu-Muslim riots if you don't want to address the permanent source of religious hatred among Muslims, the very cause of Partition, of *jihad*? But more fundamental than the identification of sources of irrational hatred in the core texts of Islam is the question how Islam came into being, which defects of human consciousness made it possible? The problem of Islam is rooted in a universal problem of human inadequacy.

Secondly, Gujarat has not been "claiming" attention all by itself. An intensive effort by the usual suspects has kept attention as much as possible away from other scenes of communal violence. In the past months, how many people have been killed by Christian separatists in the Northeast, by Communists in Kerala or Nepal, by Muslims in Bangladesh or Jammu? As for Gujarat itself, how many Hindus have been killed by Muslims even after Godhra? The secularists have been acting as if attacks on Muslims in Gujarat are the only communal flashpoint. This is typical of hate discourse: apart from pure lies, the main technique consists in exclusively highlighting the – sometimes admittedly real – crimes of the targeted group and keeping instances of its innocent victimization out of view.

As for Godhra, I have no privileged access to the police investigation. But if you care for my speculations, I consider it merely possible that a group of Muslim hotheads recklessly vented their hatred of Hindus. They must have known that in a Hindu-majority area, they couldn't get away with more than small-scale violence. There is plenty of petty Muslim terror in Gujarat, which is how Hindus were cleansed out of entire neighbourhoods of Ahmedabad, but the trick is to apply it in small doses. At any rate, whether large or small, any initiative to violence refutes the image of the Muslims as a poor helpless minority. After all, defenceless minorities, such as the Hindus in Pakistan or Bangladesh, simply don't dare to commit even the most feeble violence against the majority. A massive strike like in Godhra, courting Hindu retaliation, either was the work of foolish hotheads, or it was prepared in advance and *calculated* to provoke a backlash. Before Partition, the Muslim League would deliberately provoke Hindu violence against Muslims in order to drive home the point that coexistence with Hindus was impossible. But today, I don't see such a motive among any section of the Indian Muslims. Only Pakistan would have an interest in fomenting this kind of trouble in India, a new front in the proxy war.

5. Was the Hindu backlash spontaneous? What role do you think the VHP played in the aftermath of Godhra?

Again, I'll mistrust the press and wait for the official findings. Home Minister L.K. Advani claims that two hundred policemen were killed, and we know of the old antagonism between Muslims and the police – not only in India, even Muslim rioters in France typically target the police. Clearly the violence was not one-sided. I just read a follow-up report about Muslim women who had allegedly been raped. Many of the women interviewed deny that rapes took place at least in their own neighbourhoods, and the only woman to maintain the allegation of mass rape was obviously tutored and her story fell through upon being questioned more closely. To be sure, that Hindu follow-up report may be just as partisan as the secularists' reports aimed at exploitation of the riots. I cannot judge either version from my armchair.

But I will agree in general terms that this was mostly a Hindu retaliation for the Godhra massacre, and for all the earlier occasions of Muslim aggression. Gujarat and especially Ahmedabad have witnessed a sustained low-level terror campaign against the Hindus. With their Gandhian tradition of fleeing and turning the other cheek, the Gujaratis have amassed considerable resentment against the Muslims, and after Godhra it all came out.

6. Are you saying that the Gandhian mentality has paradoxically contributed to the eruption of Hindu anger?

Yes. I know quite a few people of Gujarati Bania background, and I am rather uncomfortable with their tough talk. As children, these yuppies were brought up on Gandhi's extreme non-violence but they are now talking very loosely about the need to "give the Muslims a good beating", things like that. The psychology behind their evolution is that they have experienced how Gandhian attitudes of appeasing the aggressor and turning the other cheek simply don't work, and then they have moved to the other extreme. In dealing with aggression, one should neither appease nor overreact.

7. In the RISA list discussion already mentioned, you were described as a defender of Gandhi's murderer, Nathuram Godse. Do you agree?

Why don't critics first learn to read? In my book *Gandhi and Godse*, I have shown how most of the arguments against Gandhi given by Godse in his speech in court were in fact very common in his day. Gandhi's erratic policies were criticized by contemporaries like Annie Besant, Sri Aurobindo, Bhimrao Ambedkar and many others. And none of them went out to kill Gandhi, so there is nothing murderous about these arguments per se. They correctly predicted that under his irrational leadership, the strategy of mass mobilization and "non-violence" would yield very bitter fruits, as it did during the Khilafat riots circa 1922 and again during the Partition. Indologists like Alain Daniélou and historians like Paul Johnson have also demythologized the Mahatma. One of the perverse effects of the murder was precisely that in India this criticism of Gandhi suddenly became taboo, and that the myth of his centrality in the achievement of independence became unassailable.

8. Was the English media reaction to Godhra predictable? If so, how? If there are cases of balanced reporting/analyses, from whom?

By all means, preserve the Godhra articles and columns in a special folder, one day they will be the object of a spectacular case study in the human capacity for doublethink. Though disgusting, it was at the same time quite funny to watch the extreme inventiveness of the secularists in blaming the victims. They were very annoyed that the Gujarat carnage was so unambiguously started by Muslims with their massacre of Hindu pilgrims, mostly women and children. So, they falsely started describing the victims as "extremists" and inventing stories of how these Hindu children had kidnapped a Muslim woman into their riding train. That canard was borrowed from an Islamist website. There is never much difference between secularist reporting and Islamist propaganda anyway, which is why Indian theocratic Islamists call themselves "secularists". The latest is their "report" claiming that the Hindus in the train had themselves lit the fire, in a gigantic mass suicide. Well, I suppose free speech includes the right to spread nonsense.

On the bright side, I noticed Vir Sanghvi's article pointing out the crass double standards of his colleagues in their

Godhra reporting. When a white missionary is murdered by tribals in Orissa, we are expected to recoil in indignation, but when Hindus are murdered by the dozens for the umpteenth time, we are expected to agree that they had it coming. Even the wave of media hate against the Hindus and the BJP has a bright side. It eloquently disproves any suspicion that the BJP is in any way a "fascist" party. Under a fascist regime, such anti-government writing would have provoked a severe punishment. But in reality, writing against the BJP is still a good career move.

2.3. Hindutva and the minorities

9. Kanwal Rekhi and Henry Rowen have proposed that the recipients of donations from American Hindus, meaning especially the VHP, are out to "destroy minorities", and that the Indian government should "deal a severe blow to such covert causes by simply labelling them as terrorists".

Even entrepreneurs like Rekhi display the typically secularist nostalgia for Soviet methods when it comes to dealing with Hindu activism. A democratic government doesn't "simply label" an organization as terrorist, it must establish proof that will stand up in court. And when it comes to proof, there is a long list of cases where much-touted secularist proof fell apart under scrutiny. What happened to the evidence for the VHP's involvement in the murder of the missionary Graham Staines? It is increasingly clear that acts of anti-Muslim or anti-Christian violence are often the handiwork of desperate but unorganised locals. Membership of an organization like the VHP, by contrast, offers them the hope of participating in a larger countersubversive strategy and thereby keeps acts of desperation in check.

10. Do you see any major changes in the RSS strategy for dealing with minority issues in India? Any hopeful outcomes from RSS leaders meeting with minority leaders?

My criticism of the Sangh's position regarding the minorities remains the same since more than a decade: it is both too hard and too soft. Ideologically, it is too soft. It deflects any serious criticism of Islam or Christianity into a matter of national versus anti-national loyalties: "Islam is OK, but it must be Indianized". On universal grounds of truth and morality, Islam is not OK, not even in Arabia where it is cent per cent patriotic. Recently, awareness of the hate-mongering impact of the Quran has become so widespread that VHP spokesman Giriraj Kishore felt compelled to address the issue. But instead of being logical and asking Muslims to renounce the Quran, he requested them to "amend the Quran". How can you change the Quran and still call it the Quran? And what blasphemy to change the supposed word of God Himself! The Hindu attitude to Islam, from Gandhiji to Giriraj Kishore, is one of total confusion. Meanwhile, the Sangh may well be too hard on the minorities in practice. To say, as several Sangh leaders have done, that "the Muslims' best guarantee of safety lies in winning the trust of the Hindus", implies that they would be endangered if Hindus have cause to mistrust them. I can understand it if Muslims read that as a threat. The correct position is that Muslims are people quite like the rest of us, and that they should be treated equally with Hindus; but that Islam as an ideology should be subjected to inexorable criticism.

10. Teesta Setalvad, Kamal Mitra Chenoy and others testified before the U.S. Commission for International Religious Freedom accusing the Modi government and the VHP of conducting a "pogrom" against the Muslims. Should Indian citizens testify before commissions of inquiry set up by foreign governments?

You mean the commission which swallowed John Dayal's long-refuted allegation of a gang-rape of four nuns in Jhabua by "Hindu activists", who turned out to be Christian themselves? And which still believes that Hindus committed a series of bomb attacks on churches, though the culprits have been caught and identified as members of the Pak-based *Deendar Anjuman*? Genuine social activists like Swami

Agnivesh have refused to appear before that commission, on the correct plea that India is a sovereign and democratic nation which needs no lessons from the US.

Democracy has brought the BJP to power, and the enemies of democracy try to overrule the voters' verdict by appealing to higher powers such as the US. The term "pogrom" applies neatly to what Muslims did to Hindus in Godhra. A retaliation, by contrast, is not normally called a pogrom, unless you want to imply that the Jews who suffered in the Russian pogroms had asked for it. But there is no doubt that Hindus have massacred Muslims in Gujarat. I for one don't need a US commission to prove that to me. What remains unproven, though, and in my opinion most unlikely, is that the VHP would have organized it. The only ones with a vested interest in preventing riots are the Hindu nationalists, for they invariably get the blame. That is why in UP, Congress and Samajwadi governments have seen a much higher incidence in communal violence than BJP governments. Conversely, riots are the very life-blood of secularist politics.

11. How so?

The secularists had made all these shrill predictions that a BJP government would open gas chambers for Muslims, throw them in the ocean etc. But for four years, in spite of numerous massacres of Hindus by Muslim terrorists, the Indian Muslims were left alone. Islamic terrorists killed forty BJP activists, allegedly "Hindu Nazis", in Coimbatore. What would real Nazis do in that case? Well, in November 1938 a young Jew killed a German diplomat in Paris, and the Nazis reacted by attacking all the Jewish shops in Germany and killing nearly a hundred innocent Jews. So that's Nazism for you. By contrast, the BJP did not retaliate at all. Hindus were being killed with great frequency in Jammu, even the parliament buildings in Srinagar and Delhi were attacked, yet the Muslims remained unharmed. So, the secularists were losing credibility day by day. They needed the Gujarat carnage, they thanked Allah when it finally materialized.

They were suddenly back in business, getting invited all the way to Washington to tell their scare stories.

2.4. My role in all this

12. You have avoided theoretical framing of issues. Why? Modern scholars, including all the talked about Indian academics use a lot of Marxist, postmodern, and feminist theory to argue their cases. You don't. Explain.

What real knowledge of the religio-political situation have those theories ever added? Read those books and you will see that "constructs" and "conceptual tools" fill the pages that should have contained real information instead. Such scholars collect just enough primary information to prove that they did get in touch with their topic, or more often they borrow even that minimum of information from like-minded publications, and then they put these raw data through the theory machine, yielding a theory sausage peppered with a few data selected for their fitting into the theory's expectations. Most of them borrow not just data, but also opinions and judgments without critically examining them. At the same time, they manage to disregard pertinent data which stare every normal observer in the face. Thus, practically every Hindu activist whom I have interviewed between 1990 and 1998 brought up the plight of the Kashmiri Pandits, murdered or expelled from their homeland, as a telling illustration of the true religio-political power equation in India. But most publications purportedly analysing Hindu nationalism in the 1990s manage to overlook this expulsion of Hindus from a part of India. They have to if they want to uphold the image of India as dominated by an overbearing Hindu majority threatening a hapless Muslim minority.

13. Some scholars like Thomas Blom Hansen and Ashis Nandy have been dismissive of your work.

They would, wouldn't they? If I am right then they are wrong, so their prestige may stand or fall with the elimination of my position from the debate.

14. Nandy ("Creating a Nationality", p.5) writes: "For the moment, we bypass the dishonesty and moral vacuity of the likes of Koenraad Elst on this issue". How do you respond? Are they contemptuous because you don't do fashionable theorizing?

That is one element which stamps me as an outsider. Another is that I don't belong to their institutional network. In my young days, anti-authoritarianism was all the rage, and I have retained some of that scorn for arguments of status and authority. In the communalism debate, however, the snobbish argument of status is the one most commonly used. Remember the "eminent historians"? But most importantly, Nandy simply disagrees with my general position, which is OK. Only, when he cannot prove me wrong with arguments, he resorts to name-calling. In the present power equation, he doesn't risk a reprimand for stooping to that level. By the way, don't you admire Nandy's rhetorical cleverness? He pushes the allegation of "dishonesty and moral vacuity" all while "bypassing" the burden of proof.

As for "dishonesty", I try to avoid uttering that allegation, at least against individuals. The secularists easily resort to sermonizing and finger-wagging rather than arguing things out with facts and logic. But I will accept in every individual case that they may be honest in their beliefs. By contrast, secularism *as a movement* must be branded as a unique achievement in dishonesty.

25. In hostile writings, you are routinely classified among the Hindu nationalists.

I am neither a Hindu nor a nationalist. And I don't need to belong to those or to any specific ideological categories in order to use my eyes and ears. So I noticed for myself that the legitimate Hindu nationalists are thoroughly misrepresented in the journalistic and academic literature about them. I never planned to. The anomaly between their image and the reality on the ground struck me by surprise when I was in India to study philosophy. As I said, I am phasing out my involvement with communalism studies. The subject is really very simple, the problem as well as the solution. It isn't all that challenging and interesting, it only seemed that way because of the artificial obstacles thrown up by the secularists.

2.5. Secularism

15. What is your basic criticism of India's so-called secularism?

That it isn't secular. As a political framework, secularism requires that all citizens are equal before the law regardless of their religious affiliation. That is a definitional minimum. An Indian secularist would therefore first of all be found on the barricades in the struggle for a common civil code, against the existing legal apartheid between Hindus, Muslims, Christians and Parsis. But the only major party to demand the enactment of a common civil code, as mandated by the Constitution, happens to be the BJP. On election eve, the others run to the Shahi Imam to pledge their firm commitment to the preservation of the Shari'a for Muslims. In the West and in the Muslim world, the upholding of religion-based communal legislation is rightly called anti-secularist.

I have often discussed this point with Indian secularists. Their usual argument is that, you see, India is a peculiar case, the uniform civil code issue has been "hijacked" by the Hindus, and for now the country *needs* these separate civil codes. I am not convinced, but even if we concede that India is better off with the present system, that still doesn't make it secular. The opponents of the common civil code, the upholders of discrimination against the Hindus in education and temple management, the defenders of a special status for states with non-Hindu majorities,— they should have the courage of their conviction and call themselves "anti-secular". Incidentally, this is one thing you have to concede to Ashis Nandy: he has criticized the very notion of secularism.

16. Don't you think that secularism is more than just an institutional arrangement, that it is also an intellectual attitude?

Alright, as an intellectual movement, secularism means that religion is treated as a human construct rather than the product of a divine revelation. It implies a frank and critical investigation of the claims of religion. In this respect, the failure and dishonesty of Indian secularism is even more complete. Its discourse on religion is extremely and wilfully superficial. It shields from criticism even the most obscurantist religious beliefs or institutions, provided they are non-Hindu. For instance, almost every self-styled secularist, from the exiting president to the editors of the newspapers, has sworn by the story that Christianity was brought to India by the apostle Thomas. In the West, not just secularists but even Catholic universities like the one where I studied have dropped this myth. But in India, the secularists are its most determined upholders.

Indian secularism is systematically dishonest in its assessment of the religions hostile to Hinduism. Thus, after the Staines murder, which apparently resulted from the well-attested resentment of the tribals against the divisive effect of conversion on their communities, the secularists massively denied that the Christian missionaries are in India for purposes of conversion. In reality, the project of converting all mankind is intrinsic to the Christian religion. In Catholic school, I always learned that the missionaries provide medical and educational services primarily in order to make the targeted communities receptive to conversion. Staines' own bulletin to his Australian sponsors proved he was doing conversion work. The Southern Baptists reconfirmed in 1999 that Hindus are doomed unless they become Christians. The Pope himself came to Delhi to say in so many words that the Church intends to "reap a harvest of faith" in India. Yet this self-evident fact is still dismissed by vocal secularists as a figment of Hindutva paranoia. In parenthesis: since my critics are fond of misquoting me, let me say explicitly that I disapprove of murder as a way of protesting against the nuisance of conversion campaigns.

Or take a more fundamental item, the core belief of Islam: that Mohammed is God's prophet. Suppose one of your colleagues told you one day that henceforth you have to obey his every word, as he has become God's spokesman receiving exclusive messages from above. Presumably you would guess he had developed a serious mental problem. Well, that's exactly what Mohammed's contemporaries thought, as the Quran itself testifies a dozen times. It is also what modern psychologists have said: Mohammed suffered of a classic case of paranoia, a grand delusion about himself nurtured with audiovisual hallucinations. A real secularist is skeptical of the defining belief of Islam and feels sorry for all those Muslims trapped in it. So there you have a properly secularist point to take up with the Muslims: do you want to continue regulating your lives after the injunctions of a 7th-century Arab businessman who heard voices? Do you want to base wars, states and laws on the unsecular belief in Mohammed's deluded claims? Instead, the only thing the secularists ever discuss with Muslims is a joint strategy against the Hindus.

2.6. Islam and conversion

17. Is that your view of Islam: that Muslims had better be talked out of it?

Here I agree with V.S. Naipaul: the non-Arab Muslims suffer from the conflict between their ancestral cultural roots and their imposed religion. Every Muslim is an abductee from the civilization to which he once belonged. Where I differ with the Nobel-winning author is that I would apply the same diagnosis to the Arabs. Though they did not have to adopt foreign customs and language, which made the transition to Islam less disruptive, they too were cut off from their original culture. Either way, Muslims would do well to take a critical look at the basics of their religion. I don't think anyone else can do it for them, and I expect little from VHP conversion campaigns among them. I expect more from state policies ensuring that Muslim children are exposed to a wide spectrum of ideas rather than being locked up in the *Madrassas* which have produced the *Taliban*. But ultimately, the Muslims have to come out of the mistaken belief system of Islam themselves. They will then enter the same vacuum where post-Christians like myself are struggling to see the light. But that uncertainty is quite alright. I can personally testify that there is life after apostasy.

18. You yourself said that conversion has a divisive effect in tribal villages. Do you imagine the conflict in the Muslim world, nearly 1.5 billion people, if a good number among them turned against Islam?

The proper comparison is not with the Christian conversion campaigns, nor with Communist campaigns against religion, but with the spontaneous secularisation which has taken place in ex-Christian Europe. I can see the beginnings of the de-Islamization already. For example, I invite your readers to take a look at the www.faithfreedom.org or www.secularislam.org website. Maintained by Muslim-born West- and South-Asians, it tells Muslims all about the good reasons for outgrowing Islam. And think of writers like Anwar Sheikh, Ibn Warraq or Taslima Nasrin, who are showing the Muslims the way out towards Enlightenment. Of course, many such writers have been murdered, but their voice is penetrating ever deeper. The information revolution has a big role to play here. Even in the harems in the remotest parts of Arabia, TV and internet are breaking open the narrow horizon of Islam.

19. Many Hindus take an alarmist view about the numerical growth of Islam through high birth rates and migration. In support of that doomsday scenario, some of

them cite your 1998 booklet *The Demographic Siege.* What are your views about that now?

This alarmist view is even stronger in Europe, with its low birth rates, than in India. The impressively higher Muslim birth rate is a plain fact, which is why the secularists are so zealous in denying it. Admittedly, birth control is now catching on in countries like Iran and Turkey (not in Pakistan), but Iran's population is still expected to double before reaching zero growth. If you extrapolate present trends, it is certain that Islam will take over Europe in fifty years, India and the US in a hundred at most. And yet, it is even more certain that the threat of Islam will disappear even faster. Firstly, there is the intellectual effort of the school of writers just mentioned. Secondly, Muslims are increasingly aware that Islam is a factor of failure. Look at Malaysia, where the Chinese and Hindu minorities have achieved an economic breakthrough which the Muslim majority can only skim off with forced redistribution.

The recent UN report on the Arab world has confirmed what any visitor there can see for himself: a stifling atmosphere and a lack of dynamism. Secularists always blame Muslim backwardness in India on some kind of invisible Hindu conspiracy, though the Muslims actually enjoy a number of privileges tending to reinforce their Islamic identity. The Arab case, with Muslims in a majority and in power, and with an immense affluence to support any policy they may choose to pursue, shows that Muslim backwardness is due to Islam itself. In the oil monarchies, most of the labour is done by Western and Asian guest workers, and the available capital is not used to build self-reliant industries. The day oil loses its value, they will have to go back to tending camels, unless they shake off their religious obscurantism. I am confident that the Arabs and other Muslims will understand this in time. It will probably happen in two phases: a vanguard disowns Islam entirely, the masses follow at a distance with attempts to reform Islam and water it down to conform to modern values.

Am I too optimistic? I admit that in 1920 already, Bertrand Russell and others diagnosed the young Soviet Union as bound to fail, yet it took a whole human lifetime before it actually collapsed, and the Russian born in 1920 is now an old man suffering the lingering after-effects of the Soviet experiment. So likewise, the mathematical certainty that Islam too will implode need not exclude that it can still cause serious problems. But I have a hunch that Islam will end the way it began: with a bang.

20. What is the view in Europe about Islam?

Let's scan the political spectrum. The extreme Right cherishes fantasies of a Euro-Islamic alliance against the American-Zionist world hegemony. The fast-growing populist Right, by contrast, takes an alarmist view of Islam, though in many cases this is only a rhetorical cover for an anti-immigration drive regardless of the religion of the immigrants. The declining Old Left with its militant secularist tradition is in no mood to make concessions to Islam, witness the recent anti-Islamic statements by Leftist journalist Oriana Fallaci. In the extreme Left, some see Muslim immigrants as a substitute for the proletariat as a force capable of destroying the system. But the important factor is the centre, the business Right and the fashionable multiculturalist Left. In the 1990s, they blocked all criticism of Islam. Careerwise, the rare active critics of Islam, including myself, paid a heavy price. In Amsterdam, the Pakistani Islam critic, the Muslim-born Mohamed Rasoel, was even sentenced to a heavy fine for "anti-Muslim racism", whatever that may mean. In the last two years, the mood has changed considerably, witness the open dismissal of Islam as backward and inferior by Italian Prime Minister Silvio Berlusconi and postmodernist writer Michel Houellebecq. September 11 confirmed that change of mood. Recently, the Syrian-born German professor Bassam

Tibi spoke for most Europeans when he stated that he didn't want to see Europe islamized.

21. How do you rate the American government's reaction to September 11, particularly regarding South Asia?

After that event, general Perwez Musharraf seriously counted with an Indo-Israeli attack on Pakistan's nuclear capability, even with the destruction of the Pakistani state. So he saw no way out but to offer his services to the US. But he made it clear, in an Urdu speech to his people, that he was not becoming America's friend. He related how the Prophet Mohammed had used alliances as stratagems in order to eliminate other allies: using the Jews to eliminate the Pagans of Medina, than befriending the Pagans of Mecca to eliminate the Jews, and finally breaking his treaty with the Meccans to defeat them. But since the CIA has explained that none of its employees know Arabic, I guess they didn't pick up those Urdu hints either. Just imagine, in the war on terrorism they don't care to learn the two languages most commonly used by terrorists. Musharraf is taking the Americans for a ride. I understand that President Bush wants to keep the Muslim world divided by enlisting some Muslim regimes in his own crusade, but I doubt he will outwit them. I think he is in for a serious humiliation. I admit this sounds like the old European armchair skepticism of American interventionism. But let's face it: American foreign policy is utterly confused, and mere muscle-flexing cannot be a substitute for a coherent vision.

2.7. Hindus and Muslims

22. Abdul Kalam is now India's president. Rafiq Zakaria wrote an op-ed piece in the *Asian Age* arguing that Kalam is not a "true" or "real" Muslim. Will Kalam help in liberating the Indian Muslim from the mental-ghettoes constructed by the likes of Zakaria?

Along with the secularists, I used to laugh at the BJP notion that Indian Muslims should see themselves as

"Mohammedi Hindus". But I was wrong: the BJP has at long last discovered its Mohammedi Hindu. And because he is such a rarity, they have at once given him the top post. I certainly hope he serves as a guide for the Indian Muslims out of their ghettoes and into the bright daylight of India and the modern world.

23. How do you compare Atal Behari Vajpayee with other Prime Ministers?

My favourite among Indian Prime Ministers is definitely Narasimha Rao. He undid the Nehruvian legacy and stemmed the rising tide of the fateful consequences of Nehru's follies. He actually implemented the BJP programme, just as Atal Behari Vajpayee is now implementing the Congress programme. Rao started liberalizing the economy, lifting the stifling socialist controls. He opened diplomatic relations with Israel. He defeated the Khalistani terrorists, nipped the beginnings of Tamil Tiger separatism on Indian soil in the bud, and pushed back Kashmiri terrorism to the point where the Kasmiri people stopped supporting it so that it is now manned entirely by foreign mercenaries. And he allowed the demolition of the Babri Masjid.

24. Are you saying that the demolition was a good thing?

At the level of historic justice, I consider it perfectly normal that a Hindu sacred site is adorned with a Hindu temple. Hindus shouldn't overemphasize the history of Islamic destruction, the current victimhood culture is quite foreign to the Hindu spirit, but for once this focus on a temple forcibly replaced with a mosque has been instructive. At a more pragmatic level, from the viewpoint of saving lives, certainly a more pressing concern than the rights and wrongs of history, the demolition was a good thing, on balance. In the preceding years, India was tormented by communal riots over all kinds of issues, most of them unrelated to Ayodhya. The demolition led to a brief round of Muslim revenge actions plus the Shiv Sena retaliation in Mumbai, but then rioting stopped for nine long years. The demolition clearly had a cathartic effect on the rioters. To be sure, Islamic terrorism has continued, but Hindus refused to be provoked. They did not take out their anger on their Muslim neighbours after the Mumbai blasts of March 1993, nor after any of the numerous massacres of Hindus and Sikhs in Jammu and Kashmir, nor after the bomb attack in Coimbatore, nor after the attacks on the parliament buildings. Hindus have shown remarkable restraint.

At the most fundamental level, however, I am not too enthusiastic about the whole idea of campaigning for the liberation of historical temples sites from Muslim occupation. It is a well-attested fact that most historical mosques were built on the site of non-Muslim places of worship. This is true of thousands of mosques in India, but also of the Ummayad mosque in Damascus, the Aya Sophia in Istambul, and even the Kaaba itself, where Mohammed smashed 360 idols venerated by the sanctuary's rightful owners, the Arab polytheists. But trying to pull these sites out of the hands of the Muslims is the wrong approach. The Ayodhya campaign had the merit of drawing attention to this historic injustice, but henceforth the energy spent on it had better be redirected to a more fundamental objective. We should help the Muslims in freeing themselves from Islam, and then they themselves will release these places of worship. Every Muslim is a Sita, an abductee who must be liberated from Ravana's prison.

2.8. Here's what's going on

[This is a reply, written on 31-12-2002 to a critique of the above interview by Marion O'Callaghan in the Trinidad newspaper *Newsday*, 28-12-2002, www.newsday.co.tt]

Marion O'Callaghan's article "Hindutva history – Hey what's going on here?" follows a pattern sadly familiar to all those who have come in the firing line of Hindu-baiters worldwide: personal attacks, misattribution of viewpoints, amalgamation and double standards. O'Callaghan appeals to our bleeding hearts concerning India's minorities but objects to my mentioning the numerous Hindus killed by Christians in Northeast India, as this would only "feed into the 'victim' cycle". But what else than victimhood indulgence is his rehashing of the long-refuted canard that "nuns have been raped" by Hindu activists? If we are to weep for Graham Staines, it is only right to pay attention to the Riang tribals ethnically cleansed from Mizoram for refusing to convert, or to the 22 Hindus killed by Christian Bodo militants last week.

Apart from getting the book title *Update on the Aryan Invasion Debate* wrong, O'Callaghan manages to misrepresent my positions in every single particular. Thus, he ludicrously alleges that my book "rehashes the Aryan race myth". In fact, it contains a critique of that myth, long dead among scholars but kept alive in a vocal fringe of the Dalit movement. Though this new version of the myth recasts the Aryans as the bad guys, it still agrees with Hitler in accepting the Aryan Invasion Theory (AIT). As for the assertion that "Blacks ain't Aryan", I have repeatedly pointed out that in the Ramayana, both Rama and his opponent Ravana are described as Aryan and as dark-skinned.

I am said to "announce that Proto-Indo-Europeans 'went out from what is now Punjab, Haryana and Western Uttar Pradesh', to the astonishment of archaeologists, linguists and ancient Indian historians". O'Callaghan seems unaware that most Indian archaeologists reject the AIT because their spade fails to find any proof of it. On the other hand, leaving aside the Marxists who have always subordinated history to their political agenda, I acknowledge that linguists have good non-political reasons to prefer the AIT. There are two legitimate sides to this debate, as I explained in my book:

"One thing which keeps on astonishing me in the present debate is the complete lack of doubt in both camps. Personally, I don't think that either theory, of Aryan invasion and of Aryan indigenousness, can claim to have been 'proven' (...) Many seem to think that all the questions have been answered, that only mad or evil people can still adhere to the rivalling school of thought (...) but what I see is that at least many parts of the question are still waiting for an answer." (p.331)

Thus, the hypothesis that Harappa belonged to "Dravidians and not Aryans", about which O'Callaghan is so cock-sure, is rejected even by pro-AIT scholars like Michael Witzel, who proposes "para-Munda" as Harappa's language instead. Scholars simply can't be sure yet.

A common technique in disinformation campaigns is *amalgamation*: create an impression of unity between the targeted person and others who are already notorious. Thus, my name is juxtaposed to the claim that "Hindutva history declared both the Red Fort in Delhi and the Taj Mahal to be not built by Muslims, but by Hindus". My repeated expressions of contempt for that nonsense exist in cold print.

Another example: "Dr. Elst puts in question another minority often targeted by the VHP — Christians. It is the VHP which led the agitation against the Pope's visit to India". I never had anything to do with that agitation, and I consider the Pope's performance in Delhi as a great boon. After the secularists had denounced any talk of Christian proselytizing as "mendacious hate propaganda", the Pope declared explicitly that the Church's intention is to "reap a great harvest of faith". With one sentence, the Pope flushed down a ton of secularist lies.

O'Callaghan defends "the present Indian Secular State", with *secular* meaning that "neither citizenship nor rights within state or society is linked to religion". By that criterion, India with its many religious discriminations (religion-based Civil Codes, autonomy for non-Hindu-majority states, educational privileges for the minorities, *Hajj* subsidies etc.) is not a secular state at all. But I am in favour of making it one.

Unlike the VHP, I agree that secularism "implies the freedom to convert or to be converted", e.g. to convert Christians and Muslims out of their irrational belief systems.

As a convert from Christianity to secular humanism myself, I can testify that conversion may be an improvement.

Marion O'Callaghan's article is not entirely inaccurate. It correctly quotes me as alleging that the so-called secularists "are wilfully superficial and shield from criticism the most obscurantist religious beliefs or institutions provided they are non- Hindu". Indeed, they avoid evaluating Christianity or Islam in the light of modern scholarship, which has proven that the Bible is not God's revealed word but a literary elaboration of older myths and doctrines; and that Mohammed was mentally afflicted with a self-delusion nourished by recurring hallucinations. Don't fear the doomsday threats of the Bible or the Quran, they are mere human confabulations. Any genuine secularist would hasten to inform the public about these liberating findings, secular par excellence.

3. The Saffron Wave

[This book review was written just after the book's publication in 2002.]

Though milder in tone, the latest academic book on Hindu revivalism suffers from the same shortcomings as most others. Ever since Craig Baxter's fairly objective and well-documented book *The Jana Sangha*, already thirty years old, and Walter Andersen and Shridhar Damle's *Brotherhood in Saffron*, already twelve years old, all the Western Hindutva watchers have chosen to rely on partisan secondary accounts, and to watch Hindutva through the coloured glasses which the so-called secularists have put on their noses.

The book *The Saffron Wave: Democracy and Hindu Nationalism in Modern India* (Princeton) by Professor Thomas Blom Hansen from Roskilde, Denmark, is no exception. Since the book has already been praised as "brilliant" by Prof. Peter Van Der Veer, I may concentrate on its less brilliant aspects. As usual, most quotations are from secondary and generally hostile sources: Bipan Chandra, K.N. Panikkar, Partha Chatterjee, Christophe Jaffrelot, Asghar Ali Engineer (a hard-boiled Islamist whom Hansen and others naively mistake for an enlightened Muslim), Sudhir Kakar, Gyan Pandey.

In the bibliography, we find Savarkar's *Hindutva*, mercifully, but none of his statements from his time as Hindu Mahasabha leader; only one title by Balraj Madhok, none by Girilal Jain or Arun Shourie; nor we do not find Ram Swarup or Sita Ram Goel mentioned there. On the Ayodhya controversy, most of the publications presenting the temple evidence (Harsh Narain, R. Nath, S.R. Goel) are left unmentioned, while the official VHP evidence bundle is mentioned but was clearly left unread.

Hansen's entire information on the Ayodhya debate is confined to anti-Hindu sources, esp. S. Gopal's Penguin booklet *Anatomy of a Confrontation* (1991), which had already succeeded in keeping all serious presentations of the temple evidence out of view. That is how he can write the following howler: "In all cases this evidence has been refuted and contested by most of the serious authorities of archaeology and medieval Indian history." (p.262) If that is so, Prof. Hansen, I challenge you to a public debate on the Ayodhya evidence. Let's make it an open-book exam: you may bring all the arguments provided by S. Gopal and his comrades — but you may find upon closer reading that far from refuting the pro-temple evidence, they have adroitly left most of it undiscussed. And like his sources, Hansen keeps the relevant context of the Ayodhya affair, viz. the history and underlying theology of Islamic iconoclasm, out of view.

By relying on a partisan selection of secondary sources, Hansen, whose good faith we will continue to assume, is led by the nose by one of the warring parties into relaying its own version of the facts, all while believing that he is giving a neutral observer's account of the conflict between Hindu revivalism and the Marxist-Muslim combine. In a footnote, Hansen describes the present writer as "a Belgian Catholic of a radical anti-Muslim persuasion who tries to make himself useful as a 'fellow traveller' of the Hindu nationalist movement". (p.262)

I strongly deny having ever been "anti-Muslim", for I make it a point to frequently insist that "not Muslims but Islam is the problem". However, I do readily admit to being a "fellow-traveller" of Dharmic civilization in its struggle for survival against the ongoing aggression and subversion by well-organized hostile ideologies. Only, I must add that in

Hindutva-watching publications of the past decade, I have never encountered any journalistic or academic "expert" who was not a fellow-traveller of one of the warring parties.

Hansen himself makes no secret of his partisanship, as when he describes the BJP as "evil" (p.235) and as "swadeshi fascism" (p.235), though he subjectively tries to be fair by mitigating this denunciation with the rightful comment that both secularity and democracy have not been well served by the Congress establishment either. His partisan and prejudiced attitude leads him to ignore or misinterpret important trends within the Hindutva movement. Thus, he dismisses the inclusion of some Muslims in the Vajpayee cabinet as follows: "Like all other measures taken by the BJP in this regard, these were also symbolic gestures devoid of any content or seriousness." (p.267) Would you allow such a clearly partisan sentence in a thesis about any other movement (say, Indian secularism) by your own students, Prof. Hansen? At any rate, the dismissal is mistaken.

From the inclusion of a green strip in the BJP flag (1980) onwards, the BJP has always consistently courted the Muslim community, so that it now has thousands of Muslim members, who even have their own "minority cell". Even before that, the Hindu nationalists in the Janata government were party to a number of pro-Muslim steps, including the creation of the intrinsically communal and anti-Hindu "Minorities Commission". Dattopant Thengadi and others have told me how the shared time in jail with Jamaat-i-Islami activists during the secularist Emergency dictatorship had kindled sympathy for the Muslims. However that may be, in the 1990s, there is just no denying the RSS-BJP tendency to what they themselves used to denounce as "Muslim appeasement".

Even in the Ayodhya campaign, from which Hansen chooses to remember only the hard-line rhetoric of a Sadhvi Ritambhara, the emphasis was again and again on Rama as a "national" (as opposed to "Hindu") hero, and on Babar as a "foreign invader" (as opposed to "Islamic iconoclast"), who had been fought "by Indian Muslims and Hindus jointly". Anyone familiar with non-Sangh Hindu activism should have noted the criticism of the Sangh's pro-Muslim line, e.g. in Abhas Chatterjee's book *Concept of Hindu Nation* (1995, not in Hansen's bibliography). One of the more disturbing and sterile approaches which Hansen has borrowed from his secularist sources, is the tendency to psychologize, and to bury hard facts under a cloud of psychobabble: "construct", "identities built around a threatening other", "domesticating public spaces", "myth of Hindu effeminacy".

To Hansen, the Hindu perception of Islam is unconnected with any historical facts about Islam, it's all self-generated psychic images whose only basis in reality is non-religious sociological phenomena such as the "inferiority complex" of the "vernacular middle class" vis-à-vis the Anglo-secularist "mandarins" (p.181). Facts about Islam are mostly kept out of view, otherwise ridiculed (Kashmiri "insurgency", p.168; "Bangladeshi infiltration", p.199) or dismissed as "myth", e.g. that Muslims have "many wives and secret links to rich Arabs" (p.211), or (repeatedly) that Muslims oppose birth control.

It is a straight fact that the Muslim birth rate is much higher, that they participate much less in India's effort at birth control, and that this is also the intention of Islamic leaders, expressed clearly in a number of pamphlets and firmly based on Islamic scripture (vide K. Elst: *The Demographic Siege*, 1998, and for a far more thorough and up-to-date account: A.P. Joshi, M.D. Srinivas and J.K. Bajaj: *Religious Demography of India*, Centre for Policy Studies, Chennai 2003). Time and again, in order to explain a community's assertiveness, Hansen relies on the voguish term "the other", which carries unspoken Auschwitz connotations (it was popularized by the French-Jewish philosopher Emmanuel Levinas in his reflections on the Holocaust), and he makes those connotations explicit, e.g. "The community is weak, sinful and unfulfilled. The only way to remedy this is by destroying the other, whose very presence (as threat qua temptation and fascination) weakens and prevents the inherent discipline, strength and manliness in the community from blossoming." (p.211) What an impressive string of words, only a pity that its relevance to Hindu nationalism is non-existent. There is no Hindu plan for "destroying the other".

The Islam problem in India has nothing to do with Muslims being a resident "other" who undermines the Hindu morale, a calque on the Nazi perception of the Jews as agents of immorality corrupting the German people, for unlike the well-integrated (and consequently influential) Jews of Germany, the Muslims are a highly separate community whose chief crime is not the influence they might have on Hindu society, but the direct threat which their doctrinal hatred of god-pluralism poses to Hinduism, especially through the medium of violence against both symbols and followers of the Hindu religion. "Otherness" discourse is totally unable to throw any light on the Hindu perception of Islam, for Hindus have proven during long millennia that they have no problem with "others", as when they provided asylum to refugee Syrian Christians, Jews and Parsis. By contrast, Hindu feelings about Islam are comprehensively explained by their experience of Islam in action, as during the Partition (I may have missed something, but I don't recall Hansen seconding the common secularist dismissal of Muslim guilt for Partition as yet another "myth") or the East Bengal genocide of 1971.

Eye-sore buildings like the Babri Masjid (until 1992) or the Gyanvapi mosque in Varanasi stand as permanent testimony to Islamic hatred of Hindu god-pluralism. Also, the usual implication that an "other" is set up as a bogey to concentrate a community's attention and thereby strengthen its unity, does not apply. All the factors of the communal conflict, far from being the creation of Hindutva strategists, were in place from the day the first Islamic invader set foot in India. Contrary to the secularist claim that "Hinduism" and "the Hindu community" are recent inventions, the Islamic invaders united all non-monotheistic Indians under the new label "Hindu", meaning any Indian unbelievers, they showed their deep awareness of their own Muslim identity, and they proved through word and deed the essential and inescapable antagonism between Islamic and Hindu identities.

All the primary sources, the medieval Persian writings of Muslim conquerors and their court chroniclers, prove that Hindu-Muslim antagonism was not generated by colonial machinations or post-colonial mobilization in an effort to "domesticate public spaces". This conflict was unilaterally imposed on the Hindus by Muslims. The immunization of Hindutva-watchers against factual discourse on Islam is so thorough that in some cases, factual statements by Hindus about Islam are not even criticized, as if their mere quotation will suffice to evoke scorn and laughter for so much evil nonsense, e.g. RSS weekly *Organiser*'s entirely correct view that "the supreme Islamic mission is to convert the Hindus, one and all" (p.179), or Sadhvi Ritambhara's accurate statement that "the Quran teaches them to lie in wait for idol worshipers, to skin them alive" etc. (p.180). Well, the Quran does say that, and it does say that the war against the infidels is on until the whole world is Islamic, which implies the conversion (or death) of even the last Hindu.

Likewise, no discussion is opened against the denunciation of the "secular intellectuals" as "alienated pseudo-secularists full of contempt for the true Hindu culture" (p.181), though the concept "pseudo-secular" is central to the whole controversy, and proves to be entirely valid when you consider that those "secularists" defend all kinds of religious discrimination, e.g. religion-based civil codes, against the genuinely and quintessentially secular system of equality of all citizens before the law regardless of their religion. Hansen's book is full of interesting information about Hindutva campaigning in the 1990s, but conceptually it is quite superficial.

Some minor remarks to conclude. The book contains some of the familiar tricks known from the M.J. Akbar school of Hindutva-smearing, e.g. just as Akbar once cleverly described Veer Savarkar as "a co-accused in the Mahatma murder trial" without mentioning that Savarkar was fully acquitted and not even indicted again in the appeals trial, we find Prof. Hansen casting suspicion on L.K. Advani by describing him as "indicted in a massive corruption scandal in 1996" (p.266) without mentioning that the investigation cleared him completely of the charges (which were minor, the "massive" scandal mainly pertaining to dozens of Congress secularists, as Hansen fails to explain). There are also minor mistakes, sometimes clearly printing errors (Rajendra Singh becoming sarsanghchalak in "1944" instead of 1994, p.182), sometimes indicators of limited familiarity with Hinduism ("Ramahandi" for Ramanandi, p.262).

But many Hindu nationalists will be glad to read Prof. Hansen's acknowledgment of the diplomatic success achieved with India's nuclear tests, which have "forced western media and decision makers to recognize India as a major power". (p.266) You may quote that whenever *Frontline* alleges that BJP rule in 1998-99 was a foreign policy disaster.

4. The struggle for India's soul: A reply to Mira Kamdar

[This article was written in December 2002.]

The article "The struggle for India's soul" by Mira Kamdar (*World Policy Journal*, fall 2002) exemplifies the confusions bedevilling the communalism debate, especially among avowed secularists and their NRI friends. In the present paper, I will not propose any new thesis but merely draw attention to the logical fallacies and factual mistakes so typical of secularist polemic against Hindu nationalism.

4.1. "Hindu fascism"

Mira Kamdar tells us about a paradoxical combination of opinions in her father: "My immigrant Gujarati father is both a liberal Democrat and a supporter of Hindu fascism. This is not as unusual as one might think."

Before discussing this paradox, we need to focus on the use of a single word which does more in conditioning the mind of the non-specialist reader than any thesis developed at length in her paper: "fascism". If the Hindu ideology under consideration were really "fascism", then its combination with liberal anti-racism would be highly unusual and problematic, requiring a thorough explanation which Mira Kamdar's paper fails to offer. Of course, if some of the groups concerned were to call themselves "fascists", it would be normal if we were to do likewise. But that is not the case at all: they describe themselves as "Hindu nationalists", "Hindu revivalists" or "genuine secularists". So, in a scholarly paper, as opposed to a partisan political pamphlet, the decision to describe them as "fascists" can come only at the end of an analysis showing how in spite of their own self-description they really do satisfy the definition of "fascism". But no such analysis has been given here. The term "fascism" is thrown in at the outset without any justification, in an obvious attempt to condition the unwitting reader into a mood of hatred against the targeted Hindu activists.

I have analysed the discourse on "Hindu fascism" in detail in my book *The Saffron Swastika* (Voice of India, Delhi 2001), and will offer a few arguments against the notion below. For now, I may limit the explanation of my skepticism about it to the following observation. The Hindu nationalists, presently in power in Delhi, are not "fascists", and the best proof is the very fact that this allegation is made so routinely. In an age in which this is the ultimate insult and the most terrible allegation, no authoritarian government would let opposition voices get away with uttering it day in and day out. Yet, for today's Indian intellectuals, levelling grim allegations against the Hindu nationalists, including that of "fascism", does not entail a risk of landing in prison or in a torture chamber, not even of being censored or fired. On the contrary, it is a very smart career move. It can get you a job with prestigious media and institutions, and it will earn you invitations to the American lecture circuit. Get rich quick!

Farther down in her paper, Mira Kamdar continues in the same vein: "The president should condemn strongly the genocide in Gujarat and attacks elsewhere against India's Muslims." Killing "2000" people is terrible, but in a population of millions, can you seriously call it "genocide"? This kind of hyperbole betrays a purely polemical rather than scholarly purpose behind her paper. Or the prevalence of the polemical mode against Hindutva to such an overwhelming extent that scholars sheepishly adopt it even without having the intention of straying from scholarly deontology.

She also writes the following line about Ashutosh Varshney's latest book: "Varshney presents, almost *sotto voce*, a secondary line of argument where, I believe, he more accurately nails the beast of Hindutva to the wall." Another brief remark on terminology is in order here. Communism killed over 100 million people, yet, what academic journal would accept a paper describing Communism as a "beast"? Anyone using such terminology would at once be derided as "McCarthyist" and worse. But in writing on Hindutva, the normal rules are suspended.

4.2. Inequality, racism and Islam

Mira Kamdar doesn't seem to realize that she is providing a good entry point into a justification of the "anti-Muslim anti-racism" paradox where she details her own family's anti-racist commitment: "Even our parents' 'mixed marriage'—my mother is Danish American—was to be understood not so much as a love affair as a salvo in the war on racism."

Well, there you have an excellent starting-point for a little meditation on the similarities between racism and Islam. If Mira Kamdar's father was in favour of mixed marriages, he had necessarily to be an opponent of Islam. For, Islam forbids mixed marriages, viz. between a Muslim and a non-Muslim. Such marriages are only allowed if the non-Muslim partner first converts, so that it is no longer a mixed marriage but a purely inter-Muslim one. This rule is strictly enforced (and even in Western countries, Muslim social pressure to this effect is very strong) in case of a union between a Muslim woman and a man of non-Muslim origin: Islam as a system of domination does not tolerate a Muslim partner submitting to the authority of a non-Muslim *pater familias*. In the reverse case, there is more scope for accommodation: care must be taken that the resulting children are raised as Muslims, but in specific social circumstances the non-Muslim identity of the wife may be respected. This asymmetry is exactly like in the racist equation in the American Old South: no white father would ever allow his daughter to go with a black man, but he might allow himself to have a black mistress. The idea is that the natural order is respected as long as the dominant male partner belongs to the dominant class. To be sure, this attitude is not exclusive to Islam or to racism, it appears in most groups pretending to some kind of collective superiority. But at any rate, it helps explain why an anti-racist could logically also be an anti-Islamist.

The combination of liberalism and anti-Islamism has recently been illustrated by the case of the Dutch politician Pim Fortuyn, murdered during his spectacular election campaign in May 2002 by a Dutch leftist. This ultra-liberal sociology professor and avowed homosexual had criticized the illiberal elements in Islam, particularly regarding women, homosexuals and non-Muslims. He was not against Muslim immigration per se ("I have nothing against Muslims, I go to bed with them") but he favoured a controlled slowing of immigration in order to facilitate the full assimilation of the Muslim immigrants, away from their physical and mental ghettoes. When he turned this position into a political programme and stood for elections, he rapidly gained the support of a veritable rainbow of different opinion segments, including emancipated ex-Muslims, native critics of immigration or of Islam, and most remarkably, some of the non-Muslim immigrant groups, especially the Hindu community immigrated from Surinam in the 1970s. There has never been anything particularly right-wing in the voting behaviour of these Hindus, and Fortuyn was not really a rightist anyway, but they certainly were ready to sympathize with the first politician to speak out against the more unpleasant aspects of Islam.

Another group that combines liberalism and anti-Islamism is the growing circle of enlightened apostate Muslims. Unlike in India, in Muslim countries it takes a lot of courage to be a secularist. It is these brave champions of freedom and humanist values who are shot in the back by the slanderous identification of anti-Islamic positions with "fascism". To be sure, these Muslim-born liberals probably don't hate their compatriots who have not yet outgrown Islam (though in many cases, it is painful personal experiences with true Muslims that made them question the faith in the first place), but that makes little difference. Indian "secularists" treat any and every criticism of Islam, no matter how experience-based, no matter how factual or scholarly, no matter how humanist and liberal, as "hate" and "fascism".

4.3. The perennial Aryans

The following sentences appear to be an attempt by Mira Kamdar to reinterpret her father's anti-racist sarcasms as actually an expression of secret Nazi sympathies, which in turn are implicitly linked to his anti-Muslim feelings: "More boldly, and more rarely, he would allude to the Nazis' linkage of Indians with Germans in one vast Aryan family. I always took these remarks to be tongue-in-cheek observations that no one, least of all my father, really believed, remarks designed more to provoke than to express his true views."

The key phrase concerns Whites and Indians jointly being "Aryans". Since the mere mention of the term "Aryan" tends to cause hysteria in the general public, and utter confusion among Indian secularists, a little explanation is in order. According to the Aryan Invasion Theory (AIT), cherished by British colonialists, Nazis and Indian secularists alike, and questioned by a variety of scholars as well as by the present generation of Hindutva activists, much of the Indian population is of "Aryan" or effectively of European origin, immigrated through Central Asia into India in the 2nd millennium BC. In the early 20th century, this theory was used by some Indian emigrants in demanding equal rights with Europeans on grounds of common ancestry or racial identity, both in South Africa and in the United States. While racial equality for all was still considered a long shot, the more limited goal of lifting Indians out of the "coloured" and into the "Aryan" or "White" category did seem feasible, at least rhetorically if not legally. That is why Mira's father had a point in turning the concept "Aryan" against its White originators by using it to claim equality.

Her Soviet-style willingness to denounce her father and think the worst of him is chilling in itself. But she need have no doubts that his use of the expression was indeed "tongue-in-cheek", for he clearly didn't seriously accept the notion of "Aryan" as a racial concept. It had nothing to do with any secret Nazi convictions, much less with his opinion about Muslims.

4.4. Hate, the concept

That opinion, we are told, amounts to nothing less than hate: "So it has been a great and sad shock to me to realize that my father, who loved Martin Luther King, hates Muslims. He hates them blindly, viscerally, categorically. (...) in any discussion where Muslims, the Middle East, Bosnia (not to mention Pakistan) comes up, he is wont to fly into an apoplectic rage, turn red in the face, shout until spit begins to pool at the sides of his mouth, shake his fists. The culmination of these fits is always the same. He bends over, seizes the cuff of the right leg of his pants, and pulls it up to show off a series of diagonal dents marching up his shin, scars from a back-alley encounter decades ago with a gang of bicycle-chain-wielding Muslim youths. 'This is what Muslims did to me! This is what Muslims do!'"

Here it is said without ambiguity: this man hates Muslims because he personally suffered under Muslim aggression. No Hindutva indoctrination needed, just a lesson from reality. This is not to say that hatred, even if based in real experience, should be condoned. But hatred is an emotional category, not a political one. I hope we won't deny a rape victim the right to hate her rapist. It might be desirable if she managed to rise above this emotional reaction, forgiveness being the cardinal

Christian virtue, but it is not something we can demand of her. It would have been magnanimous of Mr. Kamdar to rise above his vengeful feelings against his Muslim assailants, but his daughter is in no position to condemn him for failing to do so. As long as his hatred doesn't lead him to violence or other illegal behaviour, his hatred is purely a matter of freedom of opinion.

Likewise, most Hindus have generally restrained the expression of their indignation and even of their hatred to verbal utterances between relatives and neighbours, or in letters to the editor, rather than physically taking it out on Muslims. What is always overlooked in a discussion of the Gujarat carnage, is how exceptional this type of Hindu retaliation to a Muslim act of aggression (the Godhra pogrom, cfr. infra) turns out to be once we take a larger perspective. There was no Hindu retaliation to the Mumbai bomb blasts of March 1993; to the numerous group killings of Hindus in Jammu and Kashmir; to the mass killing of Hindu activists in Coimbatore in February 1998; to the frequent reports of pogroms on Hindus in Bangladesh; or to the attacks on the Parliament buildings in Srinagar and Delhi in the autumn of 2001. Even the Gujarat carnage remained confined to a few cities in one state, and when Islamic terrorists killed more than thirty Gujarati Hindu worshippers in the Akshardham temple in Gandhinagar only a few months later, there was no Hindu retaliation, in accordance with the old pattern. By and large, Hindus have shown remarkable self-restraint in the face of violent provocation, a fact for which they are given insufficient credit. Likewise, even Mira Kamdar's father, for all the intense resentment attributed to him by his daughter, is not reported to have taken any kind of revenge upon the community he is said to hate so much.

However, one intellectual failing in Mr. Kamdar's opinion as conveyed by his daughter is the sweeping generalization implicit in it. From what a handful of Muslims did to him, he deduced that "this is what Muslims do", i.e.

Muslims in general, all Muslims. This is an unwarranted leap of logic, and a dangerous one too. In his case, it apparently hasn't led him to taking out his anger on other Muslims, but in many other cases, that is precisely what happens: numerous communal riots in India start with Muslim goondas attacking Hindus, followed by (the affected as well as other) Hindus retaliating not against the original aggressors but against any Muslim in sight.

But Mira Kamdar thinks there is more to the latest rioting than an expression of pent-up resentment finally boiling over: "Until quite recently, I believed my father's hatred of Muslims to be a particular affliction, the result of an attack whose emotional scars go far deeper than the physical ones. I realized in 1992–93, when Hindu-Muslim riots raged throughout India in the wake of the destruction of the Babri Masjid (mosque) in Ayodhya by Hindu militants, that my father's views were, if not a universal plague, at least a widespread distemper. A decade later in 2002, it has become chillingly clear that Hindu-Muslim conflict in India is no longer — if it ever was — a natural malady, the unfortunate inheritance of an ancient people beset by too much history and too many conquerors: it has become a weapon of political engineering wielded by Hindu militant leaders bent on transforming India from the secular democracy its founders envisioned 55 years ago into a Hindu religious state, sanitized of Muslims and other minority groups."

This is a fashionable view, but it is given here without any evidence. It is quite unclear how in the past decade, something has happened to disprove the impression created by Mira Kamdar's father, viz. that Hindu hatred of Muslims is the reaction to a deep scar based in real experiences of Muslim violence. The causes of communal feelings haven't really changed since 1992. Talk to the average Bajrang Dal activist or Shiv Sena voter, and you will verify that the hatred is real, but that it is most certainly "the unfortunate inheritance of an ancient people beset by too much history and too many conquerors". Even a more restrained observer like V.S. Naipaul gives precisely that reason for his view that India is a "wounded civilization" and for his concomitant criticism of Islam as an alienating and destructive force. In very many cases, Hindus also have personal experiences which directly explain their hatred of Muslims,— which admittedly is true of many Muslims vis-à-vis Hindus as well. I have interacted with and taken interviews of numerous Hindutva activists and leaders in the past fifteen years, and one constant among those who expressed anti-Muslim views (by no means all of them) was the reference to actual Muslim aggression, whether during Partition or in Kashmir or in local communal confrontations.

This is not to deny that some politicians, by no means only of Hindutva parties, may have whipped up these pre-existing emotions in specific contexts where communal polarization seemed useful to them. But to explain the widespread negative feelings of Hindus about Muslims as the effect of politicians' propaganda amounts to a far-fetched conspiracy theory.

4.5. The Hindutva programme

Hindu nationalism is accused of aiming at "transforming India from the secular democracy its founders envisioned 55 years ago into a Hindu religious state, sanitized of Muslims and other minority groups". But in fact, the BJP has never included anything of this kind in any of its programmatic statements, quite the reverse. Its 5-year performance in government confirms the truth of its statements: it has not even expelled any of the millions of illegal immigrants from Bangladesh, something which is perfectly within its legal power to do (every sovereign state by definition reserves itself the right to control the access to its territory); let alone the legitimate Muslim citizens of India.

But a polemicist can always circumvent such refutation by the facts: "The BJP plays the role of the moderate, mainstream entity, friendly to multinational capital and mature enough to lead India onto the global stage of the great powers, against the RSS's frankly fascist youth corps activities, the VHP's worldwide propaganda machine, and the Bajrang Dal's street-level enforcement and terror gangs."

So now the BJP is no longer accused of Muslim-cleansing, but the party is part of a broader network with a division of labour, so that it can leave the truly dirty jobs to other affiliates of the network. However, even "the Bajrang Dal terror-gangs" haven't expelled any Muslims from India. Of course, the secularists can then fall back on their next line, which is that of a "threat", a prediction that after further radicalization, this is what the Hindutva forces will do. If today the facts stand in the way of their alarmist thesis, tomorrow will prove them right, *mañana mañana*... But meanwhile, the stark fact is that the continuous trickle of Hindu refugees from Pakistan and Bangladesh is not reciprocated by a symmetrical phenomenon of Muslim flight from India. On the contrary, even in BJP-ruled India, even in Mumbai a.k.a. Shiv Sena City, there is a continuous influx of Bangladeshi Muslim fortune-seekers. They vote with their feet to refute Mira Kamdar's alarmist stories.

For half a century, all official statements of the BJP and its predecessor Jana Sangh have emphasized that the party does not want to "transform India from the secular democracy its founders envisioned 55 years ago into a Hindu religious state", but that, on the contrary, it wants genuine secularism. Rather than being a hollow slogan, this position is articulated in the form of precise proposals for reform of an impeccably and undeniably secularist nature. Thus, the proposed abolition of the special status of Kashmir (Art. 370 of the Constitution) is nothing but the abolition of a religion-based privilege: no Hindu-majority state enjoys the special privileges accorded to Muslim-majority Kashmir. Likewise, any genuine secularist would abolish the existing anti-Hindu legal discriminations in matters of temple and school management and the subsidizing or taxing of pilgrimages.

The BJP proposal to enact a Common Civil Code in replacement of the existing religion-based Personal Law systems is the very quintessence of secularism. Today, contrary to Mira Kamdar's claim, India is not a secular state, for unlike genuinely secular states, India has no equality before the law regardless of religion. Thus, getting a divorce is extremely difficult for a Christian, is a matter for judicial proceedings in the case of Hindus or of Muslim women, and is the unilateral exercise of an unfettered right of repudiation in the case of a Muslim man. What the BJP wants is to bring India in line with the secular states of the world by enacting a common law equally applying to all citizens. The qualification of the self-styled secularists as "pseudo-secularists" is definitely justified by the fact that they support the continuation of legal religion-based discrimination all while vilifying the only political force willing to secularize Personal Law.

4.6. The Godhra carnage

In her paper, Mira Kamdar defends the well-known position of a fraction in India's ideological landscape which calls itself "secularist". It will be clear by now that this so-called "secularism" is a deeply flawed political identity, but I will give Ms. Kamdar credit for being rather more even-handed in her presentation than is common in secularist sources. Thus, she writes:

"On February 27, a train carrying Hindu militants back from a trip to Ayodhya, where they had gone to press anew for the construction of a temple on the site of the razed Babri mosque, stopped in the small town of Godhra, near Ahmedabad, in Gujarat. What happened next is not entirely clear, except for the fact that a Muslim mob set fire to the train, killing 58 people, mostly women and children."

Most Hindutva sources, searchable on the internet but otherwise quite unreported in the Western media, have emphasized that most victims were "women and children", implying a big question-mark over the description of the Godhra victims as "militants". Because of this inconvenient implication, most authors propagating the "secularist" viewpoint before ignorant Western audiences have simply left out the detail that the victims were "mostly women and children", so as to make the allegation of "militancy" more credible, along with the justifying suggestion that those fanatics had it coming to them. Well, it is to Ms. Kamdar's credit that she didn't play this game of deception. But it weakens her plea against Hindutva, for it amounts to an admission that the whole Gujarat carnage started with innocent Hindus being victimized. And in the blame game, it remains crucial which side is in a position to say: "You started it!"

Just how crucial, is illustrated by Mira Kamdar's attempt, later on, to depict the Muslim participation in the subsequent riots as "retaliatory", a characterization withheld from the Hindu retaliation: "Once the violence got underway, there were retaliatory attacks by Muslims on Hindus." It all depends at what moment you start counting. That is why many "secularist" references to the Gujarat riots now simply leave the initial Godhra episode unmentioned, just as most secularist accounts of the Mumbai riots of January 1993 pass over the initial Muslim attacks in silence. This is like letting World War II start with the Allied "aggression" in Normandy in 1944, opposed by German "defenders of Europe".

But if in the case of Gujarat the Muslim initiative cannot be denied, it can at least be minimized and even, to some extent, justified: "Conspiracy theories aside, when a trainload of Hindu militants stops in a Muslim area, when taunts and insults begin to fly, it doesn't take much to imagine how the situation can get badly out of control." While this sentence deals with an attack of Muslims on Hindus, note how the author manages to describe the Hindus, and only the Hindus, as "militants". And note that whereas the subsequent Hindu violence is attributed to the VHP, the Bajrang Dal, Chief Minister Narendra Modi and other named agents, the initial Muslim attack is not ascribed to conscious agents but reduced to an impersonal fact of life: "insults begin to fly", "the situation gets out of control". It seems that jihad really is the work of Heaven, not of man.

4.7. A pre-planned butchery ?

"Everyone expected some kind of act of revenge. Attacks and counterattacks between Hindus and Muslims are nothing new in Gujarat. No one doubted that some Muslims were going to pay with their lives for the Hindu lives lost. But few anticipated what happened next. (...) Truckloads of Hindus, mostly young men — many sporting headbands in saffron, the Hindu sacred color — headed for Muslim neighbourhoods. They were armed not only with homemade gasoline bombs, trishuls (the trident-shaped weapon associated with the god Shiva), and knives but also, in some cases, with printouts from government computer databases listing the names and addresses of Muslims and Muslim-owned businesses. (...) Muslim homes and businesses were looted, and then the buildings and often the dismembered bodies of the former occupants were set on fire. Neighboring Hindu homes and businesses were spared. (...) It was evident that state and local authorities not only did nothing to stop the violence but were actually complicit in orchestrating the attacks. (...) This was no spontaneous eruption of Hindu righteous outrage too deep to be suppressed, as the VHP would have it. (...) This was ethnic cleansing, designed by Hindu extremists to purge Gujarat of Muslims."

Assuming that the claim of rioters using governmental population data is correct, there is no reason to deduce that the riots were organized by a government agency, much less that they were "pre-planned" in the sense of having been planned in advance of the Godhra pogrom. It suffices that one government employee, in defiance of the rules, sent an e-mail divulging governmental data to some militant friends, and the same evening riot parties could take to the streets with weapons in one hand and the printout in the other.

But we may agree that there was planning involved, in this sense that the violence was not inflicted blindly but was carefully aimed at Muslims and Muslim property. At this point, we must agree with Mira Kamdar, both in acknowledging the capacity for violence in some Hindutva circles and in unreservedly condemning the initiative to riot. I have often listened with amazement and disgust to your typical Gujarati Bania (trader) who, after affirming Gandhian platitudes about the "equal truth of all religions", waxes eloquent on how "Muslims should be taught a lesson". It is hardly surprising that their unreflected and simplistic anger would at some point boil over into an actual carnage.

In my opinion, part of the reason for this is the total rejection, both by secularists and Hindutva organizations, of any critical study of religions. The superficial approach, typical of secularism and equally practised by the would-be secularists of the BJP, merely sees Muslims staging a pogrom in Godhra. The more sophisticated approach makes the distinction between the Indians who commit the carnage and the ideology which has estranged them from and turned them against their fellow-countrymen, viz. Islam. Either you realize that the problem is not Muslims but Islam and you subject that doctrine to the appropriate critique (criticism of religion being the very start of any criticism, according to Karl Marx), or you shield Islam from criticism and remain stuck with the naked fact that the perpetrators of the Godhra pogrom were Muslims. The superficial flattering blather about Islam being a "noble faith" and "a path leading to the same goal" as Hinduism (Gandhi), about "genuine Islam" being a "religion of peace" (secularism) or a respectable form of "Arab nationalism" later unfortunately "distorted by the Mullahs" (Hindutva), paradoxically leads to the non-comprehension of the Islamic phenomenon and hence to unreflected irrational attitudes and possibly to violent outbursts against Muslims.

But the capacity for violence dormant in the silly chattering of the Indian bourgeoisie is by no means confined to Hindutva or Islamist circles. Mira Kamdar herself reminds us of a secularist instance: "The attacks in Gujarat recalled quite starkly the state-facilitated, retributive attacks on Sikhs in New Delhi following the assassination of former prime minister Indira Gandhi by her Sikh bodyguards in 1984." While Hindutva activists (including the later Prime Minister A.B. Vajpayee in person) tried to save the Sikhs, the pogrom was conducted by the youth wing of the Congress Party, secularist par excellence. Three thousand Sikhs killed, that was secularism in action.

Contrary to a very common recent claim, the Gujarat carnage was by no means the biggest-ever since Partition. In death toll it was rivalled, for example, by the Bhagalpur riots of 1989. Yet, there was a new element this time around: "Certainly, the Hindu victims in the train at Godhra and those who perished or lost their homes in the subsequent violence suffered no less horrible fates than Muslim victims. These attacks are as indefensible as any other, and are to be condemned. The critical difference, however, is that there was no state complicity in Muslim attacks on Hindus."

But this remains an open question. A number of private agencies, mostly foreign-based and foreign-funded, have made and propagated the allegation of "state complicity", and I don't want to rule out that they may be right. However, India happens to be a democracy with separation of powers, with a judiciary that has often proven its independence from the government of the day. As an elitist and essentially despotic movement (claiming to know better than the backward masses what is good for them), Indian secularism is naturally ill at ease with democracy, which it decries as "populism", "demagoguery" or "majoritarianism" when convenient. But much as secularist polemicists would like to privatize justice and bypass the official judiciary, only the existing courts are empowered to pass judgment on whether or not the Gujarat state government was an accomplice in the riots. In the Ayodhya temple/mosque affair, where the courts have been dragging the case for more than fifty years now, the secularists have always told the Hindus to be patient and abide by the court verdict. In the present case, there is no dearth of agencies willing to take the Modi government to court, and then it is up to them to exercise patience and wait for the judicial verdict.

4.8. Adivasi participation

The "tribal" question is another reality check for the intellectual grip of the secularists on the communal problem: "For the first time as well, large numbers of Adivasi tribals participated in the attacks. (India terms indigenous ethnic groups who do not traditionally practice Hinduism or any other of the country's main religions and who have no place in the Hindu caste hierarchy 'tribals'.) They were trucked into target areas and plied with liquor to put them in the right ransacking mood. For some years, the VHP and other allied groups of the Sangh Parivar have been working to convert the tribals, who have their own animistic beliefs, to Hinduism and enlist them in anti-Muslim efforts. In Gujarat, Adivasis were reportedly used against the Muslim moneylenders to whom they were indebted, in order to eliminate the competition for local Hindu moneylenders."

A series of allegations is made here which are all in need of proof. Clearly, secularists doubt the capacity of tribals to make their own decisions, even consequential decisions such as participating in pitched battles with Muslims. While Hindus are wily manipulators with an agenda of their own, tribals have to be "plied with liquor" before acting. In reality, enmity between tribals and Muslims is a long-standing sociological phenomenon, based on deep cultural differences (including a propensity among tribals to eat pork and drink the liquor already mentioned, unclean practices from a Muslim viewpoint) and de facto conflicts of interests, including the said problems with moneylenders. One such objective conflict of interests is the settlement of illegal Bangladeshi immigrants on tribal lands, which in 1983 in the Northeastern district of Nellie led to clashes between native tribals (many of them Christians) and Muslim settlers, exacting a death toll of thousands. In 2002, Christian tribals in Nagaland organized in the *National Socialist Council of Nagalim* have decreed that no further Muslim encroachment on their land, nor attempts by Muslims to marry tribal women, will be tolerated, the penalty being death. So, tribal-Muslim clashes are nothing new and don't necessarily require the intervention of Hindutva agitators.

At some point in most debates on Indian religions, secularists with Hindu names will claim the right to speak as Hindus and to be judges of what "real" Hinduism is, as against the Hindutva fanatics who have "hijacked Hinduism for their own un-Hindu purposes". But let them continue, and you will find that they are unable to pass even the simplest test of knowledge of Indian religions. Typically, they will display all the misunderstandings which people from a Christian background bring to the debate, projecting categories from Western religious history onto the Indian situation. Case in point: Mira Kamdar claims that the VHP is "working to convert the tribals, who have their own animistic beliefs, to Hinduism". This is purely a projection onto the Indian socio-religious continuum of the typically Christian division of mankind into box-like groupings defined by separate belief systems, with one trying to swallow or destroy the other through conversion of its adherents.

India never had the notion that "tribal animism" and "Hinduism" were separate religions. Hinduism itself has been described (e.g. in the preamble to the 1901 Census Report) as "animism refined by metaphysics". To Muslims and Christians, even the most isolated and least "sanskritized" Indian tribals are Heathens of the same hell-bound kind as Hindus: idol-worshipping polytheists unfamiliar with Mohammed c.q. Jesus. When the Muslim invaders introduced the Persian term *Hindu* (originally a purely geographical term, "Indian"), they applied it to all native religionists, to all Indian Pagans, from Brahmins and Buddhists to tribal "animists", precisely because the most important religious trait was one which they had all in common, viz. their unbelief in prophetic monotheism. The relevant definition of "tribal" is not by belief system but by sociological and geographical position.

Even then, it is not true that the tribals, or rather *Aṯavika*-s, "forest-dwellers" (modern *Vanavāsī*-s, "forest-dwellers", or in Gandhi-speak *Girijan*-s, "hill people"), "have no place in the Hindu caste hierarchy". Traditional Hindu society was conceived as a number of concentric circles, with the narrowest circles comprising the Vedic specialists, the next one the higher castes collectively, then the whole population in so far as it abided by basic Vedic norms such as the taboo on cow-slaughter, and finally the whole of India including marginal groups not observing Vedic purity rules: people performing unclean professions or suspected of having loose sexual morals, eating beef etc. Even at worst, the tribals at least fall within the last circle, peripheral but certainly part of Hindu society. In particular, the institution of caste, which secularists obsessively identify with Hinduism, is an essential feature of Indian tribal life. A tribe is an endogamous group, the very definition of caste. Indeed, it has been observed (by Dr. Bhimrao Ambedkar among many others) that caste is nothing but the continuation in literate Hindu society of tribal identities: as tribes all over India got integrated into the expanding Vedic civilization originating in India's Northwest, they retained their collective identities as endogamous groups. The traditional Hindu term for both castes and tribes is *jāti*, "birthgroup", while the first British colonizers used the term "tribe" for both tribes and castes, e.g. the "Brahmin tribe".

What VHP workers perform in tribal communities is not "conversion", meaning the abandonment of one religion for another, but that which sociologists have called "sanskritization". The basic structure of existing tribal religiosity is left intact: ritualism, respect for the sacred, the enacted concentration of the sacred into specific objects (sacred trees, stones, idols) for worshipping purposes, these are all practices familiar to tribals as much as to Sanskritic Hindus. Into this basic religiosity, more advanced philosophical notions and values, such as meditation and non-attachment, are infused, just as they once had to be injected into the more naturalistic culture of the Vedic kings by the first seers and renunciates. The ritual and doctrinal continuity between tribal "animism" and Vedic tradition is given a practical application by the conjunction of tribal tradition with Sanskritic culture in the schools which Hindu organizations have opened in tribal areas. "Conversion" in the real sense of the term is only performed as the undoing of a previous conversion from tribal Hinduism to Christianity. These much-publicized cases of conversion are called "home-coming" (*ghar-vāpasī*), because unlike in conversions to Christianity, the people concerned are not abandoning their native religion but are returning to it.

Contrary to what Mira Kamdar intimates, the term "tribal" is by no means a Hindu imposition; it is of course a Western colonial coinage, of the same vintage as "secularism" and "conversion". The same is true of the term she innocently uses to designate the tribals, viz. *ādivāsī*, "aboriginal", a term which falsely implies that non-tribals are not indigenous, or at least less indigenous than tribals. In many cases, the implication of tribal indigenousness is also untrue, e.g. the most separatist tribes in the Northeast, the christianized Nagas and Mizos, only immigrated into their present habitat from the East in the Middle Ages, quite late by Indian standards. Even the Munda-speaking tribals in Chotanagpur are generally considered pre-Harappan-age immigrants from Indochina, still the demographic point of gravity of their Austro-Asiatic language family. And the Dravidians are traced back by various scholars to Elam, Central Asia or even Africa, immigrating into India only in the early Harappan age. If the much-maligned Aryans perforce have to be described as "invaders", they are not the only ones, nor even the most recent ones.

At any rate, unlike the secularists, the Christian missionaries were always very clever and well-informed in religious matters, and in order to indigenize their divisive categorization of the Indian population, they invented the pseudo-indigenous Sanskrit neologism *ādivāsī*. All by itself, this little word became one of the most brilliantly successful disinformation campaigns in modern history, falsely planting the novel notion of an aboriginal/invader antagonism into all thinking about the tribal condition. And no one is more susceptible to lapping up such false notions, provided they serve an anti-Hindu purpose, as are the secularists with their gross illiteracy in all matters religious and Indian.

4.9. Rape and rumours

Mira Kamdar is right in condemning the role played by ugly rumours in generating the sparks that set cities aflame: "The threat of the violation of women is a reliable way to fire up Hindu-Muslim passions. One of the reasons given for the Muslim mob attacking the train at Godhra was the rumor of the 'molestation' and 'abduction' of a girl by Hindus on board. Following the attack on the train, the vernacular press in Gujarat ran incendiary headlines, one of which accused Muslims of lopping off Hindu women's breasts."

Yes, no words are strong enough to condemn the irresponsible rumour-mongering by the media. This includes the false allegations against Hindus in the *Times of India* or the *Washington Post* as much as the cruder below-the-belt allegations against the other community in the vernacular press, whether Urdu or Gujarati.

But Mira Kamdar is not very careful in her choice of sources. She quotes someone who clearly hasn't heard of the terrible treatment of women in the Partition carnage or, during his own adult life, in the Bangladesh war: "'I have never known a riot which has used the sexual subjugation of women so widely as an instrument of violence as in the recent barbarity in Gujarat', wrote Harsh Mander, a senior Indian Civil Service Officer who resigned his post in disgust." The number of women raped by the Pakistani army and its fundamentalist collaborators in Bangladesh in 1971 is usually estimated as 250,000, of whom many were raped dozens of times. Did our expert on communalism really not know about this?

And this is not the only thing wrong with her source. For in the meantime, the truth about Harsh Mander's "resignation" has come out. Rather than resigning and forfeiting his pension, he merely took early retirement, retaining his rights and pension. Not such a terrible sacrifice for a man employed by a wealthy British NGO, Action Aid, and serving its politico-communal agenda. He is a telling example of all those private judges insinuating themselves into the debates and investigations concerning the communal confrontation, such as "Human Rights Watch, the European Union, the British High Commission, the Citizens' Initiative of Ahmedabad, the Editor's Guild of India, Communalism Combat, Amnesty International, and India's own National Human Rights Commission", all those human-rights champions who never noticed the ethnic cleansing of Hindus from Kashmir but savour their testimony of Muslim suffering in Gujarat no end.

While we are on the subject of the Hindu-cleansing in Kashmir, this is how Mira Kamdar reports the matter: "In the late 1980s, Kashmiri Muslim political frustration erupted into a violent insurgency. The state's Hindus, who were the targets of Muslim anger, fled en masse." And she goes on to quote with approval: "'With the resurgence of the Kashmir crisis and the migration of Hindus, Hindu nationalism received a new political impetus', according to Varshney." As if the Hindus made a choice to "migrate", as if their "fleeing" was a personal decision and not the result of a concerted and deliberate Pak-backed Muslim campaign. But what is innocuously called a "migration" in the case of Kashmiri Hindus, is grimly called "genocide" in the case of Gujarati Muslims.

4.10. Gandhi

"Gujarat is also the birthplace of Mohandas Gandhi, the father of independent India and the founder of a powerful political movement based on ahimsa, or nonviolence. My own grandfather — like the grandfathers of many of the young men who participated in the killing and looting in Gujarat, no doubt — was a devoted follower of Gandhi. Gandhi stood resolutely for a secular India and for tolerance — even love — for upper-caste Hindu society's outcasts: untouchables, Muslims, landless peasants, dispossessed factory workers. His murder by a Hindu extremist discredited the RSS and the Hindu militant movement for decades. But, like the phoenix, the Hindu right has risen from the ashes of Hindu-Muslim conflict in Gujarat stronger than ever."

Indian "secularist" discourse frequently relapses into the premodern stage, where rational thought could be blocked with magical formulas. One very popular power mantra to switch off the critical faculty is "Gandhi". At least for use against Hindus, since nobody holds it against secularists like Nehru that they betrayed Gandhi in every respect, e.g. the Mahatma's insistence on economic and cultural Swadeshi, his opposition to industrialization and to the deployment of a combat-worthy army, his anti-secular emphasis on the role of religion in politics. But Hindus are expected to swallow their every argument once the name Gandhi is invoked against it.

In defiance of this secularist magic, I propose we use our critical faculty and investigate Gandhi's own role in the Gujarat carnage. It is very simple and clear-cut: by going to one extreme with enormous intensity and then failing miserably, he triggered a movement towards the other extreme. With all his soul-force, Gandhi could only make Hindus and British liberals desist from violence. He failed with the Moplahs (who killed or forcibly converted Hindus in Kerala during the Khilafat agitation in 1921) and with the Muslim League, or rather, he didn't even try. It is one thing to perform a "miracle" in Calcutta during Partition, making Hindus desist from killing Muslims, but it would have been quite another and much more spectacular miracle to stop the much more massive killing of Hindus and Sikhs in West Panjab. In the event, Gandhiji didn't try to stop it. Instead, he told Hindu refugees in Delhi to go back to West Panjab and voluntarily get killed there.

This extreme case of double standards, and the abdication by the Mahatma of his original commitment to stake his life in preventing Partition, is what made Nathuram Godse decide to assassinate him. Most Hindus, including the leadership of the Hindu Mahasabha and the RSS, had never considered physically punishing Gandhiji for his failure in stopping Partition and the concomitant carnage. However, they did retain a deep scar and a resolve to avoid repeating Gandhi's mistake. Though paying lip-service to Gandhi's memory and though temperamentally at home in the Gandhian spirit of compromise, even Gandhi's own community of Gujarati Bania-s has grown weary of the policy of "appeasement". Under the blows of frequent Muslim pestering, such as the petty terror which drove Hindus out of certain neighbourhoods in Ahmedabad (as attested by a state law prohibiting inter-community sales of real estate in the wake of communal riots, a law routinely circumvented by Muslim mafia dons using stooges), they developed a strong resentment which finally boiled over after the Godhra pogrom.

Had Gandhi piloted a grown-up approach to peace-keeping, including the formula of "peace through strength" implicitly applied by most democratic governments, his principles would still be used as guidelines in controlling communal conflicts. Instead, his extremism in insisting on meekness and refusing any and every application of force against bullies backfired and helped to generate an extremism in the opposite direction: a loose readiness to take to arms on slender pretexts.

4.11. A gift from heaven

Concerning the danger posed by Hindu nationalism, Mira Kamdar engages a rival viewpoint within her secularist spectrum of opinion: "Ashutosh Varshney, a political science professor at the University of Michigan, thinks a Hindu extremist takeover of India at the national level is highly unlikely."

What follows next is an interesting discussion of a reassuring thesis developed by Varshney in his book *Ethnic Conflict and Civic Life: Hindus and Muslims in India* (Yale University Press, 2002). But our attention is drawn more strongly by something truly weird in the introductory sentence just quoted. As late as 2002, Varshney wrote, in Mira Kamdar's paraphrase, that "a Hindu extremist takeover of India at the national level is highly unlikely",— four years after a BJP-led coalition came to power. Between the BJP's electoral breakthrough in 1989 (from 2 to 86 seats in the Lok Sabha) and its coming to power in 1998, there had been no end of warnings about the terrible things which a "Hindu extremist" BJP government would do: abolish democracy, throw the Muslims into the Arabian Sea, open gas chambers, organize mass sati, restore untouchability, crucify the missionaries, what not. After all, once you called them "Hindu fascists", such predictions followed with impeccable logic.

But none of those things materialized. Consider democracy: Hitler came to power at the head of a coalition government, just like A.B. Vajpayee, and within a year he had neutralized parliament and assumed dictatorial powers. The BJP, by contrast, after losing a confidence vote in 1999 by a margin of one, submitted to the will of the people and called new elections. On the Hindu-Muslim riots front, things remained as quiet as they had been in the preceding years (from March 1993 onwards), i.e. at a much more peaceful level than in the 1980s under Congress rule. By contrast, terrorism continued unabated. But the ones lethally targeted with great frequency by terrorists were Hindus, mostly by Kashmir-related "militants" (to use the approved secularist term) and less conspicuously also by Christian separatists in the Northeast and Communist guerrilla bands in the interior. So, the facts after a few years of BJP rule were crystal-clear: the main victims of religious violence were Hindus and there were no BJP gas chambers for Muslims. The whole anti-Hindutva industry was secretly facing acute embarrassment by the utter failure of its predictions to come true.

To offset this failure, critics of the BJP tried to make the most of a supposed wave of minor incidents between Hindu tribals and Christians in 1998-2000. There were only a handful of mortal victims, far fewer than the dozens of Christians killed in Pakistan after September 11, 2001, but with the media as amplifiers, an impression of terrible oppression of a poor hapless minority was created. Unfortunately (or rather, fortunately), the key allegations made initially under the international spotlights turned out to be untrue. Yes, an Australian missionary and his two sons died in an arson incident, but neither the governmental inquiry nor the judicial investigation could confirm the eager secularist indictment of the Bajrang Dal. Yes, four nuns in Jhabua were raped, but no Hindu activists were involved: it was an inter-tribal and inter-Christian affair. Yes, a Christian teenage girl and her little brother were assaulted, but the man turned out to be a Christian himself. Indeed, this turned out to be a pattern: all inter-Christian incidents in this period, including those between the older, quieter churches (Syrian,

Catholic, Anglican) and the intruding American fundamentalist sects, were suddenly blamed on the evil hand of the Hindus.

This game of blaming the Hindus for the suffering of Christians was so successful that it inspired a third party to try its own hand at it. A series of bomb attacks against churches in South India did take place, wounding some worshipers. It was duly blamed on the Hindutva forces, but the perpetrators turned out to be a Pak-based Muslim organization, the Deendar Anjuman. Please note the chain of guilt here: the Islamic terrorists are of course responsible for their own acts, yet they would not have committed these but for the encouragement given to them by the secularists. After all, the latter had proven that any unpleasant incident can successfully be blamed on the Hindus, and that the blame could not be washed off by any amount of official refutation, which would remain under-reported while the original allegation would go on being repeated. This way, the secularists have blood on their hands, viz. the blood of the Christian victims of these Islamic bomb attacks.

In each of these cases, the original allegations against Hindus were splashed across the front pages in India and also reported in the world press, whereas the true story, once it came out, was reported on an inside page in India and not at all abroad. Even then, Christian spokesman John Dayal repeated the discredited allegations before the US Commission on International Religious Freedom, and they keep on reappearing in secularist sources. I am not aware of a single secularist who publicly withdrew the allegations and offered apologies for his slander to the maligned Hindus. Nor of one who has drawn attention to Christian violence against Hindus in the same period, such as the abduction of four RSS activists by Christian separatists in Tripura (the four dead bodies were found two years later) or the ethnic cleansing of the Hindu Riang tribe from Christian-majority Mizoram. Even so, the propaganda line of Hindu violence against Christians is no longer pursued with the same vigour, partly because its proponents seem to be embarrassed by their crying wolf a few times too often, and partly because it remains a relatively small affair even if all the allegations had been true.

So, when the dust had settled, it became clear that the BJP government still hadn't put any minority into gas chambers. Therefore, to the anti-Hindutva campaigners, the Gujarat carnage came as a God-sent. After four years of waiting in vain for some serious BJP atrocities, at long last they could go in to photograph charred Muslim bodies and point accusing fingers at BJP politicians. The new secularist party-line was, quite realistically, that the BJP contained a moderate faction, in power in Delhi, as well as an extremist faction, best represented by Gujarat Chief Minister Narendra Modi. All the predictions formerly made about "the" BJP could now be revived as applying to the extremist faction within the BJP. And given Modi's landslide victory during the Gujarat state elections following the riots, it stood to reason that the Modi wing represented the wave of the future within the BJP. Whether that will mean more violence or just the opposite (e.g. a firm elimination of "militancy" in Kashmir) remains to be seen; and unlike Mira Kamdar, I will not hazard a prediction.

4.12. Pakistan

Though the Nehruvian state was always obsessed with the evil "foreign hand" (mostly meaning the USA), its votaries have no patience with Hindutva spokesmen raising the same bogey, especially when Pakistan is meant: "But the claim that Pakistan ordered the attack at Godhra is unproved and, in my view, has little credibility."

Along with Mira Kamdar, I am rather skeptical of allegations against a Pakistani hand behind communal riots, though it must be kept in mind that the Gujarat riots have indeed worked greatly to Pakistan's advantage. If we follow the criterion of *"Cui prodest?"* ("Who benefits?"), then Pakistan is the most likely culprit. Anti-Indian and pro-Pakistani lobbyists in Washington D.C., with the help of NRI secularists, have made the most of the Gujarat affair in order to counterbalance the fact of Islamic terrorism with the notion of "Hindu terrorism", this in order to prevent the post-9/11 indignation from serving India's and hurting Pakistan's cause. Yet, it does remain unlikely that the Pakistani Inter Services Intelligence has masterminded the Godhra carnage. But that estimation is not typically secularist, nor is its opposite typically Hindutva, on the contrary.

A reasoned anti-Islamic position would consider Pakistan as merely one realization of the Indian Muslim mind, a mentality which has remained active inside India even after Partition. Hence, in this view, there is little difference between organized Indian Islam and the Pakistani state, both being inveterately anti-Hindu and quite capable of terror against Hindus. So, when a crime has been committed by a Muslim, there is no need of claiming a Pakistani (as opposed to Indian) nationality for the culprit. Likewise, the secularist position sees little difference between organized Indian Islam and the Pakistani state: both have legitimate fears about the communal designs of the Hindus and of the Indian state which Hindus dominate, and it is up to the Hindus to be tolerant of Muslim excesses just as it is up to India to accommodate Pakistani intransigence regarding Kashmir.

By contrast, the would-be secularists who fill the leadership positions in the RSS and BJP make a distinction between the Indian Muslims ("Mohammedi Hindus") and the Pakistani state. In order to prove that they have nothing against Muslims, they will bend over backwards in order to formulate any Hindu-Muslim conflict in terms of a conflict between two states, India and Pakistan. In order to exonerate Indian Muslims, they put the blame on Pakistan, the foreign hand. Mind you, the reason behind this insistence on Pakistani guilt is not Hindutva or anti-Islamism, on the contrary: it is attempted secularism, trying to shield the Indian Muslims from suspicion.

4.13. The textbook controversy

Inevitably, Mira Kamdar brings up one of the flashpoints in the struggle between Hindutva and the Marxist-Mullah-Missionary alliance, viz. the textbook controversy: "The shaping of young minds is something the Sangh Parivar takes very seriously. Murli Manohar Joshi, an old RSS hand and India's minister for human resources, wants to 'saffronize' education in India by rewriting history textbooks to reflect Hindutva's version of India's history. Joshi has announced that all new school books will have to be cleared by religious leaders before publication."

What the BJP government claims to offer, what all scholarly historians want, and what is loathed by the Marxists who have dominated the cultural and educational establishment since decades, is *glasnost*: openness, an end to the dead hand of Marxist dogma in Indian history-writing. However, it is quite wrong to say that the Sangh Parivar takes this job "very seriously". It took three years before relieving leading Marxists of their influential positions (Prasar Bharati, NCERT, IHC). Most of its new nominees were not up to the job, some because of ill-health (e.g. K.S. Lal and B.R. Grover, both now deceased), some because they had never functioned in an academic setting. It should not be forgotten that for decades, at least since ca. 1970 when the Marxists led by P.N. Haksar and Nurul Hasan were given a lot of effective power in this sector in return for their support to Indira Gandhi, distinctly non-Marxist young historians found their access to an academic career blocked by the Marxist hegemons. Of the new textbooks, some are impeccable and are welcomed as undeniable improvements, e.g. Meenakshi Jain's presentation of the Muslim period, arguably the most sensitive and controversial part of the series. Some of the others, by contrast, have been criticized or ridiculed even by fair-minded observers.

So far, I am not aware of any of these textbooks having been submitted to the approval of religious leaders. M.M. Joshi's did make such a promise, but his statement to this effect has been pulled out of context. His point was not that henceforth Hindu clerics will decide on the contents of the textbooks so as to privilege the Hindu viewpoint, but precisely the opposite: after some commotion about a denial that Vedic seers ate beef, and after his concession to Sikh pressure in scrapping a negative comment on Guru Govind Singh, he tried to reassure Muslim and Christian critics that not only Hindu and Sikh sensibilities would be respected, but those of all religions. While definitely an improvement in the application of Indian "secularist" principles because of its even-handedness, this promise was scandalous from the viewpoint of historical scholarship. Professional source-based historiography should not be submitted to the approval of any outsider, cleric or other.

In a typical display of the RSS disdain for "sterile intellectualism", this promise not only subordinated history-writing to religious pressures but also contradicted a long-held position of the Sangh Parivar in the Ayodhya controversy, viz. that Hindus should know the truth about the thousandfold temple destructions,— information obviously risking to "hurt the sensibilities" of the Muslim community. All in all, Hindutva historiography is not worse than the Marxist variety, the kind taken for granted for decades on end by the same people who now profess such indignation; but it isn't up to the mark either.

To pepper her story and give it a Gujarati angle, Mira Kamdar adds: "In Gujarat, the textbooks have already been rewritten to teach a Hindu-right worldview. Students in Gujarat were asked on this spring's final examination to join the following five phrases in a sentence: 'There are two solutions. One of them is Nazi solution.[sic] If you do not like people, kill them, segregate them. Then strut up and down. Proclaim that you are the salt of the earth.'"

As usual, the secularists take it for granted that once they use the term Nazi (or likewise, Aryan), hysteria will take over and the public will lose its analytical faculty. In this case, they assume that the juxtaposition of the words "Nazi" and "Hindu right" in one paragraph will convince the unattentive reader that the Hindu right is Nazi-inspired and openly acknowledges it. Whether that inference is justified, depends largely on the context of the sentence quoted from (or attributed to) the textbook in question. And since Mira Kamdar, for reasons best known to herself, has withheld that context from us, we are free to speculate about it. Moreover, upon looking more closely, we acquire the impression that we won't even need the context in order to determine the thrust of the quoted sentence. For, what it says is clearly sarcastic: if we could still be led to believe that the Hindutva author wanted to tell us how he himself believes in "killing" and "segregating" as the solution, we do notice the distinctly un-Hindu identity imputed to those who "strut up and down" and "proclaim that [they] are the salt of the earth".

Those are precisely the attitudes which Hindus attribute to the monotheistic faiths. It is Christians who claim to be "the salt of the earth", as told to the apostles by Jesus himself. In Hindutva discourse, self-righteousness is precisely the central vice imputed to the Christian and Islamic conquerors. Moreover, Hindu authors like Girilal Jain and Sita Ram Goel have often made the point that in this key respect, both Marxism and Nazism are but the secularized offspring of Christianity. So, while the quoted sentence may indeed have an anti-Muslim, anti-Christian and anti-Marxist thrust, it is not intended as pro-Nazi, on the contrary: it uses the Nazi reference as the indubitably reprehensible instance of a continuum of self-righteous doctrines which also includes Christianity, Islam and Marxism. And it is these which are deemed to offer as their solution to "kill" and "segregate" and self-righteously "strut up and down" as if being "the salt of the earth". The textbook as quoted by Mira Kamdar, far from propagating this "Nazi" attitude, is actually denouncing it. It implicitly contrasts its own Hindutva with the self-righteousness of its enemies.

4.14. Targeted killings

Can we sense some disappointment in Mira Kamdar's finding that there are no anti-Jewish riots in India, and that the Hindu "hate" against the so-called Semitic religions does not extend to Judaism? Especially in an attempt to equate Hindutva with Nazism, this would have been very useful, but in fact: "There have been no attacks that I know of on Jews in India, a community with a wonderful history in that country going back centuries. This is probably because there are very few Jews left in India in the wake of substantial emigration to Israel. The Jewish community in India has no political clout and no presence as a voting bloc."

Actually, even before the migration to Israel in the 1950s, the Jewish community found in India the only society which never subjected it to persecution. That's quite unlike their experience with countries ruled by Christians and Muslims, Mira Kamdar's darlings. But since the secularists have decreed that "Hindu tolerance is a myth", we had better not repeat this too loudly. India's best-known Jew is a hero to all nationalists: General J.F.R. Jacob, who played a central role in the Indian victory against Pakistan in the Bangladesh war. In 1998, he joined the BJP.

So let's get back to the more eventful Hindu-Muslim relationship. Having discussed the phenomena of street riots and mass terrorism sufficiently for now, let us focus on a third form of communal violence: targeted killings of specified individuals. Like with terrorism, the vast majority of victims in this category of violence have been Hindus. In the months and years after the Mumbai riots of January 1993, a number of Maharashtrian politicians belonging to the BJP and the Shiv Sena have been murdered, mostly by assailants who were never apprehended. In Kerala in the 1990s, dozens of ordinary Hindutva activists have been murdered by the

Communists, the dominant party in that state. When I visited the Hindu Munnani office in Chennai in 1996, the building was really impressive, having just been rebuilt and redesigned after a bomb blast. Shortly after, it was destroyed once more in another bomb blast. In this series of attacks on the Hindu Munnani leadership, several activists were killed. And after the Gujarat carnage, the Gujarat Home Minister, Haren Pandya, was murdered by Muslims.

But Mira Kamdar's sympathies go out to someone who was not killed: the heiress and actress Mallika Sarabhai. She temporarily fled her home (or should we say: "migrated"?) when "Bajrang Dal gangs threatened to kill her and her children". But clearly, she survived these threats, just as historians Romila Thapar and D.N. Jha survived alleged death threats on which the media based grim allegations of "Hindu terrorism". You see, there is a difference between disgruntled people who write angry letters with empty "threats" and assassins who don't bother with threats because they mean business. The latter kind is apparently less interested in secularist icons.

This is what Mira Kamdar wants to share with us about BJP leader L.K. Advani: "The BJP undertook a major reshuffling of cabinet positions this past July. Most notably, Lal Kishenchand Advani, an unrepentant RSS heavyweight who personally led the effort to demolish the Babri Mosque in Ayodhya in 1992 — which ignited bloody Hindu-Muslim riots across India — has been promoted to deputy prime minister."

To any sincere observer, it is obvious that Advani did not "personally lead the effort to demolish the Babri Masjid",— he just stood there flabbergasted and with tears in his eyes when RSS discipline broke down and the crowd joined hands with a group of prepared activists who started the demolition in defiance of the gerontocrats. It is very significant that no one in the Indian English press cared to go for the scoop of the year, viz. revealing the identity of the mastermind behind the demolition. Instead, the whole media establishment abandoned the search for the facts in favour of the politically more useful stand of pinning the blame on the tallest political figure involved: L.K. Advani.

But we cannot include in this paper a discussion of the awkward dishonesty evident throughout secularist reporting, denounced so often and so thoroughly by Arun Shourie and Ramesh Rao. For now, we merely want to draw attention to what Mira Kamdar (in this context, conspicuously) omits about L.K. Advani: that he has survived several attempts on his life. The most spectacular instance took place during an election meeting in Coimbatore in February 1998, where an Islamist bomb attack failed to kill Advani because he arrived late. It did, however, kill forty BJP activists present. Not being wealthy secularists, they had never been put on alert by helpful "threats".

4.15. Things to do for Western governments

NRIs based in the USA can exercise a lot of influence on the Indian situation through their contacts with powerful American interest groups. Some seek to counter the dominant anti-Indian and anti-Hindu tendency in American politics and academe, while others try to strengthen them. The twin facts of Hindutva NRI loyalty to the Indian state and of NRI secularist disloyalty are confirmed off-hand by Mira Kamdar where she reports the testimony of an Indian diplomat in Washington: "One Indian diplomat has been heard to brag, 'I can count only on the BJP and RSS types to deliver on the Hill when we need support concerning some of our issues.'"

In the contemporary geopolitical configuration, the USA seems to have its reasons for humouring the Muslim world, even at the cost of estranging India, otherwise always flattered as a "natural ally" for being "the world's largest democracy". NRI secularists feel at home with this tendency. One of the allies of the secularists in their agitation against BJP-ruled India is Robert Hathaway: "As Robert M. Hathaway, director of the Asia Program at the Woodrow Wilson International Center for Scholars argues, 'Important

American interests, including the global war against terrorism, can be directly impacted by what the U.S. says — and fails to say — about Gujarat. At this particular moment in history, the U.S. cannot allow the impression to take hold that Americans somehow value a Muslim life less than the life of a person of another religion.'"

For those who look at facts rather than at newspaper headlines, it is obvious that there is no danger whatsoever of the US giving the impression of valuing a Muslim life less than a Hindu life. Rather the reverse, and this consistently for decades. In 1971, the Pakistani Army was butchering Hindus in East Bengal by the hundreds of thousands (many times the total number of victims of Hindutva violence since then), yet the USA stood by Pakistan and did nothing to rein their Islamic allies in. Throughout the 1990s and till today, Pak-backed terrorists have been butchering Hindus in numerous shootings and bomb attacks and ethnically cleansing them from the Kashmir Valley, yet the USA have not used their leverage with Pakistan to stop this continuous terror wave. Dr. Hathaway's misrepresentation of this highly unbalanced American policy adds insult to injury.

Mira Kamdar wants to give more body to this unbalanced attitude by making the US and other Western authorities intervene and stop the flow of money to Hindu (but not to Muslim or Christian) organizations in India. For instance: "According to Gautam Appa of the London School of Economics, the two main right-wing Hindu 'charities' in England, the VHP(UK) and the HSS (the RSS's foreign organization) 'collected nearly one million pounds in the last financial year. It is common knowledge that a large chunk of the overt and covert collection ends up in India in the hands of the Sangh Parivar.'"

Perhaps it wasn't known yet at the time of Mira Kamdar's writing, but the VHP(UK) has cooperatively submitted to an official investigation and was cleared by the Charities Commission of these allegations. But in the USA, the struggle continues, as with the Indian leftist action against the Indian

Development and Relief Fund: "Part of an appropriate response by the U.S. government should be to crack down on Hindu-right organizations operating in America that funnel money to the Sangh Parivar. According to Hathaway, 'Credible reports have recently suggested that substantial sums of money are sent from Indians resident in the U.S., and from American citizens of Indian origin, to groups and organizations... that are directly linked to the violence in Gujarat.' Testifying before the U.S. Commission on International Religious Freedom, Hathaway urged the commission to initiate 'an official enquiry into financial transactions of this nature, to ensure that U.S. laws are not being violated'."

In democratic states under the rule of law, governments have no right to harm individuals or organizations on the basis of what interested parties like to pass off as "credible reports". If an organization has been judicially convicted as practising terrorism, then such measures as Dr. Hathaway proposes may be in order. But until then, they would only be an expression of raw political power arbitrarily cracking down on those not favoured by the hegemonic vested interests.

Meanwhile, American Christian Churches are known to fund the conversion of tribals and the subsequent maintenance of christianized communities, some of which have developed separatist and terrorist activities. Given the money power of these Churches and their links with the American political class, checking the destination of American Christian funding in India should be a top priority of US politicians who take the "war on terror" seriously. Indeed, it stands to reason that the financial dependence of outfits like the Tripura National Liberation Front and the National Socialist Council of Nagalim on American funding is near-total. The US government's power to stop Pakistani-supported terrorism is indirect though real; but its power to stop Christian terrorism in India's Northeast is direct and practically complete. However, using this real power in order to stop the real suffering of Indian terror victims doesn't seem to interest Robert Hathaway or Mira Kamdar. As for the Pakistani problem, we again see no sign of an interest on their part in pressurizing the US authorities to make Islamabad stop the jihadic proxy war against India. But at least we should be grateful to the two scholars for making it so clear on what side they are.

4.16. Conclusion

I would like to conclude by apologizing to Mira Kamdar for my uncharitable critique of her paper on "the struggle for India's soul". In terms of the Golden Rule, I must admit I wouldn't like to receive this treatment and am consequently hesitant about signing my name under the present treatment given to her. My only justification for doing so nonetheless is that selfsame Golden Rule. After all, she has levelled terrible allegations against a number of Hindu individuals and groups, from linking her own father with "fascism" to blaming the VHP for nothing less than a "genocide". She seems to expect us to accept such loose hyperbole effectively smearing all kinds of people and inciting hatred against them. Well, if she gives fellow human beings that kind of treatment, she should be ready for a less than flattering response. In the present paper, I myself have tried not to cross the boundaries between critical analysis and loose or exaggerated allegations. But being far from infallible, I offer my apologies in case I did Mira Kamdar and her secularist circle any injustice. At any rate, we can safely conclude in general terms that their conception of secularism, with its excess of zeal and lack of even-handedness, is more a part of the problem than of the solution.

5. Learning from Mahatma Gandhi's mistakes

[This article was written in January 2004, originally as the text for some lectures to the general public in the West.]

Mahatma Gandhi is often praised as the man who defeated British imperialism with non-violent agitation. It is still a delicate and unfashionable thing to discuss his mistakes and failures, a criticism hitherto mostly confined to Communist and Hindutva publications. But at this distance in time, we shouldn't be inhibited by a taboo on criticizing official India's patron saint.

5.1. Gandhiji's mistakes

Without attempting to approach completeness, we may sum up as Gandhi's biggest political failures the following events:

(1) Recruiting Indian soldiers for the British war effort in 1914-18 without setting any conditions, in the vain hope that this unilateral gift to Britain would bring about sufficient goodwill in London for conceding to India the status of a self-ruling dominion within the British Empire, on a par with Canada or Australia. While it was already off line for a pacifist to cooperate in such a wasteful war (as contrasted with World War 2, to both sides a kind of holy war where fundamental principles were at stake), Gandhiji's stance was also a glaring failure of political skill, since he neglected to extract any tangible gains for India in return for the thousands of Indian lives which he sacrificed to British imperial interests.

(2) Committing the mobilisation potential of the freedom movement to the *Khilāfat* agitation in 1920-22, again a non-negotiated unilateral gift. The Khilafat movement was a tragicomical mistake, aiming at the restoration of the Ottoman Caliphate against which the Arabs had risen in revolt and which the Turks were dissolving, a process completed with the final abolition of the institution of the Caliphate in 1924. It was a purely retrograde and reactionary movement, and more importantly for Indian nationalism, it was an intrinsically anti-nationalist movement pitting specifically Islamic interests against secular and non-Muslim interests. Gandhi made the mistake of hubris by thinking he could reconcile Khilafatism and Indian nationalism, and he also offended his Muslim allies (who didn't share his commitment to non-violence) by calling off the agitation when it turned violent. The result was even more violence, with massive Hindu-Muslim riots replacing the limited instances of anti-British attacks, just as many level-headed freedom fighters had predicted. Gandhiji failed to take the Khilafat movement seriously whether at the level of principle or of practical politics, and substituted his own imagined and idealized reading of the Khilafat doctrine for reality.

(3) His autocratic decision to call off the mass agitation for complete independence in 1931, imposed upon his mass following and his close lieutenants against their wishes and better judgment, in exchange for a few puny British concessions falling far short of the movement's demands. His reputation abroad didn't suffer, but to informed observers, he had thrown away his aura as an idealist leader standing above petty politics; the Pact between Gandhi and Viceroy Lord Irwin amounted to the sacrifice of a high national goal in favour of a petty rise in status for the Congress. Also, every delay in the declaration of Independence gave the emerging separatist forces the time to organize and to strengthen their position.

(4) Taking a confused and wavering position vis-à-vis India's involvement in World War 2. His initial refusal to

commit India to the war effort could have been justified on grounds of pacifist principle as well as national pride (the Viceroy had committed India without consulting the native leadership), but it was a failure because his followers weren't following. Indian recruits and business suppliers of the Army eagerly joined hands with the British rulers, thus sidelining Gandhi into political irrelevance. By contrast, the Muslim League greatly improved its bargaining position by joining the war effort, an effect not counterbalanced by the small Hindu Mahasabha's similar strategy. The pro-Partition case which the Muslim League advocated was bolstered while Gandhi's opposition to the imminent Partition was badly weakened. Gandhi was humiliated by his impotence before the degeneration of his "Quit India" agitation into violence and by ultimately having to come around to a collaborationist position himself.

(5) Taking a confused and wavering position vis-à-vis the Partition plan, including false promises to the Hindus of the designated Pakistani areas to prevent Partition or at least to prevent their violent expulsion. He chose not to use his weapon of a fast unto death to force Mohammed Ali Jinnah into backing down from Partition, a move which cast doubt on the much-touted bravery of all his other fasts "unto death" performed to pressurize more malleable opponents. If acquiescing in the Partition could still be justified as a matter of inevitability, there was no excuse for his insistence on half measures, viz. his rejecting plans for an organized exchange of population, certainly a lesser evil when compared to the bloody religious cleansing that actually took place. Gentle surgeons make stinking wounds.

(6) Refusing to acknowledge that Pakistan had become an enemy state after its invasion of Kashmir, by undertaking a fast unto death in order to force the Indian government to pay Pakistan 55 crore rupees from the British-Indian treasury. Pakistan was entitled to this money, but given its aggression, it would have been normal to set the termination of its aggression, including the withdrawal of its invading troops,

as a condition for the payment. Indeed, that would have been a sterling contribution to the cause of enduring peace, saving the lives of the many thousands who fell in subsequent decades because of the festering wound which Kashmir has remained under partial Pakistani occupation. Coming on top of Gandhi's abandonment of the Hindus trapped in Pakistan in August 1947, it was this pro-Pakistani demand, as well as his use of his choice moral weapon (left unused to save India's unity or the persecuted Hindus in Pakistan) in the service of an enemy state's treasury, that angered a few Hindu activists to the point of plotting his murder.

5.2. Problems with pacifism

The common denominator in all these costly mistakes was a lack of realism. Gandhi refused to see the realities of human nature; of Islamic doctrine with its ambition of domination; of the modern mentality with its resentment of autocratic impositions; of people's daily needs making them willing to collaborate with the rulers in exchange for career and business opportunities; of the nationalism of the Hindus who would oppose the partition of their Motherland tooth and nail; of the nature of the Pakistani state as intrinsically anti-India and anti-Hindu.

In most of these cases, Gandhi's mistake was not his pacifism per se. In the case of his recruiting efforts for World War 1, there wasn't even any pacifism involved, but loyalty to the Empire whether in peace or in war. The Khilafat pogroms revealed one of the real problems with his pacifism: all while riding a high horse and imposing strict conformity with the pacifist principle, he indirectly provoked far more violence than was in his power to control. Other leaders of the freedom movement, such as Annie Besant and Lala Lajpat Rai, had warned him that he was playing with fire, but he preferred to obey his suprarational "inner voice".

The fundamental problem with Gandhi's pacifism, not in the initial stages but when he had become the world-famous leader of India's freedom movement (1920-47), was his increasing extremism. All sense of proportion had vanished when he advocated non-violence not as a technique of moral pressure by a weaker on a stronger party, but as a form of masochistic surrender. Elsewhere (Elst: *Gandhi and Godse*, Voice of India, Delhi 2001, p.120-121) I have cited four instances of his advice to the victims of communal violence which is simply breathtaking for its callousness in the face of human suffering. Two more instances follow.

During his prayer meeting on 1 May 1947, he prepared the Hindus and Sikhs for the anticipated massacres of their communities in the upcoming state of Pakistan with these words: "I would tell the Hindus to face death cheerfully if the Muslims are out to kill them. I would be a real sinner if after being stabbed I wished in my last moment that my son should seek revenge. I must die without rancour. (...) You may turn round and ask whether all Hindus and all Sikhs should die. Yes, I would say. Such martyrdom will not be in vain." (*Collected Works of Mahatma Gandhi*, vol.LXXXVII, p.394-5) It is left unexplained what purpose would be served by this senseless and avoidable surrender to murder.

Even when the killing had started, Gandhi refused to take pity on the Hindu victims, much less to point fingers at the Pakistani aggressors. More importantly for the principle of non-violence, he failed to offer them a non-violent technique of countering and dissuading the murderers. Instead, he told the Hindu refugees from Pakistan to go back and die. On 6 August 1947, Gandhiji commented to Congress workers on the incipient communal conflagration in Lahore thus: "I am grieved to learn that people are running away from the West Punjab and I am told that Lahore is being evacuated by the non-Muslims. I must say that this is what it should not be. If you think Lahore is dead or is dying, do not run away from it, but die with what you think is the dying Lahore. (...) When you suffer from fear you die before death comes to you. That is not glorious. I will not feel sorry if I hear that people in the Punjab have died not as cowards but as brave men. (...) I cannot be forced to salute any flag. If in that act I am murdered I would bear no ill will against anyone and would rather pray for better sense for the person or persons who murder me." (*Hindustan Times*, 8-8-1947, *CWoMG*, vol. LXXXIX, p.11).

So, he was dismissing as cowards those who saved their lives fleeing the massacre by a vastly stronger enemy, viz. the Pakistani population and security forces. But is it cowardice to flee a no-win situation, so as to live and perhaps to fight another day? There can be a come-back from exile, not from death. Is it not better to continue life as a non-Lahorite than to cling to one's location in Lahore even if it has to be as a corpse? Why should staying in a mere location be so superior to staying alive? To be sure, it would have been even better if Hindus could have continued to live with honour in Lahore, but Gandhi himself had refused to use his power in that cause, viz. averting Partition. He probably would have found that, like the butchered or fleeing Hindus, he was no match for the determination of the Muslim League, but at least he could have tried. In the advice he now gave, the whole idea of non-violent struggle got perverted.

Originally, in Gandhi's struggle for the Indians' rights in South Africa, non-violent agitation was tried out as a weapon of the weak who wouldn't stand a chance in an armed confrontation. It was a method to achieve a political goal, and a method which could boast of some successes. In the hands of a capable agitator, it could be victorious. It was designed to snatch victory from the jaws of powerlessness and surrender. By contrast, the "non-violent" surrender to the enemy and to butchery which Gandhi advocated in 1947 had nothing victorious or successful about it.

During the anti-colonial struggle, Gandhi had often said that oppression was only possible with a certain cooperation or complicity from the oppressed people. The genius of the non-violent technique, not applicable in all situations but proven successful in some, was to create a third way between violent confrontation between the oppressed and the oppressor, fatally ending in the defeat of the weak, and the passive resignation of the oppressed in their state of oppression. Rather than surrendering to the superior power of the oppressor, the oppressed were given a method to exercise slow pressure on their oppressor, to wrest concessions from him and to work on his conscience. No such third way was left to the minorities in Pakistan: Gandhi's only advice to them was to surrender, to become accomplices in their extermination by meekly offering their necks to the executioner's sword.

My point is not that Gandhi could and should have given them a third way, a non-violent technique that would defeat the perpetrators of Partition and religious cleansing. More realistically, he should have accepted that this was the kind of situation where no such third option was available. Once the sacrifice of a large part of India's territory to a Muslim state had been conceded, and given previous experiences with Muslim violence against non-Muslims during the time of Gandhi's own leadership, he should have realized that an exchange of population was the only remaining bloodless solution. The Partition crisis was simply beyond the capacity of Gandhian non-violence to control. If he had had the modesty to face his powerlessness and accept that alternatives to his own preferred solution would have to be tried, many lives could have been saved.

5.3. Robust pacifism

It cannot be denied that Gandhian non-violence has a few successes to its credit. But these were achieved under particularly favourable circumstances: the stakes weren't very high and the opponents weren't too foreign to Gandhi's ethical standards. In South Africa, he had to deal with liberal British authorities who weren't affected too seriously in their power and authority by conceding Gandhi's demands. Upgrading the status of the small Indian minority from equality with the Blacks to an in-between status approaching that of the Whites made no real difference to the ruling class, so Gandhi's agitation was rewarded with some concessions. Even in India, the stakes were never really high. Gandhi's Salt March made the British rescind the Salt Tax, a limited financial price to pay for restoring native acquiescence in British paramountcy, but he never made them concede Independence or even Home Rule with a non-violent agitation. The one time he had started such an agitation, viz. in 1930-31, he himself stopped it in exchange for a few small concessions.

It is simply not true that India's Independence was the fruit of Gandhian non-violent agitation. He was close to the British in terms of culture and shared ethical values, which is why sometimes he could successfully bargain with them, but even they stood firm against his pressure when their vital interests were at stake. It is only Britain's bankruptcy due to World War 2 and the emergence of the anti-colonial United States and Soviet Union as the dominant world powers that forced Clement Attlee's government into decolonizing India. Even then, the trigger events in 1945-47 that demonstrated how the Indian people would not tolerate British rule for much longer, had to do with armed struggle rather than with non-violence: the naval mutiny of Indian troops and the ostentatious nationwide support for the officers of Subhas Bose's Axis-collaborationist Indian National Army when they stood trial for treason in the Red Fort.

So, non-violence need not be written off as a Quixotic experiment, for it can be an appropriate and successful technique in particular circumstances; but it has its limitations. In many serious confrontations, it is simply better, and on balance more just as well as more bloodless, to observe an "economy of violence": using a small amount of armed force, or even only the threat of armed force, in order to avoid a larger and bloodier armed confrontation. This is the principle of "peace through strength" followed by most modern governments with standing armies. It was applied, for example, in the containment of Communism: though relatively minor wars between Communist and anti-Communist forces were fought in several Third World countries, both the feared Communist world conquest and the equally feared World War 3 with its anticipated nuclear holocaust were averted.

The ethical framework limiting the use of force to a minimum is known as "just war theory", developed by European thinkers such as Thomas Aquinas and Hugo Grotius between the 13th and 18th century, but in essence already present in the Mahabharata as well. Thus, waging war can be a just enterprise when it is done in self-defence, when all non-violent means of achieving the just objective have been tried, when non-combatants are respected as such, when the means used are in proportion to the objective aimed for, etc.

One of the less well-known criteria for just warfare which deserves to be mentioned here in the light of Gandhi's advice to the Hindus in Pakistan is that there should be a reasonable chance of success. No matter how just your cause, it is wrong to commit your community to a course of action that only promises to be suicidal. Once a group of soldiers is trapped in a situation from which the only exit is an honourable death, fighting on may be the best course remaining, but whenever possible, such suicide should be avoided. This criterion is just as valid in non-armed as in armed struggle: it was wrong to make the Hindus stay among their Pakistani persecutors when this course of action had no chance of saving lives nor even of achieving certain political objectives.

As the Buddha, Aristotle, Confucius and other ethical guides already taught, virtue is a middle term between two extremes. In this case, we have to sail between the two extremes of blindness to human fellow-feeling and blindness to strategic ground realities. It is wrong to say that might makes right and that anything goes when it comes to achieving victory, no matter what amount of suffering is inflicted on the enemy, on bystanders or even on one's own camp. It is equally wrong to strike a high moral posture which haughtily disregards, and hence refuses to contain or subdue, the potential for violence in human confrontations and the real pain it causes. In between these two extremes, the mature and virtuous attitude is one which desires and maintains peace but is able and prepared to fight the aggressor.

Limiting the use of force to a minimum is generally agreed to be the correct position. In this case, disagreeing with Gandhi is not an instance of Communist or Hindu-chauvinist extremism, but of the accumulated wisdom of civilized humanity. Excluding the use of force entirely, by contrast, may simply whet the aggressor's appetite and provoke far more violence than the achievable minimum. This is a mistake which an overenthusiastic and inexperienced beginner can forgivably make, but in an experienced leader like Mahatma Gandhi during his time at the head of the freedom movement, it was a serious failure of judgment. The silver lining in the massacres which his mistakes provoked, is that they have reminded us of the eternal wisdom of "the golden mean", the need for a balanced policy vis-à-vis the ever-present challenge of violence and aggression. It has been known all along, and it is crystal-clear once more, that we should avoid both extremes, Jinnah's self-righteousness and Gandhi's sentimentalism.

6. Religious cleansing of Hindus

[This is the text of a paper read in The Hague at the Agni conference on the persecution of Hindus in various countries, 7 February 2004.]

6.1. A brief overview of the problem

"Religious cleansing" is the deliberate removal of a targeted religious community from a given territory.

In India, the practice is mainly associated with Muslim rule and the persecution of the Hindus in the name of Islam, vividly remembered in its instances of West Pakistan 1947, East Pakistan 1971 and the Kashmir Valley 1990. Yet, it didn't start with the Muslim conquests themselves, from the conquest of Sindh by Mohammed bin Qasim in AD 712 onwards. Conquerors imposed Islamic rule by force, and some also tried to impose conversion to Islam on the population, but the physical removal of non-Muslims from a given region mostly took place only at a later stage, because it required the presence of a Muslim population already sharing the territory with the Hindus and participating in their expulsion. Even then, in most cases, the Hindus were not told to leave (as were the Kashmiri Pandits in 1990), but the social pressure and sometimes sheer terror against them made them opt for either conversion or emigration, which equally amounted to the liquidation of Hinduism in the region.

6.1.1. Afghanistan

The first part of South Asia to be cleansed of Hinduism was Afghanistan. The 10th century saw a life-and-death struggle there between Muslim invaders and the local Hindu population and dynasty. In this case, the replacement was not just religious, of Hindus by Muslims, but also ethnic, viz. of Indo-Aryans by Iranians. The fact of an at least partial physical replacement of the native population by invaders is attested by the linguistic shift. Until then, in much of the present-day Pashtu-speaking region of Pakistan and Afghanistan, an Indo-Aryan Prakrit was spoken (remember how the Sanskrit grammarian Panini was a native of Peshawar). It was replaced with Pashtu, an Iranian language.

The mountain range *Hindu Koh* received the nickname *Hindu Kush*, a nickname which has stuck to become the official name. It means "slaughter of the Hindus", in reference to the night in 1399 when the frost killed a hundred thousand Hindu slaves on transport to Central Asia.

In the mountainous region, however, an old quasi-Vedic Paganism persisted, which is why the region was called *Kafiristan*, "land of the Pagans". In the 1890s, with British support, the king of Afghanistan sent an expedition to convert the Kafirs to Islam by force and renamed the region *Nuristan*, "land of light". Only on the British side of the border, in the Chitral region of the Northwest Frontier Province, did some Pagans survive. Under Pakistani rule, the number of these so-called *Kalash Kafirs* has dwindled to less than four thousand. Two years ago, Jordi Magraner, a Catalan scholar settled among them and working for their cultural memory and survival, was murdered by Islamic activists. It seems that the Pakistani government now deliberately reins in attempts to convert the Kalash Kafirs because they can serve as a human-rights showpiece and as a tourist attraction.

During the era of British but especially that of Soviet influence, the cities of Afghanistan saw a certain amount of immigration of Hindu entrepreneurs, eventually amounting to several tens of thousands. Most of them were expelled again by the Mujahedin who chased out the Soviets in 1992, or after 1996 by the Taliban. Under Taliban rule, the remaining hundreds of Hindus in Kandahar, who had taken to inconspicuous dress in order not to stand out among their Muslim neighbours, were forced to wear a yellow strip to make themselves recognizable.

6.1.2. Kashmir

The first part of what is now India to see the near-disappearance of the Hindu presence is probably Kashmir, where practically all castes were forcibly converted to Islam by the 14th century. Most of the Kashmiri Brahmins emigrated, some to return in quieter times, most to settle for good in Panjab and as far as Maharashtra and Goa. Those few who toughed it out, never forgave their fellow Kashmiris their so-called treason. When Kashmir reverted to Hindu control under the Sikhs and then under the Dogra dynasty in the 19th century, the Kashmiri Brahmins reportedly opposed plans by the Maharajas to reconvert the Kashmiri Muslims to Hinduism.

Their descendants were to regret this purism. In 1947, local Muslims joined hands with Pakistani invasion troops in massacring the Hindus in the Pak-occupied territories, where all traces of the hoary Hindu presence were annihilated. In 1990, a terror campaign under the motto, "kill one to expel a thousand", led by Pakistani militants but supported by a critical mass of the local Muslim population, managed to chase out practically the whole of the Kashmiri Pandit population from the Kashmir Valley. Even the supposedly Hindu-nationalist governments led by the BJP in 1998-2004 didn't achieve (nor even seriously tried to achieve) the resettlement of the Pandits in their native state.

6.1.3. Partition

The single most dramatic instance of religious cleansing took place in 1947, removing the Hindu presence completely from West Panjab, Pak-Occupied Kashmir, the Northwest Frontier Province and parts of Baluchistan and Sindh. The official number of victims, Hindus and Muslims counted together, is usually given as 600,000. We may assume that for the sake of not exacerbating communal animosity, the governments of both India and Pakistan minimized the true figure, which may well be one or two million.

After the fact, the main thrust of literary and historiographical elaborations of the Partition atrocities was to posit equal guilt between Hindus and Muslims. Of course, you could anecdotically counterbalance actual cases of Muslim cruelty with actual cases of Hindu or Sikh cruelty against Muslims. But the over-all fact remains that Partition with all its concomitant horrors was unilaterally imposed upon the unwilling Hindus and Sikhs by the Muslim League. If there was a superficial symmetry in migration patterns, there was an asymmetry in the motives of the migrants: whereas Hindus and Sikhs from West Panjab or the Northwest Frontier fled a land they had never wanted to leave, Muslims from Uttar Pradesh or Bihar moved to the promised land of their own creation. Also, the atrocities on Hindus aimed at eliminating them either by massacre or by forced emigration had started in the projected Pakistani regions months before any similar anti-Muslim atrocities started on the Indian side of the projected new border.

Another false escape clause, systematically propagated by the Congress regime, was that Partition had been the handiwork of the British rather than of the Muslim League. This is totally untrue: the last Viceroy, Lord Mountbatten, had only been mandated to organize Partition under pressure from its seeming inevitability or its emerging status as a "lesser evil" in comparison with the orgy of violence which the Muslim League was threatening to unleash. But the original British position had been articulated by his two predecessors, Lord Linlithgow and Lord Wavell, who had told the Muslim League leadership in clear terms that they were proud of their Indian empire and were in no mood to let anyone dismember it even if it were to pass out of British hands. While other parties including the British rulers and some Hindu leaders (Rajaji, Morarji Desai, Sardar Patel, Ambedkar and finally also Mahatma Gandhi) merely *acquiesced* in Partition as a lesser evil, it was purely the will and determination of the Muslim League which imposed the division of India upon an unwilling majority.

6.1.4. The Bangladesh war

On the borders of what was to become East Pakistan, Hindu-Muslim violence in 1947 was far smaller in scale. What happened there was that after a relatively peaceful transition to independence, the Partition process of religious cleansing took place anyway but drawn out over decades. During this "prolonged Partition", there has been a constant trickle of Hindu refugees from East Bengal to India, which became a flood in times of crisis. The biggest crisis was of course the Bangladesh war of 1971, when the Pakistani army and its Bengali and immigrant-Bihari collaborators hunted down Hindus along with Muslim Bengali nationalists. The official death toll as claimed by the Bangladeshi government was 3 million; foreign observers settle for 1.5 million. All disinterested observers agree that Hindus were the first and largest among the victim groups. As for the Muslim victims, they were not killed by Hindus but by Pakistanis and their Jamaat-i-Islami collaborators who killed them for not being Muslim enough.

After 1971, East Bengal made a fresh start as a secular state, and many refugees returned in the hope of a decent life. But soon Islamization policies returned to the country, along with discriminations and pogroms against the minorities. Consequently, Hindus as well as Christians and Buddhists from Bangladesh have gradually moved to India. This picture is muddied a bit by the seemingly parallel but actually quite distinct phenomenon of mass Muslim emigration from Bangladesh to India for purely economic reasons. Estimates approved by the Indian government put the number of Bangladeshi Muslims illegally staying in India at over 20 million. Most border regions of West Bengal and the North-Eastern states, originally allotted to India rather than to East Pakistan precisely because they had Hindu majorities, now have large Muslim majorities. Hindus are under pressure to leave there, too.

6.1.5. Small-scale cleansing throughout India

In many pockets of Muslim concentration in India, non-Muslims are slowly cleansed out. This is sometimes done in an unplanned manner, but in most cases one can discern the rudiments of a strategy behind it. In some southern cities, major Hindu temples have been isolated from their constituency of worshippers after Muslims strategically bought up all the real estate around the temple. In Ahmedabad, Hindus have practically been driven out of the old city.

In such an important economic centre, the planning by Muslim Gulf-based mafias was obvious. One Muslim, or his Hindu stooge, would buy up a house in a Hindu neighbourhood, overruling the Hindu owner's misgivings by offering a price far above the market value. This would eventually prove to be a very profitable investment. The next stage is that life for Hindus is made uncomfortable, initially in perfectly legal ways, e.g. a *halāl* butchery is opened in the middle of a vegetarian community where people find the mere smell of meat nauseating. Then invariably follows eve-teasing of Hindu girls, acts of disrespect to elderly Hindus, some petty but in-your-face robbery. The first Hindus now put up their house for sale, and again the mafia coffers are available to ensure a decent price, though now not much above market value anymore. Muslim youngsters start hanging out in larger numbers, holding out the threat of rape, and finally commit an actual rape. A bogus Hindu provocation of Muslim sentiments is enacted and a communal riot ensues. The conviviality of the Hindu Bania neighbourhood now good and well destroyed, Hindus start panic-selling their houses. Finally, the whole neighbourhood falls into Muslim hands for a song. The mafia dons distribute the loot among their supporters.

6.1.6. Cleansing of Hindus by Christians

Ever since their first arrival in India as refugees, probably in the 4th century, the Syrian Christians in Kerala had integrated peacefully into Hindu society. They took their place in the caste system at a fairly high rank, and never troubled their neighbours with campaigns of conversion. This changed with the arrival of the Portuguese from 1498 onwards. They made attempts to expel all Hindus from Goa and other territories they held. However, being constrained by their limited numbers and their commerce-oriented treaties with native rulers, they could never implement their plans in full and ended up tolerating a continued Hindu presence within their domains.

Under British rule, missionary activities were curtailed or kept within limits, because the administrators wanted to avoid communal conflagrations. It was only in some of the tribal regions that the missionaries were given a free hand to Christianize entire communities. Even then, they were held on a tight leash. It is only in independent India that the missionaries were given all manner of privileges to the point that they felt emboldened to participate in illegal political activities including armed separatist struggle in the North-Eastern states of Nagaland, Mizoram, Manipur and Tripura.

In Fiji, the colonial government gave a free hand to the missionaries, so that the native population was completely converted to Christianity and is now generally hostile to the Hindu immigrant population. This has led to the repeated ousting of an elected Hindu Prime Minister, to social boycotts and discrimination in job recruitment, and to frequent vandalism against Hindu temples.

The Christian-dominated parts of India's North-East have witnessed several instances of Hindu-cleansing. Hindu organizations like the Ramakrishna Mission and the RSS have been targeted for elimination from the region through pressure or violence. In the 1990s, tens of thousands of Riang tribals who rejected conversion were expelled from Christian-dominated Mizoram. The death toll of Hindus eliminated by Christian separatists dwarfs that of the much-publicized Hindu violence against Christians, which has killed only a handful since 1947, including in the supposed "wave" of anti-Christian riots in 1998-99. The killing of Australian missionary Graham Staines and his two sons by Orissa tribals who were angry at the divisive effect of conversions on their society, was front-page news in the whole world and remains a constant point of reference in the dominant discourse on communalism. By contrast, when shortly after that, four RSS workers were kidnapped by Christian separatists in the North-East and their mutilated bodies were subsequently found, it was hardly reported in the Indian press and not at all in the international media.

6.1.7. Cleansing of Hindus by Buddhists

In a bid to counter the grim and wide-ranging Hindu case against Islam as a destroyer of Hindu lives and culture, Marxist historians have propagated the claim that Hindus had done likewise to Buddhists: destroying their religious establishments and killing the inmates. This claim has gained wide currency, including in Buddhist countries where it impedes the natural solidarity between Buddhists and Hindus. However, this claim is entirely fictitious.

Even a very general knowledge of Indian history already shows that any instances of Hindu persecution of Buddhism could never have been more than marginal. After fully seventeen centuries of Buddhism's existence, from the 6th century BC to the late 12th century AD, most of it under the rule of Hindu kings, we find Buddhist establishments flourishing all over India. Under king Pushyamitra Shunga, often falsely labelled as a persecutor of Buddhism, important Buddhist centres such as the Sanchi stupa were built. As late as the early 12th century, the Buddhist monastery Dharmachakrajina Vihara at Sarnath was built under the patronage of queen Kumaradevi, wife of Govindachandra, the Hindu king of Kanauj in whose reign the contentious Rama temple in Ayodhya was built. This may be contrasted with the ruined state of Buddhism in countries like Afghanistan or Uzbekistan after one thousand or even one hundred years of Muslim rule. Indeed, the Muslim chroniclers themselves have described in gleeful detail how they destroyed Buddhism root and branch in the entire Gangetic plain in just a few years after Mohammed Ghori's victory in the second battle of Tarain in 1192. The famous university of Nalanda with its fabulous library burned for weeks. Its inmates were put to the sword except for those who managed to flee. The latter spread the word to other Indian regions where Buddhist monks packed up and left in anticipation of further Muslim conquests. It is apparent that this way, some abandoned Buddhist establishments were taken over by Hindus; but that is an entirely different matter from the forcible occupation or destruction of Buddhist institutions by the foreign invaders.

However, while Hinduism has a very good record in tolerating and patronizing Buddhism, the reverse is not entirely the case, especially in the modern age. In Myanmar in the 1960s, the Hindu immigrant population, mainly Tamil labourers and traders settled there under British rule, was formally expelled. As far as I know, this was less for religious than for ethnic and anti-colonial reasons.

Likewise in Bhutan, Nepali-speaking Hindus are being expelled in a classical instance of a sons-of-the-soil reaction against foreign settlers. The Tibetan Bhutanese explain their actions by pointing to the case of Sikkim, where Nepali-speaking Hindu immigrants had become the majority and decided democratically to liquidate the state's sovereignty and Tibetan identity and to join India. This does not justify the atrocities committed against the Hindus in Bhutan (atrocities on a scale revealed here by eye-witnesses which most of us had not deemed possible in such a seemingly idyllic nation), but it provides a sobering background to a dramatic development which would otherwise seem incomprehensible.

In Sri Lanka too, Sinhalese resentment of the Tamils, who may be either Hindus or Christians, was initially less for religious than for ethnic reasons, particularly the conflict over language policy. Under British rule, the Tamils had been privileged, and the Sinhalese tried to turn the tables on them by declaring a Sinhala-only official language regime. But Buddhist monks soon added a religious dimension to the incipient conflict by vandalizing Tamil Hindu shrines. The conflict developed into a full-scale civil war which, in spite of major recent peace moves, is not fully over yet.

6.1.8. Hindu-cleansing in Africa

Many Hindus in Great Britain and the USA are refugees from another instance of Hindu-cleansing, viz. their expulsion from the East-African countries of Uganda and Tanzania shortly after docolonization. The Hindu presence itself was perceived as a legacy of colonialism. In neighbouring Kenya, Hindus have so far been able to live with peace and dignity, though there too, some nativist political parties promise to expel them. Likewise in South Africa, the acceptance of the Hindu presence by other communities cannot be securely taken for granted. The Communist-nativist group Pan-African Congress has a slogan: "There is only one place for Indians in South Africa, and that is the Indian Ocean." Likewise, the Hindus of Trinidad and Tobago, of Surinam and of Guyana typically have a tense relationship with the (mainly christianized) Africans there.

In each of these cases, the main grievance of the Africans against the Hindus seems to be economical: the Hindus allegedly monopolize business and don't feed the accumulated wealth back into the host society. This is in essence the same resentment which exists against successful Lebanese traders in West Africa, European settlers in Zimbabwe, or earlier the Jewish communities in Europe. There may also be a cultural aspect, though. Hindus are perceived as haughty, cunning and selfish. Conversely, Hindus themselves privately describe Africans as promiscuous, disorderly, lazy and unclean,— and the Africans are sufficiently aware of this. For them, there is a markedly greater distance in lifestyle from the Hindus than from the Muslims.

6.1.9. Hindu-cleansing in Europe?

In Europe, it is oddly by amalgamation with the Muslim population that Hindus risk being expelled one day. There is little or no resentment against Hindus as such. They are practically absent from the crime statistics and they don't push any separatist or otherwise provocative political demands. Very few Europeans would ever vote for an anti-immigrant party on the basis of their experiences with their Hindu immigrant neighbours.

Islam, by contrast, is a central concern of the national-populist parties, though not in a uniform manner. The extreme Right, which by definition is only a fringe tendency, cherishes fantasies of a Euro-Islamic alliance against a perceived American-Zionist world hegemony. This is a parallel development with what you see in the extreme Left, where Muslim immigrants are considered a substitute for the proletariat as a force capable of destroying the system. Less marginally and more consequentially, the fast-growing populist Right, by contrast, takes an alarmist view of Islam and dramatizes all Islam-related "affairs" such as the ongoing *hijāb* controversies. In some cases, viz. the true-blue racists who want to send all coloured immigrants back, this focus on the problems posed by Islam is only a rhetorical cover for a more general anti-immigration drive regardless of the religion of the immigrants.

One could imagine a scenario where native resentment of the Muslim immigrant population reaches such a pitch that all Muslims are driven out, in a reversal of the expulsion of European settlers and their native "collaborators" in Algeria in 1962. In such a case of extreme polarization between native and immigrant, one could further imagine that the distinction between Muslims and other immigrant groups gets blurred, and that Hindus are cleansed out as well. For the time being, we dare surmise that this scenario remains imaginary, but if ethnic tension rises, nobody knows what can happen.

6.2. Why does nobody know or care about the plight of the Hindus?

6.2.1. Distortion of the terms underlying the information

When we want to understand a social problem, we need a language capable of expressing the data and underlying concepts describing the problem. In India, political incidents frequently pit Hindu nationalism, or even just plain Hinduism and plain nationalism, against so-called "secularism". In practice, this term denotes a combine of Islamists, Hindu-born Marxists, Christian missionaries and americanized adepts of consumerism who share a hatred of Hindu culture and Hindu self-respect. What passes for secularism in India is often the diametrical opposite of what goes by the same name in the West.

Genuine secular states have equality before the law of all citizens regardless of religion. By contrast, India has different civil codes depending on the citizen's religion. Thus, for Christians it is very hard to get a divorce, Hindus and Muslim women can get one through judicial proceedings, and Muslim men can simply repudiate their wives. The secular alternative, a common civil code, is championed by the Hindu nationalists. It is the so-called secularists who, justifying themselves with specious sophistry, join hands with the most obscurantist religious leaders to insist on maintaining the present unequal system.

Likewise, there exists a legal inequality in matters of temple management, pilgrimage subsidies, special autonomy for states depending on their populations' religious composition, and the right to found religious schools; and this inequality is defended by the so-called secularists because it is invariably to the disadvantage of the Hindus. The Hindu nationalists favour the secular alternative of equality regardless of religion.

In India, *shari'a*-wielding Muslim clerics whose Arab counterparts denounce secularism as the ultimate evil, call themselves secularists. Just as the English word *deception* differs in meaning from its French counterpart *déception* (= disappointment), the word *secularism* has a sharply different meaning in Indian English as compared to metropolitan English.

When we consider "secularism" as an intellectual movement rather than as a juridical concept, "secularism" means that religion is treated as a human construct rather than the product of a divine revelation. It implies a frank and critical investigation of the claims of religion. In this respect, the failure and dishonesty of Indian secularism is even more radical. Its discourse on religion is extremely and wilfully superficial. It shields from criticism even the most obscurantist religious beliefs or institutions, provided they are non-Hindu (and even in attacking Hinduism, its criticisms of even legitimate targets tend to be crassly superficial). For instance, almost every self-styled secularist, from former President A.K. Narayanan to the editors of the newspapers, has sworn by the story that Christianity was brought to India by the apostle Thomas. In the West, not just secularists but even Catholic universities like the one where I studied have dropped this myth. But in India, the secularists are its most determined upholders.

Indian secularism is systematically dishonest in its assessment of the religions hostile to Hinduism. Thus, after the murder of Australian Protestant missionary Graham Staines, which resulted from the well-attested resentment of the tribals against the divisive effect of conversion on their communities, the secularists massively denied that the Christian missionaries are in India for purposes of conversion. In reality, the project of converting all mankind is intrinsic to the Christian religion. In Catholic school, I always learned that the missionaries provide medical and educational services primarily in order to make the targeted communities receptive to conversion. Staines' own bulletin to his Australian sponsors (which his supporters tried to conceal from the official investigators) proved he was doing conversion work. In 1999, the Southern Baptist Church reconfirmed that Hindus are doomed unless they become Christians. In the same year, the Pope himself came to Delhi to say in so many words that the Church intends to "reap a rich harvest of faith" in India. Yet this authoritatively attested fact is still dismissed by vocal secularists as a figment of Hindu paranoia.

6.2.2. History denial

Our perception of current events is largely conditioned by our knowledge and understanding of the past. The facts concerning the persecution of Hindus in the pre-modern age were a matter of consensus until recently. For contemporary political reasons, the Congress movement under Mahatma Gandhi and especially under Jawaharlal Nehru thought it opportune to minimize or deny this painful history. They invented a history of *Hindu-Muslim bhai-bhai* totally at variance with the information given in the primary sources. The job of rewriting history in this sense was subsequently taken up in right earnest by the post-independence generation of vocal Marxist scholars, who gained firm control of the guiding history institutions under Indira Gandhi (r. 1965-77 and 1980-84).

For those unfamiliar with modern Indian history: the Marxists, already pushy for acquiring as much power in the institutions as they could grab, were handed a near-monopoly on institutional power in India's academic and educational sector by Indira Gandhi ca. 1970. Involved in an intra-Congress power struggle, she needed the help of the Left. Her confidants P.N. Haksar and Nurul Hasan packed the institutions with Marxists, card-carrying or otherwise. When, during the Emergency dictatorship (1975-77), her Communist Party allies threatened to become too powerful, she and her son Sanjay removed them from key political positions but, in a typical instance of politicians' short-sightedness, they left the Marxists' hold on the cultural sector intact.

In the old Soviet tradition, the Marxists at once set out to falsify history and propagate their own version through the official textbooks. In spite of recent instances of brutal Marxist-Muslim conflict (Iran 1979, Afghanistan in the 1980s), one of their priorities was to paint a rosy picture of Islamic rule in India, c.q. to impede criticism by blurring the very notion of "Islamic rule". This somewhat anomalous Marxist-Islamist alliance should be understood in the Indian context of a joint anti-Hindu front uniting all the minorities, a typical instance of the old Marxist "common front" policy.

After coming to power in 1998, the BJP-dominated government has made a half-hearted and not always very competent attempt to effect *glasnost* (openness, transparency) at least in the history textbooks. They ordered the writing of new history textbooks for the schools. This led the Marxists to start a furious hate campaign against the so-called "saffronization" (hinduization) of history. Most of the new textbooks have rightly been criticized for being written in poor English and riddled with errors,— the result of both the Hindu movement's long-standing anti-intellectual prejudice and the systematic exclusion of aspiring pro-Hindu scholars from the institutions by the ruling Marxists. The one major exception, however, is precisely the volume on the Muslim conquest and rule, *Medieval India* (class XI) by Prof. Meenakshi Jain, an impeccable text systematically based on primary sources.

Since some ignorant dupes of these Marxists denounce as "McCarthyist" anyone who points out their ideological inspiration, it deserves to be emphasized that "eminent historians" like Romila Thapar, R.S. Sharma and Irfan Habib are certified as Marxists in standard Marxist sources like Tom Bottomore's *Dictionary of Marxist Thought.* During the official historians' Ayodhya temple/mosque dispute in 1991, the pro-mosque team's argumentation and several other anti-temple pamphlets were published by the People's Publishing House, a Communist Party outfit. One of the recent textbook innovations most furiously denounced as "saffronization" was the truism that Lenin's armed seizing of power in October/November 1917 was a "coup d'état". And in early 2003, while they were unchaining all their devils against *glasnost*, the Marxists ruling West Bengal deleted from a textbook a passage in which Mahatma Gandhi's biographer Louis Fischer called Stalin "at least as ruthless as Hitler". Such are the true concerns of the "secularists" warning the world against the attempts at *glasnost* in India's national history curriculum.

History falsification comes in different forms and has concentric lines of defence and attack. At the time of unlimited "secularist" self-confidence and belligerence, this went as far as to deny that any Islamic persecution or oppression of Hindus had taken place. When that proved untenable, it was claimed that intolerance had admittedly existed but that it had been unrelated to Islam, that it was a general phenomenon typical of the medieval period. As if a tick of the clock, viz. the arrival of the so-called Middle Ages, could cause the widespread destruction which India suffered. In reality, the age had nothing to do with it. Tolerance remained the rule in medieval Hinduism: for all its untouchability and other flaws, it did tolerate Syrian Christians, Parsis and Jews in its midst (who, unlike in their countries of origin, also learned to tolerate one another in India), and the lively debates between its own numerous sects rarely if ever spilled over into physical confrontations. The problem was not the age but the Islamic doctrine of conquest and self-righteousness. Unfortunately, secularists have developed a habit of staring past uncomfortable historical facts, particularly those disturbing the newly claimed progressive image of any anti-Hindu group or movement or religion.

6.2.3. False reporting

When it comes to contemporary religious conflict, the same refusal to face facts is in evidence. Distortive or even totally false reporting on communally sensitive issues is a well-entrenched feature of Indian journalism. There is no self-corrective mechanism in place to remedy this endemic culture of disinformation. No reporter or columnist or editor ever gets fired or formally reprimanded or even just criticized by his peers for smearing Hindus. This way, a partisan economy with the truth has become a habit hard to relinquish. And foreign correspondents used to trusting their Indian secularist sources have likewise developed a habit of swallowing and relaying highly distorted news stories.

Usually, the creation of a false impression of the Indian communal situation is achieved without outright lies, relying rather on the silent treatment for inconvenient facts and a screaming overemphasis on convenient ones. After the BJP came to power in 1998, India should have witnessed a genocide of the minorities, gas chambers and what not, at least if you believed the predictions made by the secularists in the preceding years. Nothing of the kind happened, and the secularists didn't dare to pretend that events were bearing out their prediction. So in the next two years the secularists tried to make the most of what few incidents did take place, giving them a significance which no sober observer could have attributed to them.

In particular, all manner of small incidents within the Christian community were at once blamed on the evil hand of

Hindu nationalism. In Kandhamal, Orissa, a Christian man murdered a girl and her little brother. At once, a cry went up in the secularist and Christian media that Hindu nationalists had perpetrated the crime. When the official investigation revealed the true story, viz. that the murderer was a Christian himself, it was reported only marginally in Indian papers and not at all in the international media, which had eagerly carried the initial allegations.

Likewise, in the Central-Indian town of Jhabua, a quarrel among mostly christianized tribals led to the rape of four nuns. With no Hindu nationalists in sight, the media decided nonetheless that this was an act of Hindu nationalist cruelty against the poor hapless Christian minority. Though the official investigation confirmed the total innocence of the Hindu nationalists in this affair, their guilt has been consecrated by endless repetition in the media. While the media in India couldn't prevent the truth from quietly making itself known, the international media have never published a correction, and the story of "four nuns in Jhabua raped by Hindu nationalists" now keeps on reappearing as an evergreen of anti-Hindu hate propaganda.

Similarly, a series of bomb blasts against Christian churches in South India was automatically blamed on the Hindu nationalists. In that version, the story made headlines around the world: Hindu bomb terror against Christians. Hindu organizations alleged that it was a Pakistani operation, a blame-shifting exercise which only earned them ridicule and contempt. Yet, when two of the terrorists blew themselves up by mistake, their getaway car led the police to their network, and the whole gang was arrested. It turned out to be a Muslim group, a section of the *Deendar Anjuman*, with headquarters in Pakistan. But this was not reported on the front-pages in India nor made the topic of flaming editorials; and in the international media, it was not reported at all. In the worldwide perception of Hindu nationalism, the false association with raping nuns and bombing churches has stuck.

So, moral of the story: feel free to write lies about the Hindus. Even if you are found out, most of the public will never hear of it, and you will not be made to bear any consequences. Striking first is what counts. Any second round in which the truth comes out, will hardly be noticed. Indeed, conditioned by the initial lie, many readers and viewers will deride the correction as an attempt at "denial" of the grim facts which "everybody knows well enough". And the audience abroad will never even be informed that there has been a correction.

6.2.4. Riot vultures

These days, noisy secularists lie in waiting for communal riots and elatedly jump at them when and where they erupt. They exploit the anti-Hindu propaganda value of riots to the hilt, making up fictional stories as they go along to compensate for any defects in the true account. John Dayal is welcomed to Congressional committees in Washington DC as a crown witness to canards such as how Hindus are raping Catholic nuns in Jhabua, an allegation long refuted in a report by the Congress state government of Madhya Pradesh and more recently in the court verdict on the matter. Arundhati Roy goes lyrical about the torture of a Muslim politician's two daughters by Hindus during the Gujarat riots of 2002, even when the man had only one daughter, who came forward to clarify that she happened to be in the US at the time of the "facts". Harsh Mander has already been condemned by the Press Council of India (decision 14/106/02-03 dd. 30 June 2003, Dr. Krishen Kak vs. *Times of India*) for spreading false rumours about alleged Hindu atrocities in his famous column *Hindustan Hamara* (*Times of India*, 20 March 2002). Teesta Setalwad has reportedly pressured eyewitnesses to give the desired incriminating testimony against Hindus in the Gujarat riots.

All of them have given exaggerated death toll figures ("more than 2,000 Muslims", in reality about 800, next to over

250 Hindus whom they never mention) and characterizations ("genocide") of the Gujarat riots, which in fact paled in comparison with the communal confrontations which took place in the two decades before the cathartic post-Demolition riots of December-January 1992-93. With their depiction of India as a country where the minorities live in constant fear for their lives, a story eagerly believed abroad, these riot vultures do a lot of damage to their country.

Dealing with communal confrontations at face value has never solved the problem. Most secularist writings on the Gujarat riots manage to leave *madrassa* education unmentioned. How serious are you about weeding out Hindu-Muslim riots if you don't want to address the permanent source of religious hatred among Muslims, the very cause of Partition and of *jihad*?

Secondly, Gujarat has not been claiming attention all by itself. An intensive effort by the usual suspects has kept attention as much as possible away from other scenes of communal violence. In the past months, how many people have been killed by Christian separatists in the Northeast, by Communists in Kerala or Andhra or Nepal, by Muslims in Bangladesh or Jammu? As for Gujarat itself, how many Hindus have been killed by Muslims even after Godhra? The secularists have been acting as if attacks on Muslims in Gujarat are the only communal flashpoint. This is typical of hate discourse: apart from pure lies, the main technique consists in exclusively highlighting the – sometimes admittedly real – crimes of the targeted group and keeping instances of its innocent victimization out of view.

But I will agree in general terms that this was mostly a Hindu retaliation for the Godhra massacre, and for all the earlier occasions of Muslim aggression. Gujarat and especially Ahmedabad have witnessed a sustained low-level terror campaign against the Hindus. With their Gandhian tradition of fleeing and turning the other cheek, the Gujaratis had amassed considerable resentment against the Muslims, and after Godhra it all came out.

By all means, preserve the Godhra articles and columns in a special folder, one day they will be the object of a spectacular case study in the human capacity for doublethink. Though disgusting, it was at the same time quite funny to watch the extreme inventiveness of the secularists in blaming the victims. They were very annoyed that the Gujarat carnage was so unambiguously started by Muslims with their massacre of Hindu pilgrims, mostly women and children. So, they falsely started describing the victims as "extremists" and inventing stories of how these Hindu children had kidnapped a Muslim woman into their riding train. That canard was borrowed from an Islamist website. There is never much difference between secularist reporting and Islamist propaganda anyway, which is why Indian theocratic Islamists call themselves "secularists". The latest is their "report" claiming that the Hindus in the train had themselves lit the fire, in a gigantic mass suicide. I suppose free speech includes the right to speak nonsense.

For four years after the BJP's accession to power in 1998, in spite of numerous massacres of Hindus by Muslim terrorists, the Indian Muslims were left alone. Hindus had often refused to be provoked into taking their anger out on their Muslim neighbours, e.g. after the Mumbai blasts of March 1993, all remained quiet. Hindus again showed remarkable restraint after Islamic terrorists killed forty BJP activists, allegedly "Hindu Nazis", in Coimbatore in 1998. But unlike the Nazis in 1938 with their *Kristallnacht* killing nearly a hundred Jews in reaction to the murder of a single German diplomat, the BJP did not retaliate in kind at all. Hindus have been killed with great frequency in Jammu, even the parliament buildings in Srinagar and Delhi were attacked, yet the Muslims remained unharmed. So, the secularists were losing credibility day by day. They needed the Gujarat carnage, and they thanked Heaven when it finally materialized. They were suddenly back in business, getting invited all the way to Washington to tell their scare stories.

6.2.5. Foreign complicity

Most of the foreign India reporters borrow not just data, but also opinions and judgments from their Delhi contacts without critically examining them. On top of these borrowed distortions, they themselves also manage to disregard pertinent data which stare every normal observer in the face. Thus, practically every Hindu activist whom I have interviewed between 1990 and 1998 brought up the plight of the Kashmiri Pandits, murdered or expelled from their homeland, as a telling illustration of the true religio-political power equation in India. But most publications purportedly analyzing Hindu nationalism in the 1990s manage to overlook this expulsion of Hindus from a part of India. They have to if they want to uphold the image of India as dominated by an overbearing Hindu majority threatening a hapless Muslim minority.

The foreign correspondents also systematically misunderstand and misrepresent the relationship between Hindu vanguard organizations and the common people. It is increasingly clear that genuine acts of anti-Muslim or anti-Christian violence are often the handiwork of desperate but unorganized locals. Membership of an organization like the Vishva Hindu Parishad, by contrast, offers them the hope of participating in a larger countersubversive strategy and thereby keeps acts of desperation in check.

It has to be admitted, however, that Hindu nationalist organizations have played into the hand of the disinformation campaigners. For too long, they have spurned the intellectual and mediatic struggles. On the plea that "you don't need arguments to love your mother", meaning Mother India, the Hindu nationalists had always neglected intellectual work and favoured a mindless activism. Instead, they have adopted a boy-scout attitude of doing one's best and disregarding the opinions of the inactive and the hostile people. This way, they have left the field wide open for their sworn enemies, who have been getting away with their hate-mongering accounts for decades. Correcting this deeply uneven power equation in the control over public opinion proves to be a hard and long-term job.

6.3. Conclusion

The problem which Hindus face when they want to mobilize support for their oppressed brothers and sisters, is that nobody even seems to have heard of any oppression of Hindus. The news about this large and widespread problem gets sidetracked and minimized and ultimately silenced somewhere along the way. Yet, whether the story is heard in the international media and especially in the centres of power, is a very consequential matter. Thus, a country like Bangladesh is heavily dependent on international aid, and is therefore susceptible to being pressured into correcting its human-rights performance if only the donors knew about the human-rights violations there. Getting the information across to world opinion is, thus, of vital importance. That is why I would like to thank the organizers for at least making a serious effort to that end by holding this conference.

7. What if Rajiv Gandhi hadn't unlocked the Babri Masjid in 1986?

[This article first appeared in the online version of the newsmagazine *Outlook India*, 23 August 2004.]

In 1985, Prime Minister Rajiv Gandhi gave in to Muslim pressure in the Shah Bano affair. Overruling a secular court's decision that the repudiated wife Shah Bano was entitled to alimony from her ex-husband, he enacted a law abolishing the alimony provision in conformity with the Shari'a. Since India, unlike secular states, already had religion-based Civil Codes, this concession merely brought the minor matter of alimony under the purview of the prevailing arrangement. More importantly, it prevented riots.

Only months later, Gandhi restored the balance by giving the Hindus something as well: he ordered the locks on the Ram Janmabhoomi Babri Masjid in Ayodhya removed. Until then, a priest had been permitted to perform puja once a year for the idols installed there in 1949. Now, all Hindus were given access to what they consider as the birthplace of Rama, the prince posthumously deified as an incarnation of Vishnu.

Fundamentally, this decision didn't alter the Ayodhya equation. Architecturally, the building was and remained a mosque, while functionally, it had been and continued to be a Hindu temple. That is why in my opinion, not taking this decision wouldn't have changed the Ayodhya developments except in their timing. The different players, their strategies and goals, and their resolve to pursue these, all remained the same. The Babri Masjid Action Committee and the Vishva Hindu Parishad would have gone about their "business" just the same.

However, the VHP would have been forced to continue pushing the rather petty demand for removing the locks, rather than move on to the more ambitious and more mobilizing next step of planning the construction of a new temple. Most probably, the BJP would likewise have reaped smaller dividends from such a campaign. In 1989, it might not have jumped to as high as 86 Lok Sabha seats. Conversely, Congress might not have lost the North-Indian Muslim vote to the Janata Dal. In 1989, it could have remained just strong enough to cobble together a coalition rather than leave the initiative to the unwholesome and unstable Janata-BJP-Communist combine. So, at the level of party politics, Rajiv Gandhi's decision may have made a big difference.

On the other hand, the presence or absence of locks might have made little difference to the Kar Sevaks who brought the building down in 1992. Then again, with a Rajiv Gandhi government returning to power in 1989, there might have been no reason for this extreme move. The Hindus might by then have gotten their sacred site without a fight.

After all, in a situation where both Hindus and Muslims were laying claim to the site, Gandhi's decision in 1986 was important because it allowed for only one interpretation: he favoured the Hindu claim. This was logical, for the site has a sacred significance for Hindus as the putative birthplace of Rama, while it had no special status for Muslims. Historical documents confirm that Hindus continued to go on pilgrimage to the site all through the centuries of Muslim occupation, while no Muslim ever went on pilgrimage there.

Admittedly, a Muslim lobby had been formed which insisted on reoccupying this Hindu sacred site. However, the existing Congress culture notoriously knew how to deal with such problems: give the Muslim lobbyists some ministerial posts, some public largesse for their institutes or a raise in the Hajj subsidies, and they will come around. A small application of this approach was the annulment of Syed Shahabuddin's announced march on Ayodhya in 1988 in exchange for the governmental ban on Salman Rushdie's freshly-released book *The Satanic Verses.* A similar but bigger concession might have annulled the Muslim claim on the Ayodhya site. It would not have been the most principled policy, but it would have avoided a lot of communal blood-letting.

This pragmatic approach was thwarted midway. It is not often that intellectuals play a crucial role in politics, but this time they did. After the locks had been removed, India's Marxist intellectuals unchained all their devils in order to prevent the full restoration of the site as a Hindu pilgrimage centre. In particular, they started insisting that there had never been a Hindu temple at the site before a mosque had been imposed on it.

This was a strange claim to make, for two reasons. Firstly, it was untrue. Until then, all parties concerned had agreed that the mosque had been built in forcible replacement of a temple. What is nowadays rubbished as "the VHP claim" was in fact the consensus view. Thus, in court proceedings in the 1880s, the Muslim claimants and the British rulers agreed with the Hindu claimants on the historical fact of the temple demolition, but since it had happened centuries earlier, they decided that time had sanctioned the Muslim usurpation and nullified the Hindus' legal claim. Further, numerous documents and several archaeological excavations confirmed the history of the temple demolition (with the court-ordered excavations of spring 2003 removing the last possible doubts). The sudden denial of this history by a circle of Marxist historians was not based on any new evidence but purely on political compulsions. It seems that their long enjoyment of a hegemonic power position in academe had gone to their heads, so they thought they could get away with crude history falsification.

Secondly, the question of the site's history was beside the point. The decisive consideration for awarding the site to the Hindus, both for the Hindu campaigners themselves and for Rajiv Gandhi, was not the site's sacred status in the Middle Ages, but its sacredness for Hindus today. It is the Hindus of

1986 or indeed of 2004 who have been going on pilgrimage to Ayodhya, and they are as much entitled to find a Hindu atmosphere there, complete with Hindu architecture, as Muslims are entitled to find an Islamic atmosphere in Mecca. The VHP has been blamed for politicizing history, but it was its opponents who complicated matters by bringing in history, and false history at that.

Nonetheless, the Marxist historians had their way. In their shrill manifestoes, these secular fundamentalists slandered the genuine historians who stood by the facts, and they denounced the Hindus' perfectly reasonable expectation that a Hindu sacred site be left in the exclusive care of the Hindus. They did this with such titanic vehemence that the pragmatists were thrown on the defensive.

Rajiv Gandhi didn't give up, though. In 1989, he allowed the Shilanyas ceremony, in which the first stone of the planned temple was put in place. In 1990, as opposition leader, he made Chandra Shekhar's minority government organize a scholars' debate on the history of the site, obviously on the assumption that this would confirm the Hindu claim. And so it did, for the anti-temple historians showed up empty-handed when they were asked to provide evidence for an alternative scenario to the temple demolition. In a normal course of events, i.e. without the interference of secularist shrieks and howls, this would have set the stage for the peaceful construction of a new temple in the 1990s, with some compensation for the Muslim community, and the conflict would have been forgotten by now. Instead, the sore has continued to fester. In 1991 Rajiv Gandhi was murdered, and his successors didn't have the good sense to continue his equitable and pragmatic Ayodhya policy.

8. No Hindu justification for Islamic iconoclasm

In early November 2004, I found myself involved in a weblist debate on the question whether Hindus were forced to pay *jizya* or "toleration tax" under Muslim rule. Someone argued that: "As Romila Thapar's recent book on Somnath has so clearly demonstrated, we cannot always take the boasts of Islamic court 'historians' at face value. Richard Eaton's investigation into this matter, in general, corroborates the Thapar position as presented; the results were presented in two articles in *Frontline* in 2000. Eaton argues that there is no evidence to support the assertion that temple desecration/ destruction was undertaken wholesale in the Indian subcontinent by Muslim rulers, and that the rhetoric of temple destruction was just that: rhetoric. (...) by destroying temples patronized by rival kings, new rulers asserted their authority over the realm in a manner, Eaton argues, that was established well before Muslim rulers came to the subcontinent; new rulers continued this practice."

Both on jizya (about which, do consult Harsh Narain: *Jizyah and the Spread of Islam*, Delhi 1990, entirely based on Arabic and Indo-Persian sources) and on iconoclasm, we are dealing with a sizable and coherent testimony of dozens of Muslim authors spanning seven centuries. Eventhough some Muslim rulers had their reasons (esp. to trump their opponents in the endless infighting within the Muslim elite) to accommodate their Hindu subjects and vassals by suspending jizya and allowing temple construction, nonetheless iconoclasm and the imposition of jizya appear as rule and not as exception in the history of Muslim regimes in

India. If the chroniclers all describe truthfully a normative Islamic practice, it is only normal that their accounts are similar.

But while truth is one, untruths can be many (if I may espouse a secularized-monotheistic assumption), and if a large set of authors all convey the same untruth, the researcher needs to find an explanation for their remarkable consensus. Someone eager to be convinced may accept the conspiracy theory that, in collectively conveying the same lie, those authors were all motivated by one and the same collective motive, i.c. boastfulness. This would at least prove that in their common cultural framework, iconoclasm was consistently deemed a praiseworthy practice, though this in turn raises the question why this praiseworthy ideal of iconoclasm was never put into practice by Muslim rulers eventhough their scribes all egged them on to it. Anyway, why assume a conspiracy when Occam's razor points to a far simpler explanation? They all mentioned jizya and iconoclasm because that happened to be the reality they witnessed.

It was interesting to see how many modern academics, esp. in India's ongoing "detoxification of history" effort, were ready to sweep such a body of evidence aside as "just rhetoric" and mere "boasts". The only dissenting voice in the forum was Delhi University art historian Prof. Bharat Gupt:

"If the historians of Islamic courts were 'boasting' for 700 years and all their descriptions of conquest, plunder, slave-taking and massacres were exaggerations, then we have nothing to rely upon for medieval India. All other evidence such as archaeological, literary and folklore does not show that it was boasting but was close to the truth."

In sharp contrast with this voguish rejection of the chroniclers' solid testimony (which happens to be corroborated by other types of evidence, including the material remains of temples in numerous mosques, e.g. very visibly in Varanasi's Gyanvapi mosque, formerly the Kashi

Vishvanath), do note the uncritical eagerness with which the testimony of a mere handful of Hindu sources concerning alleged acts of inter-Hindu iconoclasm has been seized upon, in particular by Prof. Richard M. Eaton. In the latter case, no hypercritical questions are asked about their possible boastfulness.

The dominant ideological school in India, ably represented by the Communist fortnightly *Frontline* (yes, a paper which applauds North Korea and the Chinese occupation of Tibet in its cover stories can safely be termed "Communist"), is quite enthusiastic about Prof. Eaton's revisionist hypothesis that Islamic iconoclasm came about as a continuation of this inter-Hindu iconoclasm, and clearly doesn't want to spoil its own fun by going through the motions of normal critical reflection on it. To be sure, the fact that currently hegemonic ideologies such as Nehruvian secularism exploit a scholarly hypothesis for their own ends doesn't disprove the hypothesis, just as the Aryan Invasion Theory's long-standing exploitation by colonialism and racism doesn't disprove the theory itself. In the very brief format of an internet debate, I could only draw the forum's attention to five problems with Eaton's thesis.

Firstly, nobody seems to have noticed that the crucial evidence which might have proven this hypothesis is entirely missing: any reference by a Muslim iconoclast to an earlier act of inter-Hindu iconoclasm as his justification. In the theory and practice of Muslim law, the precedents and rules of *Jahiliyya* or pre-Islamic society (including even the well-codified and well-known Roman law in ex-Byzantine territory) were not accepted as justification anyway.

Secondly, there is a big elephant in the room which the revisionist school somehow manages to keep outside the discussion: the tradition of Islamic iconoclasm established outside India well before Ghaznavi, Ghori and their successors. What *is* accepted as justification, unlike pre-Islamic precedent, is *Sunna* (tradition) precedent from the

Prophet himself and the Rightly-Guided Caliphs. When mosques replaced demolished Christian churches (e.g. the Mezquita in Cordoba) or when churches were transformed into mosques after removal of their idols (e.g. Ummayad mosque in Damascus, Aya Sophia in Istambul), this was in emulation of precedents set by the Prophet himself, e.g. his very own mosque in Medina was built on a Pagan shrine after removal of buried corpses and chopping down of sacred trees. Most importantly, the Kaaba itself was a Pagan shrine until Mohammed broke its idols with his own hands. This is in cold print in the core texts of Islam as one of its great founding events, and the Taliban can cite it to all those people who allege that the destruction of the Bamian Buddhas was "un-Islamic". No Islamic court could sentence iconoclasts like the Taliban for their iconoclasm unless it were willing to denounce Mohammed's normative behaviour itself as un-Islamic.

Thirdly, Eaton follows the convention, earlier used by Romila Thapar and the Marxist school, of contrasting "religious" or "ideological" reasons for temple plunder with "material" or "economic" or "political" reasons. Karl Marx himself would have regarded this pious Christian distinction between lowly-motivated materialistic wars and lofty idealistic wars with some skepticism; but more importantly, Islam itself doesn't recognize this distinction. When Mohammed was materially in dire straits, he organized caravan raids (82 according to one orthodox count), but Islamic scripture never discounts these as un-religious and merely materialistic. On the contrary, the Prophet himself called them *Jihād fi Sabīl Allāh*, "effort in the way of God", or more conventionally, "Holy War". In fact, they were the original Jihad, setting the model for every later Jihad. Likewise, Jizya, though a major incentive to conversion, could be described as "merely" material and political, "merely" serving the material welfare of the Islamic state,— but the creation of an Islamic state (ultimately spanning the world) in this material world was Mohammed's life work and remains the very purpose of Islam.

Fourthly, the claim that mosques were left alone because they were no centres of politics while temples were, is a textbook example of what you call special pleading. And for most temples and quite a few mosques, it is simply untrue. Many — in fact, easily most — temples had nothing to do with royal legitimacy, e.g. the numerous caste-reserved temples belonging to non-ruling castes. Of the 1000 temples recordedly demolished during the Muslim conquest of Varanasi in 1194 (an instance accepted by Eaton into his list), maybe 990 had no role in the legitimation of political power. By contrast, the number of mosques serving as an enemy power's royal showpiece or as centres of political conspiracies or palace revolution or rebellious preaching was rather more than zero, both in the Middle Ages and in the present (ask the late Shah of Iran). In such cases, Muslim rulers would try to capture the enemy leader and his clerical confidants or arrest the rebels and conspirators but still leave their mosques standing.

Fifthly, the superficial similarity between Hindu conquerors carting off the enemy temple's idol and Muslim conquerors doing the same thing actually hides a crucial contrast between the two. The Hindu conqueror installed the looted idol in his own temple as an object of worship, whereas the Muslim conqueror ceremoniously broke it to pieces or built it into walkways for treading underfoot or into lavatories for further soiling. It can be conceded that Indo-Muslim rulers continued a Hindu practice *if* anyone can show us one example of a Muslim conqueror installing his captured Hindu idol in his own mosque for purposes of worship. As Sita Ram Goel used to say: I am asking for one example, not two.

9. Wahi: the supernatural basis of Islam

[Completed in this version in 2005, an earlier version was published in instalments in the on-line magazine *Kashmir Herald*, autumn-winter 2002-03.]

In discussing Islam, most non-Muslims and ex-Muslims tend to focus on the negative achievements of Islam, such as Islamic mistreatment of women and unbelievers. However, we should realize that in its essence, Islam is only secondarily an ethical system with a characteristic record of conduct. In the first place it is a belief system, a truth claim. The Islamic religion stands or falls with the truth or untruth of two assertions: (1) there is no God but Allah, the Creator of the universe; and (2) Mohammed is the final spokesman of Allah, who through him passed on to mankind a series of messages assembled in the Quran. This Quranic communication is understood to have been a constant process of "revelation" from AD 610, when Mohammed was 40, until his death in AD 632.

The first belief is a theological claim which Islam has in common with some other monotheistic religions, and which, if subjected to cunning interpretation, could even be reconciled with some schools of polymorphous-theistic Hinduism ("the wise call the one True One by many names"). The second belief, by contrast, is the truly defining truth claim of Islam, setting it apart from every other religion: the prophethood of Mohammed. In this essay, we will discuss some non-Islamic views of this core assertion of Islam.

9.1. The modern view of the Quranic trance

Some modern Western and even some Muslim-born scholars have diagnosed the process of Quranic revelation to Mohammed as a case of paranoid delusion. For now we shall discuss the analysis offered by the Marxist scholar Maxime Rodinson. In his Penguin monograph *Mohammed*, p.76-79, he starts out by rejecting the allegation that Mohammed's claim to receiving visions in a state of trance (*wahī*) was fraudulent. This allegation has of course been made by Christian polemicists against Islam, but also by modern leftist sympathizers of Islam seeking to recast Mohammed in the mould of a social progressive. In order to further his purported programme of social reform, Mohammed is said to have enacted the role of conveyor of God's injunctions merely to carry more conviction with an audience steeped in religion. Against this line of thought, Rodinson argues:

"Modern advances in psychology and psychiatry have made short work of such simplistic explanations of fraud, whether justifiable or otherwise. The reaction may even have gone too far in the other direction, for there have been, and still are, cases of real fraud. But their number is limited. At all events, it is now generally understood and admitted that certain individuals can sincerely believe that they are the recipients of visual, auditory and mental messages from the Beyond; and also that their sincerity is no proof that these messages really come from where they are claimed to come."

So, where did the Quranic messages come from?

"It is the concept of the unconscious that has enabled us to understand these things. (...) One has only to dip into psychology text-books to find a hundred perfectly bona fide cases of people in a state of hallucination hearing things and seeing visions which they claim quite genuinely never to have seen or heard before. And yet an objective study of their cases shows that these are simply fresh associations produced by the unconscious working on things which have been seen or heard but forgotten."

Just like a dream, a hallucination recombines old sensory and mental impressions:

"It is therefore conceivable that what Muhammad saw and heard may have been the beings described to him by the Jews and Christians with whom he talked. It is understandable that, in the words that came to him, elements of his actual experience, the stuff of his thoughts, dreams and meditations, and memories of the discussions that he had heard, should have reemerged, chopped, changed and transposed, with an appearance of immediate reality that seemed to him proof of some external activity which, although inaccessible to other men's minds, was yet wholly objective in its nature."

Throughout his career as a Prophet (except, as we shall see, at the very beginning), Mohammed genuinely believed that the visions and spoken messages which he "received" were of divine origin. His *wahī* or Quranic trance seemed to make a far deeper impression on his mind than any ordinary human experience could, and he therefore considered it supremely real.

Today, both in mental hospitals and in the cult scene, you can find numerous people who likewise believe to be regular recipients of messages from Above. In some cases, these people manage to make others believe in their claims, too. They then set themselves up as cult leaders, revered by a group of followers as their direct telephone line to God or the spirit world. It is not uncommon for people who regularly hallucinate to function fairly normally in the world, sometimes even highly successfully. Thus, Joan of Arc derived from her visions the strength to lead an army against the British invaders of France. Chengiz Khan transmuted the shamanic messages from his god Il-Tengri into a trail of battlefield victories founding a far-flung empire, which disintegrated a few generations later. In terms of durability and ultimate geographical expansion of his religio-political empire, Mohammed was the single most successful voice-hearer in world history.

It is only in a very few cases later on in his career that both contemporaries and later scholars of Islam have found reason to cast doubt on the genuineness of certain instances of his Quranic trance. These are the cases where the divine messages received during *wahī* were just a little too convenient not to look like Mohammed's self-serving fabrications. The best-known instance is when Mohammed received permission from Allah to marry Zaynab, the repudiated wife of his adopted son Zayd. Under Arab customary law, this union was prohibited, but in a timely revelation (Q.33:37, 33:50), Allah exempted Mohammed from this law. Christian polemicists against Islam have often cited the Zaynab episode as proof of Mohammed's insatiable lust, but in fact its indication of self-serving manipulation of the *wahī* by Mohammed is more damaging to the Islamic belief system.

According to Rodinson: "It is true that, later on, some disturbing characteristics did appear. Muhammad had to take day-to-day decisions, decisions of a political, practical and legislative nature, which could not wait for some unspecified moment when the spirit might see fit to breathe on him. He was constantly under fire, bombarded with questions and requests for advice. The divinely inspired nature of his replies gave them a solid basis of authority. Did he yield to the temptation to nudge the truth a little? Some of the revelations correspond a little too closely to what might have been the Prophet's own human desires and calculations. Or was it, once again, his unconscious at work? We shall never know."

These few somewhat suspect instances should at any rate not make us lose sight of the general case: "When his soul was thus plunged into the void (...) Muhammad then attained periodic states of ecstasy in which he felt that he had been stripped of his own personality, submitting passively to the invasion of a mysterious force, (...) he experienced the phenomena described above – seeing and hearing things, either inwardly or outwardly, in the mind or the imagination. We find these ecstasies and sensory phenomena in a very similar form among persons suffering from recognized mental conditions such as hysteria, schizophrenia and uncontrolled verbalization."

If anything can dispel the lingering doubt about Mohammed's genuine belief in the reality of his trance visions, it is the description of his own reaction when these psychic phenomena started. Rodinson: "A study of Muhammad's earliest messages, coupled with a perusal of accounts of the crises of doubt or despair which preceded or accompanied them, can only produce a skeptical attitude towards the theories which see them as evidence of a coolly calculated plan carried out ruthlessly from motives of either ambition or philanthropy. And these accounts do seem to be authentic. Tradition, concerned to stress the supernatural affiliations of Muhammed's personality, would not have invented from scratch such very human traits."

9.2. Mohammed's reaction to the Quranic trance

The first person to doubt the genuineness of the Quranic "revelations" was Mohammed himself. This was at the very beginning of his career, when during his *Ramadhān* (month of fasting, then always roughly coinciding with the month of March and the Christian Lent) retreat outside Mecca in AD 610, he had an audio-visual experience in which he both heard and saw the archangel Gabriel, calling upon him to "Recite!" (*Iqrā'*, from *Qara'a*, whence *Qur'ān*). Upon receiving his first "revelation", Mohammed thought he was going mad, or in the parlance of those days, that he was getting possessed by an evil spirit.

He didn't want to spend the rest of his life as Mecca's village idiot, and so, preferring death to disgrace, he decided to throw himself from a high rock: "Now none of God's creatures was more hateful to me than an ecstatic poet or a man possessed: I could not even look at them. I thought, Woe is me poet or possessed — Never shall Quraish *[i.e. his fellow tribesmen of the Quraish tribe]* say this of me! I will go to the top of the mountain and throw myself down that I may kill myself and gain rest." (Ibn Ishāq's *Sīrat Rasūl Allāh*, tra. Alfred Guillaume: *The Life of Mohammed*, p.106/153)

The history of Islam could have ended there and then, with Mohammed escaping the spell of the alleged evil spirit by jumping to his death. But the ghost himself came to the rescue, as Mohammed testified: "So I went forth to do so and then, when I was midway on the mountain, I heard a voice from heaven saying, 'O Mohammed! Thou art the apostle of God and I am Gabriel.'" (ibid.)

So, the vision repeated itself. We don't know if that was sufficient to reassure Mohammed about his sanity, but then another and more decisive factor intervened to save him: "And I continued standing there, neither advancing nor turning back, until Khadija sent her messengers in search of me and they gained the high ground above Mecca and returned to her while I was standing in the same place; and he *[i.e. Gabriel]* parted from me and I from him, returning to my family." (ibid.)

It was indeed his wife Khadija who saved him and helped him to accept the trance states as they became a recurring and then a regular feature of his life. Later on, she supported him when others doubted his prophetic claims: "By her, God lightened the burden of His prophet. He never met with contradiction and charges of falsehood, which saddened him, but God comforted him when he went home. She strengthened him, lightened his burden, proclaimed his truth, and belittled men's opposition." (Ishaq/Guillaume:111/155) But more importantly, she supported and soothed Mohammed in the crucial phase when he himself entertained the deepest doubts about his own sanity.

This is how she did it. When Mohammed came home, he told her: "Woe is me poet or possessed." But she replied: "I take refuge in God from that, o Ab'l Qāsim *[i.e. "father of Qāsim", after Mohammed's first son Qāsim].* God would not treat you thus since he knows your truthfulness, your great trustworthiness, your fine character, and your kindness. This cannot be, my dear. Perhaps you did see something." And Mohammed answered: "Yes, I did." (Ishaq/Guillaume: 106/153)

Certainly Mohammed had seen something, meaning that his sensory nerves had indeed produced a visual sensation. But was it a false sensation, or in the parlance of the day, the impact of ghost-possession? Khadija and her Christian cousin Waraqa b. Naufal eagerly embraced the idea that Mohammed had had a genuine vision and had been invested with the mantle of prophethood, but Mohammed himself, with his skeptical-Pagan background, still had his doubts. Fortunately, his loving wife knew a way to decide the matter and convince him of both his sanity and his new prophetic mission.

She asked him to notify her when his visitor returned, so that they could verify whether he really was the archangel Gabriel or an ordinary demon. "So when Gabriel came to him, as he was wont, the apostle said to Khadija, 'This is Gabriel who has just come to me.' 'Get up, o son of my uncle', she said, 'and sit by my left thigh.' The apostle did so, and she said, 'Can you see him?' 'Yes', he said. She said, 'Then turn round and sit on my right thigh.' He did so, and she said, 'Can you see him?' When he said that he could, she asked him to move and sit in her lap. When he had done this, she again asked if he could see him, and when he said yes, she disclosed her form and cast aside her veil while the apostle was sitting in her lap. Then she said, 'Can you see him?' And he replied, 'No.' She said, 'O son of my uncle, rejoice and be of good heart, by God he is an angel and not a Satan." (Ishaq/Guillaume: 107/154)

In modern language, this account relates how Mohammed's vision of the Archangel waned and disappeared as his wife turned up the heat of sexual arousal. Narrator Ibn Ishaq adds a second tradition (through Khadija's daughter Fatima, her son Husayn, his daughter Fatima, her son Abdullah b. Hasan) which is even more explicit in this regard, viz. that "she made the apostle of God come inside her shift, and thereupon Gabriel departed, and she said to the apostle of God, 'This verily is an angel and not a satan.'" (ibid.) The underlying assumption appears to be that a lustful demon, the kind who might take possession of a man's soul, would have stayed around to enjoy the sight of Mohammed and Khadija's sexual intercourse; whereas an angel with his ethos of renunciation would politely withdraw from the scene.

After his wife had provided him with this experimental proof of the genuineness of his meeting with the Archangel, Mohammed was cured of his doubts. He could now safely embark upon his career as God's exclusive spokesman and frequent recipient of Gabriel's messages, which were written down by a secretary and later collected into a book, the *Qur'ān*. Only on one occasion would the doubt briefly reappear, viz. during the episode of the "Satanic verses".

Frustrated at the unyielding skepticism of his Meccan townsfolk, the Prophet consciously or subconsciously devised a way to win them over to the acceptance of his prophetic claims. He would compromise on the central item in his theology, viz. the falseness of the gods of the Arabian pantheon as contrasted with the unique reality of Allah alone. Modern apologists slanderously depict the Meccan heathens as fanatics intolerant of Mohammed's innovative cult, but in reality they were always eager for reconciliation. They were pluralistic or what modern Indians would call "secular". At a meeting outside their national shrine, the Ka'ba, they proposed to Mohammed: "Come let us worship what you worship, and you worship what we worship. You and we will combine in the matter." (Ishaq/Guillaume: 165/239) They were even willing to shed some of their religious practices if those of Mohammed were to prove superior: "If what you worship is better than what we worship, we will take a share of it, and if what we worship is better than what you worship, you can take a share of that." (ibid.)

It is at this point that Mohammed received an anti-pluralistic and anti-compromise "revelation": "Say, o disbelievers, I do not worship what you worship, and you do not worship what I worship, and I will not worship what you have been wont to worship, nor will you worship that which I worship. To you your religion and to me my religion." (Q.109; note that both fools and knaves sometimes quote the latter sentence as proof of Mohammed's pluralism, when the context actually shows it to mean the exact opposite.) On another occasion, viz. around the deathbed of Mohammed's uncle Abu Tālib, the Meccans again pleaded reconciliation and pluralism with the words: "Let him have his religion and we will have ours". But once more Mohammed refused all compromise and demanded that they accept his monotheism and his claim to prophethood, nothing less. (Ishaq/Guillaume:191/278)

Yet, at one point he did give in to the tempting idea of a quick way to bring the Meccans into his fold, viz. by accepting the reality and auspicious role of the three popular goddesses *al-Lāt*, *al-Uzzā* and *Manāt*. A revelation duly arrived from heaven, saying: "Have you thought of al-Lāt and al-Uzzā and Manāt, the third, the other? These are the exalted cranes whose intercession is approved." (Ishaq/Guillaume:165/239) The Meccans were enthusiastic, prostrating along with the Muslims at the mention of the goddesses in Allah's company, and word even spread that they had converted to Islam.

But then another revelation came down, telling Mohammed that he had been deceived by Satan, who had smuggled these goddess-revering words into the channel of the prophet's *wahī* or revelatory trance, falsely making it look like a divine message on a par with all the others Quranic verses. So Allah annulled the Satanic verses and sent down the verse: "We have not sent a prophet or apostle before you but when he longed *[viz. for acceptance]*, Satan cast suggestions into his longing. But God will annul what Satan has suggested. The God will establish his verses, God being knowing and wise." (Q.22:51/52; Ishaq/Guillaume 166/239) Since then, the Quran gives a corrected reading, this one properly revealed by Gabriel himself: "Have ye seen *Lāt*, and *Uzzā*, and another, the third, *Manāt* ? (....) These are nothing but names which ye have devised, ye and your fathers, for which Allah has sent down no authority." (Q.53:19-23)

Mohammed got away with it, the indignation among a few of his followers at this lapse from orthodoxy remaining brief and inconsequential. But an objective observer cannot avoid facing the question: if the prophet could be thus deceived by Satan, how could he know on all the other occasions that he hadn't been deceived? The only answer the Islamic apologist can come up with, is the one given in the above narrative: God or Gabriel told Mohammed which revelation to believe and which one to reject as false. That way, the only guarantee of revelation is another revelation.

But at least we can sympathize with Mohammed's brief pang of conscience when he realized the deception (he "was bitterly grieved and greatly in fear of God", according to Ishaq/Guillaume:166/239). Clearly he tried to be honest and bring only genuine revelations to his audience. Unfortunately, the fullness of Mohammed's critical sense vis-ã-vis his revelations had been abandoned at the very beginning, when, safe and warm between Khadija's thighs, he had accepted the basic genuineness of the process of divine revelation through the voice and vision of Gabriel.

9.3. The yogic view of Mohammed's trance

In certain cultures, altered states of consciousness enjoy a certain legitimacy as ways of knowledge. The most systematic premodern exploration of consciousness was achieved in the Hindu-Buddhist tradition. It is there, though mostly only in the past century, that we do find a critique of Mohammed's Quranic trance.

Before the colonial age, there was hardly any Hindu evaluation of Mohammed's prophetic claims, nor even of Islamic doctrine in general. The first detailed criticism of Islam, and in particular of the Quran, was written by Swami Dayananda Saraswati, founder of the Vedic reform movement Arya Samaj in 1875. He mainly lambasted the contradictions, irrational beliefs and inhumane injunctions in Islamic scripture. Later Arya Samaj criticism of the Prophet typically focused on his dictatorial and immoral personal behaviour (e.g. Rajpal's *Rangīlā Rasūl*, about Mohammed's sex life), not on the source of his "revelations". This was all not unlike the Christian missionary criticisms of Hindu scripture and of allegedly licentious Hindu heroes such as Krishna, and it missed the point about the dubious source of the Quranic revelations.

The basis of Islam is the belief that Mohammed regularly went into a state of trance (*wahī*) and heard a voice dictating Allah's own words. In recent years, Hindu students of Islam have invoked the eyewitness testimony of Mohammed's contemporaries in support of their own skeptical rejection of the Prophet's claim of receiving divine messages: "The Meccans stood firm by their gods; their faith in the gods was not at all shaken by Muhammad's attacks. Allah reports: 'When it was said unto them, There is no God save Allah, they were scornful, and said: Shall we forsake our gods for a mad poet?' (Q.37:36/35) 'And they marvel that a warner from among themselves had come. They say: This is a wizard, a charlatan.' (Q.38:4/3)" (S.R. Goel: *Hindu Temples*, vol.2, 2nd ed., Voice of India, Delhi 1993, p.334)

It was probably Swami Vivekananda who first connected the questionable nature of Mohammed's leadership with the nature of his prophethood. Mohammed had to be ruthless in imposing adherence to his belief in his own divine mission because this belief could not stand on its own, based as it was on a delusion. If your neighbour, whom you have known for years as an ordinary businessman, tells you one day that he is hearing God's voice and that you have to obey his divine instructions from now on, would you readily give in to his demand? Rather, you would wonder what had happened to him. So, Vivekananda offered one hypothesis of what had happened to Mohammed so as to make him believe in his own selection as God's sole living spokesman.

The specifically Hindu contribution to our understanding of the Quranic revelation is to bring in the yogic experience. As an example of how yogic practice can go wrong, warning against the dangers of experimenting with yoga without competent guidance, Vivekananda mentioned Mohammed:

"The yogi says there is a great danger in stumbling upon this state. In a good many cases, there is the danger of the brain being deranged, and, as a rule, you will find that all those men, however great they were, who had stumbled upon this super-conscious state without understanding it, groped in the dark, and generally had, along with their knowledge, some quaint superstition. They opened themselves to hallucinations. Mohammed claimed that the Angel Gabriel came to him in a cave one day and took him on the heavenly horse, Burak, and he visited the heavens.

"But with all that, Mohammed spoke some wonderful truths. If you read the Koran, you find the most wonderful truths mixed with superstitions. How will you explain it? That man was inspired, no doubt, but that inspiration was, as it were, stumbled upon. He was not a trained Yogi, and did not know the reason of what he was doing. Think of the good Mohammed did to the world, and think of the great evil that has been done through his fanaticism! Think of the millions massacred through his teachings, mothers bereft of their children, children made orphans, whole countries destroyed, millions upon millions of people killed! (...) So we see this danger by studying the lives of great teachers like Mohammad and others. Yet we find, at the same time, that they were all inspired. Whenever a prophet got into the super-conscious state by heightening his emotional nature, he brought away from it not only some truths, but some fanaticism also, some superstition which injured the world as much as the greatness of the teaching helped." (Vivekananda: *Complete Works*, vol.1, p.184, from his book *Raja Yoga*, Ch.7: "Dhyana and Samadhi")

Mental disturbance as a consequence of meditative experiments had already been named as the cause of the Quranic revelations by Gisbertus Voetius, a 17th-century Dutch Calvinist theologian who trained missionaries for conversion work in Indonesia (discussed in Karel Steenbrink: *Dutch Colonialism and Indonesian Islam. Contacts and Conflicts 1595-1950*, Rodopi, Amsterdam/Atlanta 1993). Protestants who had abolished monastic institutions and were scornful of the ascetic practices of Catholic and Orthodox monks, liked to point out such dangers, and their warning seemed to apply to the case of Mohammed as well.

Most yoga manuals emphatically warn against wrongly practising the techniques of *Haṭha Yoga*, which are very powerful whether used properly or in disregard of the concomitant rules. Yogic masters can relate anecdotes of pupils or colleagues who spurned the precautions and practised dangerous forms of *prāṇāyāma* ("breath control" or "control of the vital energies") till they impaired their nerve systems. One well-known written testimony of the painful and lasting effects of erratic yogic practice is given by Gopi Krishna in his well-known book *Kundalini, the Evolutionary Energy in Man* (1967, still available in many Indian and overseas editions). Arya Samaj leader Vandematharam Ramachandra Rao told me of one case involving a friend of his who inflicted brain damage on himself and died of a stroke as a consequence of improper *prāṇāyāma* practice. Likewise, the Taoist energy-steering system of *Qigong* comes with the same warning and similar anecdotes. Many mystic phenomena the world over come about as cases of stumbling upon certain states of consciousness, which may lead to some kind of "enlightenment" but also to serious delusions. The most typical among these is megalomania, witness the self-importance of the assorted gurus and messiahs in the modern cult scene.

Hindu yogis claim to have left these dangerous mind games behind because their forebears have developed a safe and sound method laid down in such classics as Patanjali's *Yoga Sūtra.* Ram Swarup (*Hindu View of Christianity and Islam*, Voice of India, Delhi 1993, p.45-46) argues that the methodical and systematic "science of yoga" has a substantial qualitative edge over other forms of mysticism or mediumism. From this angle, it is unfair — even if fashionably in tune with the "equal truth of all religions" doctrine — to put yoga in one class with the experiments of Shamans taking hallucinogenic plants, or with the uninvited voice-hearing experiences of Mohammed.

In recent years, Ram Swarup and Sita Ram Goel have further developed Swami Vivekananda's position on the nature of Quranic revelation. Ram Swarup has elaborated on the yogic theory of *samādhī* (enstasis) states of different levels of purity, which allows for states of high concentration tainted by delusion (*Hindu View of Christianity and Islam*, p.107). S.R. Goel has pointed out the similarity between Mohammed's experiences and that of other men who combined a susceptibility to convulsive trance states with a great charisma and strategic ability, most notably Chengiz Khan (Goel, ed.: *The Calcutta Quran Petition*, 3rd ed., Voice of India, Delhi 1999, p.238-249; with reference to Ibn Ishāq: *Sīrat Rasūl Allāh*, tra. Alfred Guillaume: *The Life of Mohammed*, OUP Karachi, p.104/150-107/154).

They conclude that the Pagan Arabs had every right to reject Mohammed's claims, born from a deluded consciousness and then propagated on a war footing, but that they made the one mistake which history does not forgive, viz. the mistake of being defeated. However, "the fact that they failed to understand the ways of Mohammed and could not match his mailed fist in the final round, should not be held against them. It was neither the first nor the last time that a democratic society succumbed in the face of determined gangsterism. We know how Lenin, Hitler and Mao Tsetung succeeded in our own times." (Goel: *Hindu Temples*, vol.2, 2nd ed., p.272)

As far as I can see, the foregoing constitutes the single most radical criticism of Islam available in the world. Christian critics, no matter how fierce, usually appreciate at least Mohammed's monotheism, which does not impress these Hindu authors. They are also inhibited in criticizing the deluded nature of Mohammed's "revelations", as they profess a belief in the divine revelations to the Old Testament prophets. Though "irreverent" and "demythologizing" are among the most specious words of praise in the review columns of modern newspapers, few people have the stomach for something as irreverent and demythologizing as the Hindu revivalist analysis of the Prophet's mission.

9.4. Cultural relativism comes to the defence of Mohammed's *wahī*

There is a school in psychiatry, now well past its prime but quite strong in the 1960s and 70s, which rejects the whole notion that we can arrive at a diagnosis of mental disturbance for people from other climes and cultures. If you tell that crowd about a psychopathological diagnosis of a 7th-century Arab, they will dismiss it as cultural imperialism, as projection of modern notions onto radically different premodern cultures. In non-specialist circles, this cultural relativism is now probably stronger than ever before: postmodern intellectuals refuse to be "judgmental" about characters from other cultures, including the Prophet of Islam.

Thus, it is argued that more or less controlled and ritualized forms of ghost-possession were an established part of many cultures since thousands of years. This way, Mohammed's Quranic trance (*wahī*) could be justified as a form of Shamanic contact with the spirit world. To be sure, classifying Mohammed as a kind of Shamanic medium would still undermine his claim to a unique status as the final prophet, but it does sound better than labels like "hallucination" or "sensory delusion". Georg Feuerstein (*Holy Madness*, Arkana Books 1992, a book on the interface between religion and altered mental states, p.15) does Mohammed the honour of describing him as a "mystic".

And yet, the relativistic position is refuted by spokesmen of those premodern cultures themselves. It is simply not true that where we see pathological symptoms, the ancients merely saw a state of divine intervention. Some of the terms still in common use as names of specific psychopathological syndromes, such as *mania* and *paranoia*, originate with the ancient Greeks. Manuals of Ayurvedic and Tibetan medicine already try to classify and treat mental problems. Indeed, it is hard to find any culture which doesn't have a notion of "madness", however vague and general. In this particular case, we cannot say that the 7th-century Arabs already had an embryonic knowledge of psychiatry, but at least they were clearly of the view that there was something wrong with Mohammed's mind.

In our latest chapter, we saw that Mohammed himself initially evinced a healthy skepticism vis-à-vis the visions and revelations which he had started receiving from AD 610 onwards. It was mainly his first wife Khadija who helped him in getting accustomed to this recurring psychic phenomenon and in accepting his status of prophet. Meanwhile, most of his townsfolk in Mecca remained unconvinced. It is not modern neocolonial Western psychologists who imposed this skepticism on them, it is clearly they themselves who, within the framework of their own culture, saw sufficient reason to reject Mohammed's belief in his status of recipient of divine revelation.

The Quran itself gives more than a dozen instances where Mohammed, or the "voice" he heard, puts himself on guard against the Meccans' view that his revelations are merely the effect of ghost-possession. This is very explicit in the ten verses 15:6, 23:70/72, 34:8, 34:46/45, 37:36/35, 44:14/13, 52:29, 68:2, 68:51, 81:22. Thus: "They say; 'He suffers of ghost-possession'? No, he came to them with truth but most of them abhor truth." (23:70/72)

To this list, Mohammed himself adds several references to Biblical prophets likewise accused of ghost-possession: earlier prophets in general 51:52, Noah 23:25, Moses 26:27/26 and 51:39. It is to be noted that the Bible nowhere mentions such an allegation against Noah, Moses or most other prophets. The one exception is verse 9:7 of Hosea, a prophet apparently unknown to Mohammed: "They call the man of the spirit a madman: so great is their guilt that their resistance is likewise great". Undoubtedly, Mohammed, whose knowledge of the Bible was only sketchy, was merely projecting his own plight onto Noah and Moses.

To be sure, the Arabs were not modern psychiatrists, they had no clear-cut diagnosis though they were in no doubt that something was wrong. In a few instances, they gave the alternative explanation that Mohammed was an ambitious but fanciful poet who had merely invented it all: Q.21:5, 36:69, 37:36/35, 52:30, e.g.: "But no, they say: 'A web of dreams. He must have invented them. He must be a poet.'" (21:5) They also opined that he was "enchanted": 17:47/50, 25:8/9. Mohammed counters this by calling the unbelievers themselves enchanted (23:89/91), but mostly, we again see Mohammed defending himself with the plea that the same allegation had been made against earlier prophets: Moses 17:107/108, Shu'aib 26:185, Salih 26:153.

The argument that "I am a prophet but am not acknowledged as such by my narrow-minded contemporaries, just as the ancient prophets were not given due recognition either" somehow manages to make non-recognition into an indication of genuine prophethood. Ordinary people would start doubting themselves when confronted with general skepticism of their beliefs. But not Mohammed, whose reasoning went like this: *because* I have these revelations from above, *because* I have the exceptional status of prophet, people reject me or laugh at me, but far from shaking my belief in the divine origin of these visions, this merely proves the weightiness and genuineness of my prophetic mission, for it puts me up there in the top league with prophets like Noah and Moses. For people of the scientific temper, this subjective and self-centred rationalization of the negative feedback that Mohammed encountered, can be put aside as just that: a fallacious rationalization of a private belief easily recognized as irrational.

9.5. Herman Somers' diagnosis of Mohammed

Ever since Mohammed's first preachings, people have tried to pinpoint the psychic ailment accounting for his prophetic self-delusion. Thus, some Christian polemicists described him as an epileptic, citing episodes in which he foamed at the mouth and rolled on the floor. This was a meritorious guess, but its explanatory power was limited because the neurological disorder of epilepsy need not be accompanied by hallucinations and an enduring self-delusion. However, now that psychopathology has matured into a scientific discipline, a more accurate diagnosis is available.

The Flemish psychologist, Dr. Herman Somers, formerly a Jesuit who became a religious skeptic after discovering psychopathological elements in the utterances of some Biblical prophets, has elaborated the first technical diagnosis of Mohammed's behaviour. So far, it is only available in Dutch: *Een andere Mohammed* ("A different Mohammed", Hadewych, Antwerp 1993), but I will give its general outline in English. The basis of this diagnosis is the elaborate description of Mohammed's personality and conduct provided by the Quran and by the *Hadīth* (traditions of the prophet, grouped by theme) and *Sīra* (chronological biography) literature.

As for the nature of these sources, it is worth noting the contrast between Jesus and Mohammed. Jesus is a composite literary character made up of essentially historical reports on a wandering healer-preacher combined with religious stereotypes, partly borrowed from other traditions, and with deliberate interpolations made by the evangelists in compliance with the developing political and theological needs of the budding Church. Mohammed, on the other hand, is a fully historical character.

To be sure, we are aware of unconventional theories questioning the historicity of the entire Mohammed narrative including the Quran (vide e.g. Ibn Warraq: *The Origins of the Koran*, Prometheus, New York 1998). If these were to be accepted, Islam is in very deep trouble, for the whole edifice of Islamic belief and jurisprudence is based on the assumption of the historicity of the traditions concerning Mohammed. It is not our job to save Islam from these skeptics, but we think they are going too far.

One of the reasons why the tradition should be given the benefit of the doubt is that it contains too many admissions against interest, accounts of less than flattering data about Mohammed and his companions (even about Mohammed being derided as a madman), clearly included because they happened to be known as factual to contemporaneous audiences and not because they served anyone's political or hagiographical interests. Another reason is that there is simply no motive for inventing most of it. In the case of certain political rules laid down by the Prophet, one could still assume strong motives on the part of later contenders for leadership to attribute this or that position to the Prophet,— though in that case, it is strange that he was allowed to remain silent on so many contentious issues, e.g. that before his death, he wasn't made to speak out on the question of how his succession was to proceed (a matter leading to a fratricidal war, the murder of caliph Ali and his son Hussein, and the Shiite schism). But the tradition contains many uncontroversial judgments and regulations and plenty of humdrum information devoid of implications for later inter-Muslim power struggles or theological system-building; it is unlikely that this was all interpolated. This is especially true when it comes to the description of the Prophet: the Ummayad- or Abbasid-age traditionists had nothing to gain from describing Mohammed's complexion, hygienic habits, sex life etc. with the information they gave rather than with any other.

Even if a lot has been added to or changed in the historical data during the editing of the core Islamic text corpus, many correct data must have been preserved. In particular, if the tradition describes a pathological syndrome entirely in conformity with modern medical knowledge unavailable to the authors, it is clear that the latter cannot have invented the description but must have been describing a real case to which they or their informants had been witnesses. Dr. Somers explains:

"The reader be warned against a strange type of reasoning by certain *doctores*, whether historians or medics. They assume that the preserved traditions have been written down belatedly, that they are hard to control, and that some clearly belong to mythology. Preparing a diagnosis on the basis of such uncertain data is clearly nonsense. (...) They forget that they are proceeding from an unproven and dubious supposition, viz. that *all* data in the sources are untrue and unreliable. (...) First of all, the tradition undeniably preserves a number of more or less reliable data. Secondly, modern science disposes of detailed information about all kinds of diseases. These information elements are called symptoms; they are bundled into syndromes. (...) What we now find, to our amazement, is that the facts passed on to us by the tradition correspond with the symptoms and syndromes known to modern science. Now, if these traditions describe the facts with such exactitude, they must be reliable." (p.18)

It is one thing if someone makes a general claim that Mister X is "mad" (as in jokes about a stereotypical madcap's hilarious behaviour), but quite another when he describes in detail the typical development of the paranoia syndrome. In the latter case, either he is a student of modern psychopathology quoting a textbook description, or he is describing an actual case to which he was a witness.

Mohammed, according to Dr. Somers, was a classic case of paranoia. The syndrome of paranoia is essentially characterized by a delusion about oneself nourished by recurring hallucinations. These hallucinations may be auditory (hearing voices), visual (seeing visions or apparitions), or purely mental (being struck with sudden "insights" of enormous and unshakable certainty, not susceptible to falsification by reality). The delusion typically puts the affected person in the centre of events: either he is the target of a ubiquitous and all-powerful conspiracy (delusion of persecution); or he is the privileged witness to a cosmic event, esp. the imminent end of the world; or he has been selected for a unique mission.

Mohammed's life-story offers only a hint at a delusion of persecution. He (and later his apologists) liked to see himself as persecuted by the Meccans, which is usually given as the reason for his migration to Yathrib/Medina. While this might have been true, the reality of his interaction with the Meccans after his migration suggests otherwise. Thus, a few months later, he lets his followers invite their families from Mecca to join them in Medina. However, if the Meccans had really been serious about confronting and "persecuting" Mohammed, it is unlikely that they would have allowed tnese relatives to leave, as they made perfect hostages of great strategic value in a grim confrontation.

The delusion of being privy to esoteric information about the approaching end of the world (though not about its exact timing, a prediction that would have been uncomfortably testable), also announced by some Biblical prophets, is already much more pronounced. The verses Q.15:85, 44:10/9 and 78:40 assure us that the end is nigh (as Jesus' apostles had also been made to believe). The description of the Final Judgment is one of the main recurring themes of the Quran. While partly based on Mohammed's hearsay knowledge of

Jewish and Christian theology, it is charged with a strong personal involvement based on his deeply impressing visions of how the Judgment would arrive, what the fate of the different categories of men would be, and what the roles of major religious beings in it would be: that of a gloriously returning Jesus, but also that of Mohammed himself.

Mohammed's central delusion, however, was his belief, first hesitant but soon becoming unshakable, that he had been selected for a unique mission of cosmic proportions. He is God's spokesman, and not just one among many, but in his age the *only* spokesman, and for the remaining interval before Judgment Day also the *final* spokesman, the "Seal of the Prophets". This unique mission forms the contents of his second "revelation" on that fateful day in the month of *Ramadhān*, AD 610. In the first "revelation", the archangel Gabriel had ordered him: "Read!" (or "Recite!", or "Proclaim aloud!"), and Mohammed had been left confused and incomprehending. Thinking that he was becoming "a man possessed", he made up his mind to go and commit suicide, but then Gabriel appeared again, this time with a very clear message: "O Mohammed, thou art the apostle of God and I am Gabriel." (Ishaq/Guillaume, p.106/153 ; Q.96:1)

This self-delusion turned the businessman Mohammed into a prophet, then a cult leader for a small secret circle, next a prominent religious leader with political ambitions, and finally the first emperor of all Arabia and founder of a conquering world religion. It forms the core of the creed pronounced by all Muslims: "There is no God but God and Mohammed is God's prophet." (At this point I won't go into a theologico-linguistic discussion of the name *Allāh*, analysable as "the God", "the deity", sometimes used by the Pagan Arabs as a generic term for any deity, sometimes as a title for a kind of *deus otiosus* at the top of their pantheon, then singled out by Mohammed as the only genuine deity.) Whereas monotheism, the belief in a single God, is espoused by several other religions beside Islam, the belief in Mohammed's prophethood, which implies the belief in the divine origin of the Quran and hence the commitment to revere and obey the Quran, is the unique and defining doctrine of Islam. Sad to say, this world religion espoused by more than a billion contemporary human beings, is based on a private delusion entertained by its founder.

9.6. Further symptoms

Of all the founders of religions, none has left a more detailed biography than the Prophet of Islam. So, what useful information about Mohammed's psyche can be distilled from the core texts of Islam in order to give more body to our suspicion of a paranoid condition?

About his childhood, admittedly the less public part of his life and hence less likely to yield information that was widely remembered, a few strange data emerge which can be interpreted as *prodromes* or pre-symptoms. As a three-year-old, he was found lying on the ground, pale and in shock, and he complained to his foster-parents (townspeople often put their children in the care of poor country folk) that two white-clad men had come and opened his belly, looking for something. His foster-mother Halima even considered returning him to his real mother, not wanting to bear the responsibility if something went wrong with the boy, and she opined to her that the boy might "have a *jinn*" or ghost. As indications of a latent mental problem, this is still pretty vague, but this much is clear that even as a boy, Mohammed was noticed as a special case.

When he became a young man and his vital powers were strong, these strange traits were not in evidence, but as he entered middle age, they returned. In the years preceding the start of the Quranic revelations, we know that his wife Khadija thought he had the "evil eye". For this reason, she sent him to exorcists for treatment. This again we only know in very general terms, but it corroborates the suspicion that Mohammed was predisposed to developing a mental problem, and that his contemporaries were aware of his unusual psychic complexion. When the prophetic trances became really serious, involving the vision of the archangel Gabriel, Khadija took him to the Christian godman Waraqa ibn Naufal, who certified the genuineness of Mohammed's visions. From that point onwards, her supportive attitude to her husband's initially desperate attempts to come to terms with his trances took on the character of a *folie à deux*: though not afflicted herself, she went along with his self-delusion. She became the first believer, the first one to surrender (*islām*) her common-sense judgment and take his claims as true.

More than these corroborative indications, however, it is the contents of Mohammed's hallucinations which clearly mark him as a paranoia patient. A loud voice localized in heaven or in a gigantic heavenly person speaks to him in the second person: *you* are the prophet, chosen to convey the words of the Creator of the Universe. He is given a uniquely central role in the cosmic scheme of things: God's final spokesman, the rightful ruler of mankind as God's vice-regent on earth, mediator for sinful mortals on the impending Day of Judgment.

The disproportion between his new self-perception and his actual social status as an ordinary businessman and later as a derided cult leader was unbearable. In fact, intolerance of others' skepticism, along with vengefulness, is a typical trait of paranoia patients. And so, we find Mohammed singling out each of his critics for assassination or execution. Not that other, more regular tyrants haven't executed critics, but it fits Mohammed's paranoid personality, and only the non-occurrence of his campaign of vengeance against his doubters would have given us reason to doubt the diagnosis of paranoia. Incidentally, not a few of these other tyrants may also have exhibited traces of paranoia, a condition which (unlike schizophrenia and some other psychopathological syndromes) is not incompatible with worldly success. Megalomania, in particular, often provides a strong motivation for the climb to centrality and power.

9.7. The physical basis of a mental problem

Mohammed's megalomania may partly have been an overcompensation for the misery he had suffered, the early death of his parents and of his little sons. Yet, this purely psychological explanation of the Freudian type cannot fully explain the strange phenomena surrounding the development of his delusion: the hallucinations and their neurological infrastructure. The denial of physical determinants in favour of purely socio-psychological explanations (for problems ranging from poor school performance to impotence), so popular from Freud down to the 1970s, has given way to a restored respect for the materiality of the human being: as a conscious subject, he may establish his freedom by skilfully sailing on the sea of his material being, but he is affected by its storms, which are not of his own mind's making. The immediate impact of psychotropic drugs on one's mental condition, for better or for worse, provides experimental proof for the relative materiality of our minds. Less sensationally, it has now been established that the sufficient or insufficient presence of certain hormones and even of certain minerals and vitamins in the body may cause good or poor concentration, aggressiveness or passivity, euphoria or depression, or other mental states.

Therefore, it may be apt to search for physical problems underlying the Prophet's mental troubles, and this is what Dr. Somers has tried to do in his book *Een Andere Mohammed*. Of Mohammed's physical traits, one which draws the attention is that he suffered of chronic headaches, which he tried to remedy by bleeding himself in two veins in his neck. While in itself not enough to indicate a brain problem, it certainly will fit that picture as soon as more indications are found.

The mention of his falling on the ground once during a trance was earlier interpreted as an indication of epilepsy, e.g. by the Byzantine author Theophanes in his

Chronographia (AD 814). But this is clearly unsatisfactory, not only because epilepsy is not typically accompanied by a permanent self-delusion, but mainly because one of its typical symptoms is the complete forgetfulness about even the occurrence of an epileptic fit after the recovery. Paranoid (or similar) hallucinations, by contrast, leave a very strong impression on the mind.

Closer to an explicit symptomatology is Mohammed's own description of the physical sensations accompanying his trance, as Somers explains. During the initial revelations, the Prophet felt the angel's presence exerting an enormous, suffocating pressure on him. To Abdullah ibn Umar he once described the sensations typically accompanying the trance: loud noise, being hit by a mighty blow, feeling outside himself. The intensity of the sound was unbearable to his oversensitive ears (or rather his auditory brain centre), which is also why he disliked live music, a dislike later emulated by Padeshah (Moghul emperor) Aurangzeb in the late 17th century and by Ayatollah Khomeini in the 1980s as a matter of piety. Somers also quotes Ibn Sa'd recording the Prophet's words: "Revelation comes to me in two ways. Sometimes Gabriel comes and speaks to me from man to man, but I forget what he says then. But sometimes he comes to me with the sound of a bell, like the roaring of many waters, so that I get into confusion. But what is revealed to me in this manner never lets go of me again."

This indicates an identifiable neuropathological basis for Mohammed's hallucinations. As a hypothetical physiological explanation of Mohammed's mental problems, Dr. Somers suggests that very near the main sensory (auditive and visual) nerves in the midbrain and on the front part of his pituitary gland, Mohammed may have developed a tumour. The descriptions of Mohammed's physical characteristics may indicate traces of acromegaly, a disorder involving a belatedly overactive growth hormone and leading to roughness of the extremities and a strong body odour (suggested by Mohammed's well-attested abundant use of perfumes), and that would only confirm this hypothesis. But this, of course, is more speculative than the well-established psychopathological diagnosis of Mohammed's paranoia condition. As both Arabic scholarship and neuropathological science continue to progress, future researchers may determine more definitely what we must leave as merely an interesting hypothesis for now. Mohammed's paranoia, by contrast, is an obvious, scripturally well-attested and diagnostically articulate fact.

9.8. Dealing with a mistaken religion

Now that science has spoken out on the true nature of Mohammed's revelations, we should explore the practical implications of this new and more enlightened understanding of Islam. How to deal with our Muslim neighbours now that we realize they are the prisoners of a gigantic centuries-spanning delusion?

(1) Distinctions within Islam

The first thing to do is to cultivate a correct understanding of Islam among ourselves. Whenever something critical is said about Islam, non-Muslims are always the first to come to its defence and to lambast the critics as "prejudiced hate-mongers" or some such unthinking hate-filled smear. Just as the so-called "anti-anti-Communists" provided the first line of defence to Communism by countering or ridiculing every serious anti-Communist argument, we are now faced with anti-anti-Islamism as the first major roadblock on the way to a candid analysis of the Islamist problem. Many non-Muslims have a romanticized view of Islam centred on Sufi poetry and vague reminiscences of civilizational successes during the bygone Golden Age of Islam. For the sake of argument, we may concede for now that these are indeed meritorious contributions of Islam. The point is then to distinguish within Islam its different components.

Charming achievements such as algebra, Arabic calligraphy or the basic and most attractive ideas of Sufi mysticism are all external to Islam. Arabic calligraphy, geometrical ornamentation on mosque walls and other non-figurative aesthetic developments were stimulated by the Islamic prohibition on the depiction of human or animal life; but they were no more than variants on art forms which have existed outside and before Islam as well. Algebra and other sciences were borrowed from India, China or Greece, as the Arab conquerors readily admitted, witness their name for the so-called Arabic numerals, viz. *rakmūl-Hindī*, "Indian numerals" (written from left to right, like the Indian and unlike the Arabic scripts). The belief that they were in possession of the true religion was enough to bolster their pride, so they could honestly concede other achievements to other nations. The central aim of Sufism, the self-extinction in the merger with God, is obviously borrowed from Buddhist and Vedantic sources. Initially the orthodox clergy persecuted outspoken Sufis like *Mansūr al-Hallāj* who said blasphemous things like *"anā'l Haqq"* ("I am the True One", Arabic translation of the Upanishadic dictum *"Aham Brahmāsmi"*) and was tortured to death for it in AD 922, because they saw through its un-Islamic inspiration; but later they adapted and domesticated Sufism into an acceptable Islamic form of devotion for both the spiritual eccentrics and the sentimental illiterate masses.

At any rate, all these attractive sideshows of Islam can be evaluated separately without judging the defining beliefs of Islam. Even within Islamic theology proper, a distinction must be made. Firstly, there is a distinction between general religiosity or ethics and the specifically Islamic innovations. Partly in order to gain respectability, Mohammed included in the Quran and in his own sayings many elements of traditional morality, injunctions against stealing, slander, child abuse or marital infidelity. This can be compared with Moses' Ten Commandments, where his own theological innovations (monotheism, taboo on idolatry, taboo on uttering the God-name, keeping a weekly day of rest) are coupled with age-old moral rules against lying, stealing, disrespect to parents, adultery etc. In both Moses' and Mohammed's case, the intention seemed to be, to confer the authority of age-old morality upon the prophet's own innovative religious ideas. The net result is at any rate that a believer in the Bible or the Quran can truthfully say that his Holy Book has taught him morality. That much in the Quran deserves respect: elements of universal ethics which are not specifically Islamic but which nonetheless have come to form a part of Islam.

Even in the theological core which defines Islam as distinct from other religions, a further distinction must be made, one which practically coincides with the two assertions of the Islamic creed: monotheism ("there is no God but Allah") and the belief in Mohammed's prophethood ("and Mohammed is the prophet of Allah"). Monotheism, the belief in the oneness of the Divine, can be deduced from different sources of inspiration, not merely the Bible or the Quran. One can discern a kind of monotheism in Aristotle's philosophy or in Stoicism, it has been claimed for Zarathushtra's religion of Ahura Mazda, and even Hindu devotionalism to Vishnu or Shiva is sometimes conceived as monotheistic. Within the monotheistic framework, Medieval and Renaissance philosophers (al-Arabi, Cusanus, Bruno, Galilei, Leibniz et al.) have developed profound conceptions of consciousness and the universe. In principle, it is possible to subscribe to monotheism without developing the allegedly typical problematic features of the major monotheistic religions, viz. their intolerance. So, if your Muslim neighbour says *"Alḥamdulillāh"* (Praise be to Allah) or some other Allah invocation, please don't jump to jihadic conclusions. He may well mean the exact same thing intended by a Hindu who invokes *Bhagwān*, or by the agnostic who utters: "Only God knows..."

The real problem arises when he understands God/Allah as exclusively the character revealed in the Quran, the collection of sayings which Mohammed claimed to have heard from a supernatural source identified as the Archangel Gabriel. The ultimate core of Islam is not Allah and monotheism, but Mohammed and prophethood. Monotheism is a fairly widespread idea, but Mohammed and his Quran are truly the defining elements of Islam. If the oneness of God can conditionally be accepted as a valid manner of speaking about the Divine, there can be no compromise with Mohammed's deluded belief in his exclusive telephone line with Heaven. Here, we hit the radically irrational and unacceptable core of Islam. Here, there is no room for sweet-talk, even if only metaphorically or figuratively intended, of a "basic unity" or "equal truth" of all religions. The defining core belief of Islam is wrong. It is nothing but the paranoid delusion of an ordinary early-medieval Arab businessman. Putting such vain self-delusion on a par with the profound insights of a Yajñavalkya, a Buddha, a Confucius, a Laozi or a Socrates, is plainly absurd.

(2) Speaking out

Speaking with Muslims about the deluded basis of Islam may initially prove to be difficult, both for non-Muslims and for ex-Muslims. Believers will not like to hear criticism of Islam from anyone, but in a paradoxical way, they will tolerate more of it from non-Muslims who enjoy the benefit of their unbeliever status. In the present world, Muslims have had to accept at least the existence of unbelievers, and an unbeliever is by definition one who doesn't believe in Mohammed's prophetic claims. After all, if he believed in Mohammed's claim to prophethood, he would accept the validity of the Quran and hence the whole contents of the Quran, and by accepting all that, he would by definition be a Muslim. So, in private conversation, subject to rules of politeness and diplomacy, a non-Muslim has a certain freedom to express his doubts about the core belief of Islam. There is no need to be intrusive with your message, as most Muslims spontaneously bring up the subject of the relative superiority of one religion vis-ã-vis another once in a while.

For born Muslims, introducing critical questions about Islam is more difficult, as it amounts to a statement of apostasy, a crime punishable by death under Islamic law. Yet, it is mainly these enlightened ex-Muslims who will do the job of opening the exit gate from Islam for their Muslim-born brothers and sisters. It is helpful and meritorious if we non-Muslims speak our minds about the fundamental questions of religion, but our influence on Muslim audiences will always be much more limited. We may work for the inclusion of properly scientific information in all general textbooks of religious history, so that Muslim children in state-funded schools will be exposed to a more enlightened view of Mohammed's prophecies; but we should expect many Muslims to distrust and reject all such information emanating from unbeliever sources. By contrast, born and bred Muslims who have shaken off the veil of the faith and exposed themselves to the light of Reason may have more impact on the Muslim masses,— which is why it is also much more dangerous for them to speak their minds.

However, I am confident that recent developments in communications technology, particularly the entry of satellite television and the internet in even the remotest harems of Arabia, will profoundly alter the mental climate in the Muslim world. So far, a lot of the authority wielded by the orthodox clergy over their flock was purely the result of the latter's ignorance about the world outside Islam. Most Muslims have grown up with caricatured enemy-images of Western and Asian cultures, which made it that much easier for them to identify civilization and morality with their own familiar Islam. In the next decade, their mental horizon is bound to widen dramatically.

Already, websites hosted by ex-Muslims centralize all the information about the dark side of Islam, about persecutions of non-Muslims and injustices to women, and more consequentially, about the irrationality and unsustainability of the core beliefs defining Islam. Books can be burned and speeches interrupted by the police, but the newer forms of communication are very discrete and can penetrate into the private rooms of every inquisitive Muslim.

(3) The alternative

Experience in the secularized West has shown that apostasy from religion can have unpleasant side-effects. On the one hand, people are better informed and more open and honest about touchy subjects. On the other hand, many people flush out ethics and self-restraint along with the religion which they have come to see as irrational and obsolete. In this sense, one can sympathize with those Muslims who fear that a weakening of Islam will lead to immorality, hedonism, crass consumerism, flaky quasi-religions (whether political, sex-centred or occultist) and a general lowering of cultural standards. If the world of non-Islam gets identified with Hollywood, McDonalds and *Playboy*, it is understandable that Muslims will cling to the devil they know rather than expose themselves to the intruding devils from the West.

This is where non-creedal or post-creedal spiritual traditions have a key role to play. They have to show the Muslims that there is life after apostasy from an irrational belief system. They have to prove that religion can be something else than a silly acceptance of some prophet's vainglorious claims about himself.

10. Let's combat communalism

[This article was written in early 2006.]

What follows is a comment on "Koenraad Elst—Sangh Parivar's Apologist", a review of my book *Decolonizing the Hindu Mind: Ideological development of Hindu Revivalism* (Rupa, Delhi 2001), by Ayub Khan in *Communalism Watch*, 13 March 2003. It is not normally done for an author to write a rebuttal of a review of his book. Since he himself has had his say for hundreds of pages in the book itself, he should leave the review pages of the papers to his critics. They don't usually get more than one or two pages of space from their editors to develop their opinions, so they are already at a disadvantage. Then again, in a brief text it is possible to write more insults and lies than could be answered convincingly in a whole book. Moreover, in many cases far more people read the reviews or the resultant polemic than the book that is their object. That is why in exceptional cases, an author may feel pressured to write a rebuttal. I will try to do justice to the Mr. Khan's effort and reproduce it in full, interspersed with my own comments.

10.1. Am I a Sangh Parivar apologist?

Ayub Khan's review was published in *Communalism Combat*. Naïve readers might understand this as "combat against communalism", but its effective editorial line lends itself better to the description: "combative (anti-Hindu) communalism". Its editor, Mrs. Teesta Setalwad, is a convert from secular Hinduism to Islam, and she has the typical zeal of the convert. She was repeatedly caught in the act of lying during the secularist attempts to exploit the Gujarat riots of spring 2002. She even went on record thinking up a justification for the Muslim arson attack on the women's wagon of a pilgrims' train in Godhra, killing 58 innocent Hindus. A Muslim girl whom she had paraded as her crown witness in her culpabilization of the Gujarati Hindus, came out to accuse her of kidnapping and of coercing her to give false testimony in court. Of course, the poor girl stood no chance against Mrs. Setalwad's well-financed media machine, so she was convicted of perjury (which she at any rate committed, but more likely when initially toeing the Setalwad-dictated line than when recanting), but Mrs. Setalwad's insulted-royalty conduct during the whole controversy clearly revealed just what type of character gets attracted by the secularist hate industry. In these circumstances, I take it as a point of honour to find myself the target of criticism in her paper.

Ayub Khan opens his attack on me in a very predictable manner: "In the past decade Belgian scholar Koenraad Elst has emerged as the most prominent advocate of Sangh Parivar in the West."

Anyone who has read my book *BJP vis-à-vis Hindu Resurgence* (1997) will be surprised to see me described as an "advocate of the Sangh Parivar". The book under review, too, contains a lot of critical observations of the Sangh, as Ayub Khan ought to have noticed. In fact, even some of my observations which secularists might consider favourable to the Sangh, are properly meant as criticisms. Ayub Khan reveals his own outlook of political activist rather than intellectual observer by brushing aside the actual contents of these criticisms, so inconvenient to the case he is making.

But then it is true that I haven't repeated the hysterical discourse so common in journalistic and academic writings on Hindu nationalism and the Sangh Parivar. Thus, before the BJP came to power in 1998, I had never written that the BJP would build gas chambers for Muslims or dump them into the ocean, which clearly put me outside the consensus of the experts. I suppose that in a world of partisan scholarship, where the party-line is scrupulously followed by activists and camp-followers alike, any attempt to remain objective must come across as counter-partisan, meaning partisan activism for the opposite side.

Ayub Khan continues: "Elst's commitment to the Sangh Parivar can be gauged from the fact that he unabashedly defended it even as the fires of Gujarat were still raging last year. (See Elst's 'Dr. Hathaway's Patronizing Conclusions' published at *Rediff.com*)."

Actually, the correct reference is: "US thinker gives unthinking support to anti-India demands. A reply to Robert Hathaway", 30 August and 3 September 2002, Rediff on the Net; also included in Ramesh Rao & Koenraad Elst: *Gujarat after Godhra: Real Violence, Selective Outrage*, Har-Anand, Delhi 2003. It was written months after "the fires of Gujarat" of March 2002 had stopped raging.

In my reaction to Dr. Hathaway's patronizing sermon on Hindu society, which in his opinion needs supervision by Americans to protect it against its own vicious inhumanity, I have merely pointed out the exaggerated, partisan and plainly false points in his attack on the BJP government of Gujarat. Like most American India-watchers, Dr. Hathaway throws all norms of research to the wind as soon as it comes to Hindu activism, for rather than critically assessing his sources of information, he has merely lapped up all the rumours spread by unscrupled "secularists" such as Arundhati Roy and Ayub Ḳhan's employer Teesta Setalwad. Thus, *Communalism Combat* and its numerous parrots have been alleging that "more than 2,000 Muslims have been killed" in the post-Godhra riots, but in the meantime the UPA (anti-BJP) Central Government's Home Ministry has officially confirmed the death toll as 790 Muslims and 254 Hindus.

Here is Ayub Khan's clinching argument for my Hindutva affiliation: "Such is his importance in Hindutva circles that L.K.Advani quoted him at length while deposing before the Liberhans Commission investigation the demolition of Babri Masjid."

Rest assured that in Hindutva circles, many people count as far more important than I. If I was the one to be quoted, it is simply because I happened to be the one who had written about the question of the exact authorship of the Ayodhya demolition. That was in reaction to the surrealistic but highly significant behaviour of the Indian media after the Demolition. Eventhough the film footage clearly shows Advani helplessly breaking down in tears when the ordinary activists took control and started the Demolition, and all eyewitnesses confirmed this (as I know from interviewing many of them), the media in unison blamed Advani and the wider Sangh leadership. Instead of doing their job and earning laurels with the scoop of the year by finding out and revealing just which mid-level Sangh activist masterminded the Demolition against the designs of the leadership, the Indian media and their parrots abroad chose the politically motivated option of doing maximum damage to Advani by accusing him. If the media and later also the academic India-watchers had done their job, Advani could have cited many commentators pointing their fingers away from him, but in the event I turned out to be the only one. No special merit, on the contrary: I only did what was normal, it's the others whose conduct was partisan to the point of being bizarre.

10.2. My critique of Islam

Like most so-called secularists, Mr. Khan isn't very good at distinguishing between various "anti-Islamic" positions: "His vociferous defence of the Hindu right is equally matched by his rabid attacks on Islam. In order to escape being branded a bigot he follows a route, which is much popular among anti-Muslim writers these days. He insists: 'not Muslims but Islam is the problem'. (See Koenraad Elst review of Thom Blom Hansen's *The Saffron Wave*)."

I wasn't aware that this line has become so popular. I haven't seen it being declaimed anywhere, certainly not in Sangh Parivar circles, nor even among Western

"Islamophobes". On the contrary, the official line, intoned across the spectrum from Guru Golwalkar in the 1950s to Tony Blair after the London blasts of 7 July 2005, is that "Islam is not the problem", only a few "misguided" Muslims are. In reality, of course, the problem *is* Islam. Many Muslims are not terrorists, but those who are, invariably cite the instructions and precedents of the Prophet of Islam as their inspiration.

I agree that many people are fanatical by temperament, no matter what religion they are brought up in; and that others are peaceful and tolerant, no matter the intrinsic fanaticism of the religion they are brought up in. But for many more, religious indoctrination does make the difference: good people are made to do evil because they are taught that this particular evil is the will of God. To repeat a comparison I've made before: some people get drunk and still drive home safely; others are teetotallers and yet are a danger on the road; but for most people, alcohol does make the difference between driving safely and causing an accident. Therefore, most acts of Islamic fanaticism, such as in the Moplah rebellion, the Partition massacres, the East Bengali genocide or the frequent bomb attacks on Hindu crowds and places of worship, are the result of Islamic indoctrination, committed by people who would never have done so if they or their ancestors had not been islamized.

Khan again: "In this book Elst tries to promote a humane face of the Hindutva fanatics while at the same time indulging in polemical attacks on Islam and Christianity."

Here I firmly disagree. Does Mr. Khan really think I would have gotten away with replacing a descriptive study of a Hindu movement with "polemical attacks" when working for a degree at a top-ranking university? In this case, moreover, it was a Catholic university that, according to Mr. Khan, awarded me the degree for what amounted to "polemical attacks on Christianity". I agree that unabashed "polemical attacks" need not necessarily stand in the way of getting a Ph.D. in Indian Studies, but that's only if they are attacks on the Hindu side. By contrast, I have had to scrupulously limit myself to a *description* of certain criticisms of Christianity and Islam. However, having been pampered and shielded from criticism for all these years, Indian Islamists just cannot tolerate the experience of merely seeing certain criticisms of Islam reproduced in print. And yes, it so happens that after hours, I agree with some of those criticisms, and have said so in other forums. Mr. Khan can try to refute them if he wants, but thus far he hasn't even tried to do so.

Moreover: "It is Elst's contention that the Muslims along with British were also colonizers of the Hindu civilization and that Nehruvian secularism and Islam are two major adversaries that are obstructing the revival of Hindu religion. Hindu thought, he argues, is finally coming into its own after 'centuries of being under the shadow of Islam and Christianity'."

At worst, he is accusing me here of slamming an open door. What is described here as my own "contention" is simply a set of obvious facts, well-known to all except the wilfully blind. Of course Islamic rule was a form of colonialism, the main difference being that the English took India's riches but also gave it railways and democratic institutions, while Islam gave nothing in return for what it took. That Hinduism has been under the shadow of Islam or Christianity is another statement of the obvious that needs no further proof. But I may have been rash in assuming that "Hindu thought is finally coming into its own".

Khan: "While the Sangh is hiding its anti-Muslim feelings Elst is more forthcoming in his animosity towards Islam and Muslims. He is smitten by the age-old biases about Islam. Two fanatical writers namely Sita Ram Goel and Ram Swarup shape his views on Islam. A careful study of these pseudo-historians indicates that there is nothing original in their works. They have just recycled the old orientalist works with the addition of inflammatory comments. For Elst however these two characters are heroes whose books all Hindu revivalists should read. He says that the Islamic civilization did not create any substantial contribution in the development of India and there is nothing special about the Indo-Saracenic architecture. He says that Muslims did not work towards the elimination of caste-system in India but only preserved it. He falsely claims that the Prophet Muhammad (SAW) never enjoined class equality. (p.398) Obviously he has not read the last sermon of the Prophet (SAW)."

The trick is already a bit worn out but secularists never get enough of it: neutralizing criticism of Islam by identifying some old-school "orientalist" (a dirty word to the followers of Edward Said, that pitiable Arab Christian *dhimmi* who ran errands for his Muslim bullies) who formulated similar criticisms, then "exposing" such criticism as some long-refuted colonial ploy. The actual refutation is never given, of course. For criticism of Islam is not the fruit of colonial "orientalism", but of the healthy sceptical human mind, which has been around since much earlier. Indeed, the Quraṇ itself reports a number of criticisms of the Prophet by his own contemporaries, and the Hadith collections relate how Mohammed dealt with critics: he had them assassinated in the night or, once he was formally in power, had them executed. To be sure, Mr. Khan is welcome to improve upon the Prophet's conduct and provide the first refutation to anything he dislikes in the criticisms cited in the core texts of Islam, or in the works of "colonial orientalists" like D.S. Margoliouth, or in the works of Ram Swarup and Sita Ram Goel.

Mr. Khan is also invited to enlighten us on Islam's "substantial contribution". Unlike the British railways, which were an unprecedented novelty that opened *new* economic (and political) possibilities for Indian society, Indo-Saracenic architecture merely replaced the ornate native building style with another. India would have lost nothing if the Muslims had left the numerous magnificent instances of Hindu architecture standing instead of destroying them and replacing them with their own predictable and monotonous architecture. The highlights of Indo-Saracenic architecture were the handiwork of Hindu artists and craftsmen anyway, e.g. the master-masons of the Taj Mahal who had a hand chopped off after finishing the job lest they do a similar job for a rival ruler. For another example of Islam's elusive contributions: the Muslim invaders destroyed all the Buddhist universities which had flourished for centuries under Hindu rule, and never built any educational institutions of similar quality and broadness of subject-matter.

As for Islam and class equality, Ayub Khan is bluffing on the assumption that most readers of the review won't read the book anyway. So, he pretends that my scepticism regarding the propaganda of Islam as the religion of equality is my own, when in fact I was only rendering, with ample quotations, the observations of several authoritative sources and the injunctions in the basic texts of Islam. Thus, summarizing a critique by the generally pro-Islamic leftist Belgian author Lucas Catherine, I refer to three Quran verses (16:71/73, 42:12/10, 43:32/31) he cites as evidence for Islam's anti-egalitarianism, in which Allah states that He has made one man rich and another poor and that it would be ungrateful for man to try to change this divine distribution of fortune.

Mohammed himself sold women and children prisoners as slaves and never questioned the institution of slavery, which remained central to the Muslim economy until the much-maligned British colonialists enforced its abolition. Islamic law regulates the institution of slavery as well as other forms of social inequality including of course that between Muslims and "tolerated" non-Muslims. And naturally, it elaborately details the unequal rights and duties of men and women. That's not all that exceptional, most if not all religions and law systems know gender inequality, but here again the claim that Islam introduced equality is proven to be false.

In India, the Muslim conquerors never interfered in the caste divisions of Hindu society and the converts largely retained their caste identities or acquired new forms of inter-Muslim stratification based on affiliation with various sects or ethnic lobbies of the conquerors. Caste-like stratification in Indian Muslim and Pakistani society has been described by sociologists, though secularist convention is to pretend otherwise in order to magnify Hindu inequality by contrast. All this is a matter of general knowledge but Khan tries to pass it off as figments of my imagination.

As for Mohammed's last sermon, given during his last pilgrimage to Mecca shortly before he fell ill and died, here again Mr. Khan is bluffing. The few readers who may take the trouble of looking up the text of that sermon, as given in Ibn Ishaq's *Sīrat Rasûl Allāh* (Alfred Guillaume: *The Life of Mohammed*, OUP, Karachi, p.650/968-652/969) will find that it contains no imposition of equality. To be sure, Mohammed abolishes usury, which is not a bad thing. And yes, he enjoins his men to be kind on their wives, but the reason given is that women "are prisoners with you having no control of their persons". That's hardly equality. He also says that "every Muslim is a Muslim's brother", but he conspicuously fails to deduce from this vague sentiment that they are legally equal, let alone entitled to socio-economic equality. Equality with or among non-Muslims is of course nowhere in the picture.

Khan: "Elst narrates with relish the myth about the execution of 900 Jews at the order of Prophet Muhammad (SAW) in Madina without realizing that this has been debunked long time ago by classical Islamic scholars like Ibn Hajar and Imam Malik and recently by Barakat Ahmed in an article in *The Journal of The Royal Asiatic Society*."

The execution of the Banu Quraiza tribe is narrated in authoritative Islamic sources such as Ibn Ishaq's *Sīrat Rasûl Allāh* (Guillaume: *Life of Mohammed*, p.464/690) and hinted at in others. I have read Barakat Ahmad's attempt at whitewashing the Prophet's record regarding the Jews (*Muhammad and the Jews, a Re-Examination*, Delhi 1979), and I haven't come across an actual *refutation* of that narrative. But if there were such a refutation, it would be even worse for Islam. Mr. Khan is of course allowed to bring in the critical method pioneered by modern Bible scholarship, but then he should accept the consequences. After all, if the orthodox sources of Islam can lie to us about that particular event, what else could they be lying about? What else will be "debunked"? The whole edifice of Islamic doctrine and law comes crashing down if the authoritative reports on the Prophet's words and deeds turn out to be unreliable. It's the Islamic theologians and jurists themselves who tell us that Islam is a "seamless garment": pull out a single thread and the whole fabric comes apart.

Khan: "Similarly other arguments made by messrs. Sita Ram Goel etc. have been refuted but Elst would care less. In the bizarre world of Elst and his Hindutva fellow travellers Islam is to be blamed for all the ills of the Indian society as well as the world. From child marriage, caste inequalities to violence and poverty."

Where and when have Mr. Goel's arguments about Islamic doctrine and history been "refuted"? The Marxist and Muslim polemicists have consistently given him the silent treatment because they knew they didn't stand a chance against him. There have been a few swearwords *ad hominem* by Romila Thapar and maybe some other "eminent" academics, but that leaves Goel's arguments perfectly intact. Ayub Khan seems to have a rather airy and self-serving understanding of the precise logical concept of "refutation".

I have often argued against Hindu apologists who claim that caste, sati and child marriage were the result of Muslim oppression. Like the Arya Samaj reformists, I am convinced that Hindu society became intellectually poorer and socially harder in the post-Vedic age. The marriage age for girls was lowered to the onset of puberty in order to maximize the use of her womb (like in Muslim society) and to minimize the cost of the girl's education (not yet of the dowry, which mainly became a problem during the colonial age), deemed a waste to her family as she was going to spend her married life in another family anyway. Caste discrimination was hardened, witness the insertion into the Ramayana of the Shambuka episode, in which Rama kills a Shudra for having practised austerities, whereas the core Ramayana had described Rama's carefree relations with non-Dwija tribal populations. The taboo-based institution of untouchability, probably originating in neolithic cultures in South India (according to George Hart: *The Poems of Ancient Tamil*, 1975, OUP Delhi 1999, p.119 ff.), was unknown in Vedic society but was adopted throughout India well before the Muslim age. As for *satī*, this is an ancient Indo-European custom attested even among the Germanic and Celtic members of the Indo-European world, pre-dating Islam by thousands of years and described in Hellenistic sources about India still predating the Islamic invasions by a millennium.

All the same, Islam did a lot to aggravate these social problems. Marrying off your daughter at the onset of puberty became a sensible safety measure once unaccountable Muslims soldiers and rulers were on the prowl for girls. Caste reform couldn't become a priority as long as Hindu society was on the defensive and forced to focus on sheer survival. Upper-caste Hindus also didn't escape the human tendency of weighing more heavily on their subordinates when they themselves were under the boot of the Muslim occupying forces.

Khan: "In his maniacal zeal Elst hopes for a similar destruction of Islam as had happened to Communism. He wants the Parivar to concentrate more in attacking the Islamic belief systems. He writes: 'But the implosion of Soviet Communism has alerted people to the possibility that giants on clay feet can crumble surprisingly fast, and in particular, that Pakistan and the rest of the Islamic world may soon see the collapse of their dominant ideology from within.' (p.591) It looks like he needs a refresher course in world history. Islam has survived much more destructive scenarios (civil wars, Mongol invasion, dismantling of the Caliphate, etc) in its history than the one it is currently facing. If Elst and his fellow daydreamers think that they can destroy Islam by indulging in pedestrian attacks they are simply fooling themselves."

European Christianity has survived many fratricidal wars and violent onslaughts by Islam and Communism, but it suffered far greater and deeper losses under the impact of the modern rational inquest into its doctrines. Ayub Khan gives us a glimpse into his own Islamic mindset by changing the subject to military confrontation, when my stated position in the past seventeen years has always been that Islam will implode under the rising impact of critical thought and healthy scepticism among its own followers. Even in the lines quoted by him, I mentioned a scenario in which "Pakistan and the rest of the Islamic world may soon see the collapse of their dominant ideology *from within*".

Khan: "With regards to Indian Muslims, Elst once again repeats the many urban myths that they are a pampered lot, always start riots, are multiplying at an alarming rate etc. If these claims are true then why are Muslims still so downtrodden and impoverished?"

In Malaysia, the Muslims are still poorer than the Indian and Chinese non-Muslims. The latter are more productive and generate wealth, which the Muslims then redistribute to themselves under various *bhumiputra* schemes of "positive" discrimination. Muslim culture promotes business to some extent, but its work ethic is poor and it doesn't foster inventiveness and dynamic innovation. That is why even in a position of legal privilege and a numerical majority, Muslims still lag behind. This is sufficient explanation for the "impoverished" condition of many Muslims in India.

But "downtrodden" they are not, for they enjoy many legal privileges. But it is in the nature of Islam that those very privileges become factors of backwardness. Muslims enjoy the anti-secular privilege of a separate civil code, but this only puts them under the domination of obscurantist clerics. So they send their children to medieval Islamic schools, dooming them to backwardness in terms of modern skills and job prospects. To the extent that Indian Muslims are impoverished, they have themselves to blame. Or rather, they have Islam to blame.

10.3. What is Hindutva?

Ayub Khan makes much of certain terminological issues: "Based on his Ph.D. thesis, Elst's *Decolonizing the Hindu Mind* is a study of the history and ideological development of the extremist Hindutva movement, which he prefers to call 'Hindu Revivalism'."

This choice of terminology is justified. Not all Hindu activists would accept the label *Hindutva*, a coinage by V.D. Savarkar ca. 1923 embraced by the Hindu Mahasabha and later the RSS. Conversely, the insistence on labelling all Hindu activism or all Hindu discourse critical of Islam and "secularism" as *Hindutva* is an undisguised attempt to distort the picture by blurring the distinctions within the broad Hindu spectrum of opinion. The term "Hindu revivalism" is well-established, and it has the advantage of emphasizing the continuity between the 19th-century Hindu Renaissance, which was already described as "revivalism", and the 20th-century political movements in the service of Hindu interests.

Khan: "He rejects the charges of fascism, fundamentalism, extremism, etc. lobbed against the Hindu supremacist movement, instead opting for the voguish 'revivalism'."

Once more, Mr. Khan seems to have spotted a trend that has totally escaped me. Having read plenty of academic and journalistic literature on Hindu activism, I have hardly seen anyone using the term "revivalism", which most treat as obsolete and apply only to the pre-Gandhian phase of modern Hindu self-assertion. I thought I was restoring a term that had deliberately been discarded. He himself ends up admitting as much:

"This 'revivalism' is not a recent phenomenon but began in the early stages of the British rule of India by groups like Arya Samaj and Brahmo Samaj under the leadership of influential reformers like Vivekananda, Dayananda Saraswati and Swami Shraddhanand. Nor is this revivalism limited to those within the Sangh Parivar or other similarly oriented organizations. According to Elst 'the most interesting formulations of Hindu revivalist thought have been provided by individuals outside the said organizations, from Bankimchandra Chatterjee and Sri Aurobindo to Ram Swarup , Sita Ram Goel and their younger friends'. (p.584)"

That's correct. Hindutva is a fairly crude ideology, borrowing heavily from European nationalisms with their emphasis on homogeneity. Under the conditions of British colonialism, it was inevitable that some such form of Hindu nationalism would arise, but I believe better alternatives have seen the light, more attuned to the genius of Hindu civilization.

10.4. Choice of sources

Ayub Khan alleges: "While charting the history of this movement Elst relies almost exclusively on sources associated with Hindu groups giving only partial and that too mostly negative consideration for the other viewpoints."

My job was not to survey other people's opinions about the Hindu movement. That would have been an interesting exercise, especially if it is called by its name, viz. a survey of outsider opinions, and not (as many such academic publications are) falsely presented as a study of the Hindu movement itself. By contrast, I endeavoured to get beyond the secondary—source and mainly hostile-source "research" that has so disastrously filled up this field of study, and focus on the primary sources instead.

The primary sources of Hindu revivalism are obviously going to be pro-Hindu. I knew that, and the reader may be expected to know that. It is perfectly normal to discuss a pro-Hindu movement by analysing its pro-Hindu publications. What is rather less normal, though it is very much the done thing, is to discuss a pro-Hindu movement on the basis of almost exclusively anti-Hindu publications. But that is what Mr. Khan is demanding of me.

Next allegation: "Elst accuses other India watchers of not meeting any Hindutva leaders in their research while at the same time he himself has not interviewed any Muslim to get his viewpoint. Not one Muslim, not even the BJP ones, figures in his long list of people that he has interviewed. His hostility towards the Muslims is evident when he describes the mild-mannered Syed Shahabuddin as a 'proverbial fanatic'. Compare this with that of Elst's description of Advani whom he calls a 'soft-spoken gentleman' who had tears in his eyes when his vandals destroyed the Babri Masjid. Expectedly Advani's tears were shed not at the demolition of the Babri Masjid but at the 'breakdown of RSS discipline'. (p.175)"

Most people who ever met Mr. Advani will confirm that he is a soft-spoken gentleman. That does not make him either a fanatic or a non-fanatic, which is a different matter. The Sudanese Islamist ideologue Hassan al-Turabi comes across as a soft-spoken gentleman, though his writings and his record in government would also stamp him a fanatic. As for Syed Shahabuddin, I have tried to meet him at his office sometime in 1990, but he sent his assistant to keep me waiting under various unconvincing pretexts, the last one of them being that he had to leave. So I left without meeting him. Similar scenario in 1996 with V.T. Rajshekar, editor of *Dalit Voice* in Bangalore, who had first agreed to receive me. As for BJP Muslims, I have interviewed Sikander Bakht, but then I realize that some Indian Muslims refuse to recognize him as a Muslim after his marriage to a Hindu lady who didn't convert.

10.5. The murder of Swami Shraddhananda

At long last, Ayub Khan leaves the sweeping generalizations of the usual secularist discourse behind to get down to specifics. It is about the murder of Swami Shraddhananda, a leader of the movement for *Hindu Sangathan* (self-organization) and *Shuddhi* ("purification", conversion to Hinduism), applied on a sizable scale to the Malkana Rajputs, a community that had been islamized under duress in centuries past but wanted to return to its Hindu roots. The Muslims on their part intensified their perennial effort of *Dawah*, missionary work:

"He writes that Arya Samaj leader Shradhhananda became active in Shuddhi work only after discovering *Dai-e-Islam*, the so-called 'secret' pamphlet of Khwaja Hasan Nizami, which called upon Muslims to engage in Dawah work. Elst doesn't mention the fact that the activities of Khwaja Hasan Nizami and other luminaries of the Tabligh/Tanzeem movement were a reaction to the massive conversion efforts of Arya Samaj and not vice versa. The *Dai-e-Islam* was not a 'secret' pamphlet but was distributed widely in the public. The year 1923 alone, in which it was first published, saw three editions of the book. By 1925 it has already seen its fifth edition. Does any book that was supposed to be secret, ever published on such a massive scale? Additionally Elst doesn't mention that there were similar allegations of a 'secret' Shuddhi book from the Muslim side. Tabligh leader Ghulam Bhik Nairang had claimed that the Kashmiri ruler Maharaja Ranbir Singh had commissioned a 21-volume Hindi encyclopaedia by the name of *Ranbir Karit Prayaschit Mahanibandh* (Ranbir's Great Essay on Repentance), which suggested strategies for converting to the Hindu fold many neo-Muslim communities in India. This encyclopaedia was alleged to have been secretly circulated among prominent Hindus so that the Muslims remain unaware of the plot. An unbiased scholar should have mentioned this allegation as well but may be that is too much to expect from a person like Elst."

Frankly, I had never heard of this latter counter-allegation. From the information which Ayub Khan provides, it sounds like a totally ludicrous allegation: a Hindu encyclopaedia of no less than 21 volumes was to be kept secret, but not a brief Muslim pamphlet? There is little need to enumerate all the instances of secularist double standards, but this one can certainly join the list. Indeed, the counter-allegation sounds as just that: a futile attempt to counter an allegation not with a refutation but with an echo allegation. Typically the impulsive reaction of someone who knows he has been caught in the act. As I have observed before (viz. in the conduct of the anti-temple historians in the Ayodhya debate), liars often aren't very creative, so the lies they think up are transparent of the truth. In this case: the allegation of a Hindu secret encyclopaedia was made by people conscious of their own involvement in circulating a Muslim secret pamphlet, who thought in terms of secret propaganda and couldn't think up an allegation except one in those same terms. Mr. Khan may justifiably hold it against me if I am unaware of pertinent facts, but not if I have failed to hear about some silly rumour.

At any rate, within my thesis, the background information to the murder of Swami Shraddhananda, involving the "secret" pamphlet, was exactly that: part of the background. I had no particular message about these events nor claims of an original finding, they were just part of the story's thread. Therefore, I considered it safe to rely for that on one of the most authoritative secondary sources on his life and on Arya Samaj history: Prof. J.T.F. Jordens' book *Swami Shraddhananda, His Life and Causes* (OUP, Delhi 1981). Jordens writes:

"The Urdu pamphlet *Daī Islām* by Khwaja Hasan Nizami came into his hands. He immediately wrote in answer a pamphlet, the title of which clearly expressed his violent reaction: 'The Hour of Danger: Hindus, be on your guard! The order has been given to attack and destroy the fortress of your religion in the hidden dead of night!' (...) The Swami found out that the pamphlet was in fact only the introduction to a larger volume called *Fātamī Dawat-i-Islām*, which had been published as early as 1920, years before the *shuddhi* of the Malkanas started. In this the Swami saw proof that the Muslim reaction of the day was not merely against the *shuddhi* and *sangathan* movements, but rather was part of a sinister plot hatched years earlier. In his pamphlet the Swami went on to show how Nizami in his own introduction referred to his consultations with many Muslim leaders, including the Aga Khan, and how all had agreed that the publication of his work should remain a carefully kept secret within the Muslim community. The single purpose of the pamphlet was to describe all the means, fair and foul, by which Hindus could be induced to become Muslims. (...) In the conclusion of his own booklet, the Swami suggested some ways in which the Muslim threat could be countered. The openness and ethics of his methods stood in strong contrast with Nizami's tactics." (p.140-141)

It is the word of the top-ranking scholar Jordens, a Christian and as such no sympathizer of Hindu revivalism, against that of the Islamist militant Ayub Khan. Whom should I believe?

10.6. Hedgewar's and Golwalkar's record

Ayub Khan writes: "One cannot but help notice Elst's attempts to whitewash the horrible heritage of the Hindutva movement. He defends RSS' less than patriotic record during the freedom movement by creating lame excuses. Hence RSS founder Hedgewar kept his outfit away from Gandhian agitation 'partly for safety reasons, not to endanger the young sapling, and partly because he had a metapolitical project in mind'. (p.145)"

It is simply a fact that through K.B. Hedgewar, the RSS was an offshoot of the freedom movement. He himself had been involved with the revolutionary wing of the freedom movement in Bengal, and had drawn his lessons about the needs of Hindu society on the eve of the (by then increasingly inevitable) transition to freedom. The RSS uniform was originally the uniform of a safety squad guarding a conference of the Indian National Congress, which had felt the need of extra security after the Khilafat riots against Hindus because most politicized Muslims saw Congress as a Hindu phenomenon. Hedgewar's successor M.S. Golwalkar had been a teacher at Benares Hindu University, a centre of nationalist agitation. So, through different tributaries, the RSS was entirely rooted in the freedom movement, in both its Gandhian and revolutionary wings. For a "less than patriotic record", Mr. Khan may look to the Muslim League, which firmly collaborated with the British and received the overwhelming majority of the Muslim votes in the 1945-46 elections on the single-point programme of rejecting the secular state in favour of Islamic separatism.

And then, Mr. Khan throws what must be the perennial trump card in the secularists' deck: "We have often read this infamous statement of Golwalkar from his book *We, Our Nationhood Defined*: 'From this standpoint, sanctioned by the experience of shrewd old nations, the foreign races in Hindusthan must either adopt the Hindu culture and language, must learn to respect and hold in reverence Hindu religion, must entertain no idea but those of the glorification of the Hindu race and culture, i.e. of the Hindu nation, and must lose their separate existence to merge in the Hindu race; or may stay in the country, wholly subordinated to the Hindu nation, claiming nothing, deserving no privileges, far less any preferential treatment — not even citizen's rights'. Elst explains it away as a 'juvenile mistake' on the part of Golwalkar and that he (Golwalkar) himself withdrew it and that a majority of Hindu nationalists have never read it. One only needs to look at the statements of current RSS chief

Sudarshan where he routinely asks Muslims and Christians to Indianize (read Hinduize) to realize the falsity of this argument."

It is simply a matter of record that the RSS has chosen not to reprint Golwalkar's booklet *We* after the seizure of its remaining stock in the police crackdown on the RSS in the wake of the Mahatma murder in 1948; and that the post-1948 generations of RSS workers have had no exposure to it. That it was Golwalkar himself who "withdrew" the booklet is not only the unanimous testimony of a number of Sangh activists I interviewed, but is also a matter of simple logic: in the much-maligned hierarchical structure of the RSS, the decision not to reprint his own booklet was obviously made by the top leader, and could at any rate not have been made against his will.

None of this is refuted by the correct observation that the theme of "Indianization" of the minorities has remained a central concern from (before) Golwalkar down to K.S. Sudarshan. The latter didn't need the former's booklet for reiterating this most central and founding concern of the organization. But this concept of Indianization need not mean that citizen's rights are denied to the minorities. Contrary to Khan's intimation, there is no continuity on this point from the young Golwalkar down to Sudarshan, who has never expressed such an opinion. Indeed, there was not even such a continuity between the younger and the older Golwalkar (d. 1973), whose later writings and communications were a lot more conciliatory than his maiden attempt, *We*, written in 1938.

10.7. BJP secularism

The BJP's term in government has confirmed my prediction that the party doesn't mean business when it comes to redressing specific Hindu grievances. Mr. Khan emotionalises this impeccable observation, but otherwise is correct in rendering my viewpoint:

"If we are to believe Elst, the Bharatiya Janata Party is more secular than other parties and that RSS is Boy Scouts like organization whose members think that it deserves a Nobel Peace Prize for their 'constructive work'. (p.155) According to him BJP has outdone even the Congress and other secularist parties in reaching out to the Muslims. He criticises the BJP ministers for not introducing even an ounce of Hindutva when they are in power. They are simply too nice. (p.245). They have gone soft and are acting like the 'secularists'. The growing militancy of Parivaris is simply not good enough for him. He is pained by the token gestures that BJP makes towards Muslims. Downplaying RSS' shrewd tactics he says it is a 'big dinosaur in a small brain'. (p.234) He is exasperated with the RSS' culture of 'anti-intellectualism' and argues that other parties profit from this scenario."

Mr. Khan imputes to the Sangh Parivar a very clever strategy, though he fails to cite any actual successes that would prove this cleverness. Has cow-slaughter been banned? Has the Ayodhya temple, of which the first stone was laid in 1989, been built by now? Has the special status of Kashmir been abolished? Has a uniform civil code been enacted? Anyway, he wants me to pay more attention to dishonest propaganda emanating from the Sangh Parivar, which includes the BJP's apparent pro-Muslim gestures:

"A glaring omission from the book is the analysis of RSS' propaganda machinery. It is really surprising how Elst could miss the Sangh's masterful use of catchy slogans, provocative art and inflammatory rhetoric. The RSS is anything but innocent when it comes to propaganda but Elst blissfully ignores it. Anyone with some familiarity with the Sangh's tactics knows that all these gestures of goodwill towards Muslims are just a façade to mask its real dangerous intentions and to gain acceptability in the populace. Elst himself hints towards this when he writes that the shift from 'Hindu' to 'Indian' in the formation of BJP was not due to conviction but to fear. (p.158) At another place he admits that 'anti-Muslim feelings are hiding just beneath the surface of Muslim-friendly statements'. (p.362)"

Yes, fear, or less dramatically the calculated avoidance of conflict with the secularist opinion hegemons and with Muslim muscle power, is the explanation of many of the Sangh Parivar's positions and moves. I have often noticed that Hindus have a double discourse regarding Muslims: privately hostile but full of praise in public. That may not be very brave, but it does indicate a power equation. If the Hindus were really the powerful and overbearing majority to which *Communalism Combat* always alludes, this fearful double discourse wouldn't be needed.

As for catchy slogans, I agree that some of them have been right on the mark. Thus, *"Hindu India, secular India"* correctly drives home the message that Hindu society guarantees "secularism" in the sense of tolerance and pluralism. My problem with the RSS is rather that its thinking rarely gets beyond the level of slogans.

10.8. Eaton's book banned ?

Ayub Khan takes issue with a minor remark I made in passing: "In discussing the alleged Indian Muslim power to ban books Elst makes a patently false claim. He says that Richard M. Eaton's *Sufis of Bijapur* is banned in India because in it 'a few marginal sentences cast an unfavourable light on the Sufi tradition.' (p.318) According to Dr. Richard Eaton this book was never banned. As a matter of fact when the book went out of print with its original publisher, Princeton University Press, it was picked up by Munshiram Manoharlal in New Delhi and is still available from them."

On the matter of the alleged banning of Eaton's book, I concede that closer inquiries do contradict the received wisdom I had taken for granted. I had heard from a number of different contacts in Delhi that *Sufis of Bijapur* (1979) had been banned. It now appears that the story can be traced to a single, usually well-informed source, viz. the late Girilal Jain.

When he was editor of the *Times of India*, he often had private meetings with Indira Gandhi and Rajiv Gandhi. Sometimes he was privy to their discussions with close advisers, often more important in the decision-making process than formal cabinet meetings. It was on such an occasion that Indira Gandhi, freshly reinstated as Prime Minister, took up a suggestion to ban Eaton's book.

Unfortunately, Girilal Jain has passed away, and so have the others most likely to have been present. Consequently, it is impossible to get at closer details, unless some notebook of one of them turns up. I suppose it must have been Nurul Hasan or P.N. Haksar who brooked the idea, Indira's confidence men who changed the face of India by handing complete power in the cultural and academic sectors to the hard Left. But it was only the idea of a few anti-Hindu intellectuals, not a demand made on the streets by marching Muslim crowds, so it seems the Prime Minister didn't consider the matter very urgent. While Mr. Jain came away with the knowledge that she had okayed the plan of banning the book, it seems she didn't care enough to go out of her way and actually implement the ban. So, nothing came of it.

This turns out to be one case where inside information can be misleading, and I'll take it as an interesting learning experience. The dangers of misinformation against which reporters and historians must be on their guard are numerous and of many different types.

10.9. The demolition

Mr. Khan thinks that I am trying to shield the BJP from the blame for the Ayodhya demolition. Given the trouble it has predictably caused the BJP, it is indeed entirely rational to consider the BJP an unlikely culprit. But that's still some distance from blaming arch-secularist V.P. Singh:

"Regarding Babri Masjid Elst continues his blame game by pointing fingers towards Narasimha Rao and V.P.Singh. He writes: 'I was told at the BJP office that Prime Minister

V.P.Singh had suggested to Advani that he create some public opinion pressure on the Government concerning Ayodhya. That way, V.P.Singh (who rejected the claim that the disputed building was a 'mosque') could explain to his Muslim supporters that in the face of such mighty pressure, he would be unable to keep his promise to give them the disputed site. So, possibly that is how the BJP decided to have the Rath Yatra.' (p.174) V.P.Singh has always denied this charge."

He would, wouldn't he? But here again, the suspicion is perfectly rational, entirely logical with V.P. Singh's interests and tactical constraints. To avoid misunderstandings, this does not mean that he contrived to have a wild demolition as took place on 6 December 1992. Like Rajiv Gandhi before him, he merely wanted a hand-over of the site to its legitimate owners, Hindu society, in exchange for some favours to the Muslim leadership. As a pragmatic way of calming tensions, such political deals are respectable and not a cause for "blame". As for the actual demolition:

"With regards to Narasimha Rao's government's involvement in the demolition of the Babri Masjid Elst writes: 'Consider the matter from his (Narasimha Rao's) viewpoint: as long as the 'mosque' (for the BJP, 'the disputed structure'; for commentator Girilal Jain, 'the non-mosque') was standing, the BJP could use it as a rallying-point, a visible 'sign of national humiliation imposed by the invader Babar' kept in place by the 'pseudo-secularist' Congress Government. On the other hand, if the building was demolished in a BJP-related action, this could be used against the BJP and the whole Hindu movement, viz. as a reason to dismiss the BJP state governments and ban the Hindu mass organizations. This is at any rate what effectively happened; the Ayodhya theme was killed as a BJP vote-getter, and the BJP's march to power was temporarily reversed'. (p.175)"

That still sounds like a correct assessment of the considerations factored into Rao's decisions. Of course, his intimate thoughts are a black box to me, but the output from that black box, viz. his actual policy, seems to fit my hypothesis nicely. Let me also mention that I have had the privilege of meeting Mr. Rao, near the end of his life at some India event hosted by the State Department in Washington DC, and telling him in person that I consider him India's best Prime Minister to date (Yes, I'm a sycophant). Unlike Atal Behari Vajpayee, he actually implemented a serious part of the BJP programme.

10.10. Conclusion

Fortunately, Mr. Khan hasn't wasted his time reading my book. He found some useful information in it:

"Apart from Muslim-bashing, *Decolonizing the Hindu Mind* throws up some interesting side notes as well. For example that one of the nieces of L.K. Advani converted to Islam and married a Muslim man with his blessings. According to Gurudatt Vaidya, a prominent Arya Samaji and Jana Sanghi, Shyama Prasad Mookerjee, Jan Sangh leader, died of a heart attack in his prison cell because he ate two chickens against his doctor's orders. So much for Sangh's advocacy of vegetarianism."

To be sure, the latter account is based only on a personal testimony (though the medical records may yet confirm it), but I considered it important enough to at least not let it go unmentioned, if only because it provides a down-to-earth counterpoint to the exalted hagiography surrounding historic Sangh leaders. Personal anecdotes are not my main line of interest, but a different type of historian may take up this lead and explore the matter further. Meanwhile:

"In short Elst is a very useful writer for the Parivar even though he admits that the relationship has soured because of his criticism of RSS. But despite that it appears that the Parivar is taking him seriously. The very selective appointments of Sangh oriented individuals in scientific, educational, cultural and literary councils, and attempts to re-write the history, aggressive campaigns against Muslims and other minorities, all indicate that slowly but surely Elst's recommendations are being implemented. The relationship between the two is mutually beneficial. The Parivar gets a seasoned and ardent advocate for its agenda in the West and Elst (a self confessed apostate from Christianity and one whose sole source of income is writing) gets an ideology to hold on to, apart from the material benefits that come along with it."

I wonder on what planet Ayub Khan has been living lately to think that a pro-Hindu stance could be lucrative. If lucre and career prospects had been my motivation, I should have joined the anti-Hindu camp, which controls all the appointments and grants in the Indian Studies field. At the very least, that choice could have landed me a job with publicly-funded outfits like *Communalism Combat*, the organ of combative communalism.

11. Dhimmitude in Eurabia

The ills of Nehruvian secularism have now taken root in Europe as well, where the doctrine goes by the name of "multiculturalism". Quite frequently now, European authorities give in to demands by Muslim lobby groups, sometimes even when these demands are only being anticipated. The Jewish-Egyptian historian Bat Ye'or has termed this attitude "dhimmitude" (after *dhimmi*, a non-Muslim who accepts his subordination to Islam) and analysed it as the beginning of a new Islamic-dominated Europe, "Eurabia". An important test case was the Danish cartoon affair. In autumn 2005, when the culture editor of the leading Danish newspaper *Jyllands Posten* discovered that artists were reluctant to provide an illustration for a Muslim children's story about the life of Mohammed, he invited several dozens of them to send in their idea of a Mohammed cartoon. These cartoons became the flashpoint of Muslim riots and even triggered several murders in revenge for this "insult to Islam". I wrote a few columns on these and related incidents in the Belgian conservative on-line paper *Brussels Journal.*

11.1. "Don't take liberties with freedom"

[Originally published in www.brusselsjournal.be, 2 Feb. 2006, under the title: "Thank God for the Danish cartoons".]

On 31 January 2006, the British House of Commons has defeated, 283 against 282, the New Labour government's *Racial and Religious Hatred Bill*, intended to prohibit speech or artistic expressions deemed insulting by religious communities. This is a narrow yet historic victory for freedom of expression as well as a victory for Parliament against a despotic-minded Government. Liberal-Democratic spokesman Evan Harris commented: "The Government just failed to understand that they can't take liberties with freedom of expression."

This parliamentary vote may also boost the morale of the Danish government and media besieged by Muslim governments and pressure groups promising dire consequences if no action is taken against the cartoons of the Prophet first published in the daily *Jyllands Posten*. The Danes could use a bit of support now that they are also attacked, openly or indirectly, by an international establishment speaking through the mouth of Bill Clinton, the Council of Europe and various EU bureaucrats. Their exercising the freedom of expression is blackened as "Islamophobia", a notion introduced by Tariq Ramadan (the media-savvy face of radical Islam, also grandson of Hassan al-Banna, its Egyptian ideologue) and now promoted and inserted into international policy by people such as Karel De Gucht, Belgium's Foreign Affairs Minister and current Chairman of the Organization for Security and Cooperation in Europe. So far, the Danish Government and the *Jyllands Posten* editor have, all while making some conciliatory gestures, stood firm against all this pressure. A few European newspapers, including *France-Soir* and *Die Welt*, have expressed their support by republishing the offending cartoons in their own pages.

On the occasion of the House of Commons vote, familiar maxims on liberty have aptly been invoked in various debates, e.g. against the British Government's plea that the bill was "necessary" to make multicultural coexistence possible (an argument invoked by governments across Europe to impose similar censorship laws), William Pitt the Younger was quoted: "Necessity is the plea for every infringement of human freedom; it is the argument of tyrants;

it is the creed of slaves." Regarding the argument that this curtailment of freedom of speech is only a small concession to an acute societal need, Edmund Burke's words are repeated: "The true danger is when liberty is nibbled away for expedience and by parts."

Finally, against the argument that many things people say about other religions are ill-informed or prejudiced, Mahatma Gandhi was quoted: "Freedom isn't worth having if it does not connote the freedom to err." But the utterances about religions that really cause offence are of course not those that are in error but those that are undeniably right on the mark. Depicting Mohammed with a bomb in his turban, as in one of the contentious cartoons, hurts because it is so obviously apt. Mohammed himself organized dozens of armed raids on caravans, took hostages for ransom, permitted his men to rape the hostages, ordered the assassination of poets who mocked or criticized him, and had his prisoners of war massacred or sold into slavery. He didn't have modern bomb technology, but his most dedicated followers have no problem interpreting his precedent as a warrant for terrorism. Indeed, in spite of all the reassuring comments by ignorant and dishonest outsiders that "Islam prohibits terrorism", the perpetrators of most recent acts of Islamic terror, from 9/11 suicide hijacker Mohammed Atta to Theo van Gogh's assassin Mohammed Bouyeri, have explicitly affirmed that they were motivated by their zeal for Islam and by the teaching and precedent of the Prophet.

Does a scholarly paper patiently documenting this link between the Prophet and terrorism, or indeed a cartoon making the same point in an eyewink, hurt the feelings of all those peace-loving ordinary Muslims? Quite possibly, but that's where George Orwell's observation applies: "If liberty means anything at all, it means the right to tell people what they do not want to hear." Millions of Muslims have constructed for themselves a version of Islam that reconciles a veneration for the Prophet and the Quran with an acceptance of more enlightened values of pluralism and tolerance. To them, it may come as a shock to see their sweet delusion pin-pricked. But that kind of shock therapy is a healthy thing. Those Danish cartoonists are among the greatest benefactors the Muslims have ever had.

11.2. How to criticize the Prophet

[Published in the *Brussels Journal*, 11-2-2006.]

For the upcoming breed of Muslim politicians in Europe, the cartoon crisis has been a golden opportunity in terms of public relations. They suddenly found themselves courted by journalists eager to find the "voice of moderate Islam" or, alternatively, fishing for a sensational quote encapsulating Islamic extremism in some novel way. One of the Muslim politicians capably giving voice to the "moderate" position is Turkish-born Mr. Ergün Top, a lawyer, town councillor in Antwerp and one of the coming men in the Flemish Christian-Democratic Party. His future is bright, for his party badly needs its handful of Muslim candidates to counter the large Muslim presence in the Socialist Party in the contest for the fast-growing Muslim electorate.

I can personally testify that Mr. Top is a nice fellow, a model of integration, and quite a contrast with some of the Turkish-born politicians in the Francophone Socialist Party. Thus, you may have heard of Mr. Emir Kir, one of the heavyweights in the regional Government of Brussels, who ensured the non-implementation of our laws regarding slaughter during the latest Islamic Sacrifice Day (*Eid-al-Kabir*), and who keeps on lobbying against any form of recognition of the Armenian genocide. I sincerely hope the voters of Turkish origin will reconsider their choices and abandon the likes of Mr. Kir in favour of more responsible politicians like Mr. Top.

In several TV debates now, Mr. Top has argued that offensive speech or cartoons are perfectly allowed legally, but are morally unacceptable, esp. if published by people who know and understand the Islamic prohibition on depicting and insulting the Prophet. It is of course commendable that he clearly accepts the legal position: newspapers enjoy freedom of expression in which the Government cannot interfere. He calls on his fellow Muslims to abide by the law but to educate their non-Muslim neighbours into accepting this demand of "respect" for the Prophet.

It is often said that "integration" is a hollow concept except in so far as it means the only thing that we can demand of immigrants, like of all citizens, viz. that they abide by the law, as Mr. Top recommends. If they want to stand out by wearing funny dress and eating funny food, that is their right as long as it isn't in explicit conflict with any law. Hence, the whole fashionable discourse of "norms and values", into which the Muslims should assimilate, is beside the point: only the written law lays down the limits, for the rest anyone is free to differ from the "mainstream" in convictions and lifestyle, in norms and values, as much as Catholics are free to differ from Protestants, beef-eaters from vegetarians or hippies from yuppies.

It must be admitted that the discourse of "norms and values" is vague and politically unpractical. Yet, here we seem to be encountering a situation where these concepts are valid. To say that irreverent cartoons are "morally unacceptable" is not in conflict with our laws, but it might be in conflict with our "norms and values". Laws don't just fall from the sky, they grow in a certain cultural soil. If we have enshrined freedom of speech and of the press in our constitution, it is because we had first come to value these freedoms. That pre-existing conviction motivated a struggle for these freedoms which resulted in their adoption into our system of laws. We believe that it is morally acceptable to express your opinions, even if they hurt someone's religious sentiments. If those opinions are wrong, it is still best to see them out in the open so that we can evaluate them. So, to us, it is *good* that opinions including mistaken opinions are given free expression.

As the case of Mr. Top indicates (to the extent that his answers in the rather hurried context of a TV interview can be taken to reflect his convictions accurately), even law-abiding Muslims have not entirely embraced our norms and values. To be sure, that is their privilege, just as anarchists are welcome to reject the rule of law mentally as long as they abide by the law in practice. But it remains a point worth noting if we want to understand the problems of integration that the Muslim community is going through.

For now I'll leave that as something to think about. Meanwhile, seeing Ergün Top on TV reminded me of my first meeting with him. It was an occasion where I probably made a more irreverent attack on the prophet than all the twelve Danish cartoonists together,— and got away with it. I will relate my experience here as a case study in how and when a critique of Islam can be presented to committed Muslims without causing damage to anyone.

Mr. Top, then a law student, was one of the organizers, along with the Green Party's student section, of an Islam debate in Leuven ca. 1994. It was at his place that we had agreed to meet before walking together to the university hall where the debate was to be held. The panel featured Mr. Arif Ersoy of Turkey's Islamist party, the party currently in power in Ankara; the Muslim convert Prof. Yahyah (formerly Jean) Michot, who was to make headlines a few years later with a pseudonymously published booklet arguing that Islamic jurisprudence allowed the killing of Christian monks, then a regular occurrence in Algeria; and myself, introduced in the leftist student paper *Veto* as "the controversial Orientalist Koenraad Elst". The audience of several hundreds consisted mostly of Muslims, men and women in roughly equal numbers.

The first skirmishes were about the usual topics: Islam's record of intolerance and iconoclasm, the Crusades etc. After a while, I managed to steer the debate to more fundamental issues. When I brought up Mohammed's snatching the beautiful Zaynab from his adopted son, making the latter divorce her to make her available for the Prophet's own use, Prof. Michot replied along classical lines, viz. that it was an old Christian argument to depict the prophet as a lecher lusting after ever more women. I explained that that was not my point at all: it is of no consequence to us if a 7th-century chieftain in a far-away desert had a large harem. The real problem with this episode is that Mohammed knew he was breaking Arab tribal custom, which prohibited marriage with the ex-spouse of a legal (even if non-biological) relative, so he contrived to receive a "revelation" from Allah telling him that in this exceptional case, his marriage with Zaynab was allowed.

This means that the episode puts in doubt the genuineness of Mohammed's prophetic revelations, which he apparently conjured up to provide justification for his personal interests, less by deliberate manipulation than through a subconscious self-delusion. Likewise, when he trespassed against the existing war conventions, as by fighting during the "sacred months" (when a truce guaranteed the safety of pilgrims to Mecca) or chopping down fruit trees (a rare and precious commodity in Arabia), he always received revelations from heaven justifying his decisions. Even his favourite child-wife Aisha sceptically remarked that those revelations were always so suspiciously convenient for his all-too-human personal whims.

Indeed, I argued, the Quran itself has Allah tell Mohammed a dozen times how he should react when people disbelieve his claims of hearing a voice from heaven. His contemporaries are reported to dismiss him as "ghost-possessed", "fanciful", and even as "a mad poet". Worse, the very first person to suspect a mental disorder behind his prophetic trance was Mohammed himself. When he had his first vision of the archangel Gabriel dictating him a message, he feared he was going mad and decided to undo this shame by committing suicide. It was his first wife Khadijah who would comfort him and help him adjust to these recurring visions. From terrifying mental crises, they gradually became a familiar phenomenon and Mohammed integrated them into his new persona of God's Prophet. When Mohammed went into his trance, he vocalized what he "heard" so a secretary could write it down, and these utterances were later collected into the Quran.

The first-hand diagnosis by immediate witnesses, admittedly laymen who understood mental phenomena in terms of "spirits", has later been developed in more serious detail by professional psychologists, such as the late Dr. Herman Somers in his book *Een Andere Mohammed* ("A Different Mohammed", Hadewych, Antwerp 1993). Somers' considered verdict is that Mohammed was a textbook case of a paranoid delusion, i.c. a self-centred belief in his own unique status as God's spokesman, nurtured with recurring visual and auditory hallucinations. Contentswise, the hallucinations brought to the surface bits and pieces from Mohammed's memory bank: his own opinions on religious or worldly matters and his own very human desires, along with elements of Judeo-Christian lore which he had learned around the campfire from Jews and Christians during his business trips. There is not a single sentence in the Quran that cannot be explained from Mohammed's own socio-cultural background, nothing at all that indicates a superhuman source. Consequently, Islam as a belief system is nothing but a collective second-hand delusion, borrowed from a mentally afflicted Arabian businessman.

So, that's what I said to my two fellow panelists and to an audience of several hundred Muslims. For a moment, I was quite apprehensive about their reaction, but there was no outcry of indignation. A few mouths fell open in utter amazement, but it seemed nobody was ready for this. They all had learned the standard replies against the standard Western objections about Islam being intolerant ("it's the religion of peace") or oppressive to women ("Mohammed was the first feminist"), but this they had never heard before. When even the two Muslim panelists weren't volunteering a reply, the moderator introduced another topic. After the debate, some members of the audience joined me for a drink but no one brought up the question of Mohammed's sanity again.

Years later, I put those ideas in writing. My article *Wahi: the Supernatural Basis of Islam* (Wahi is the Arabic term for Mohammed's prophetic trance) was published in instalments in the on-line paper *Kashmir Herald* [www.kashmirherald.com] in the winter of 2002-03. A Tamil translation has been published as a booklet in India. To my knowledge, this has not led to any riots nor even to demands of censorship. Likewise, Dr. Somers was never troubled for publishing his diagnosis of Mohammed. Even Maxime Rodinson's brief critique of Mohammed's sanity, on pp.76-79 of his Penguin monograph *Mohammed*, available worldwide, never got him into trouble; apparently it wasn't even cited as incriminating evidence when his book was banned from use in some Egyptian universities (where it had been required reading, no less) a few years ago. Yet, this is a more fundamental critique of Islam than the usual arguments about terrorism or the unequal treatment of women and unbelievers.

If Mohammed is shown to be a robber chieftain on the strength of the Hadith account of his 82 attacks on caravans, Muslim apologists can always say that Arabia and the early Middle Ages just happened to be a violent place and time for everyone. If the Quran is quoted as ranking women below men, they can reply that all established religions (including those now fashionable in Hollywood, like Buddhism) happen to assume the inequality of men and women, even if in different ways. But if Mohammed is shown to have heard a voice that spoke from his own subconscious rather than from heaven, and that the Quran is nothing but a collection of all-too-human dreamspeak, the whole edifice of Islam is undermined. Not religiosity per se, not devotion to Allah, but that which distinguishes Islam from other religions, viz. the belief in Mohammed's prophethood.

I have to touch wood as I write this, but my impression is that this radical critique of Islam is much safer to utter than the more usual criticisms. It has solid academic precedent in psychological studies of non-Islamic religious figures, most famously Sigmund Freud's study on Moses, so it can hardly be put down as a device concocted to hurt Islam. More importantly, it is a less sensational topic than sex and violence, less likely to make headlines in the popular press where agitators can seize upon it. Whether in words or in images, describing Mohammed as a terrorist or a lecher or a paedophile (as Mrs. Ayaan Hirsi Ali has done, referring to the Prophet's deflowering nine-year-old Aisha), or locating his wives in a brothel (that's how many Muslims misunderstood a scene in Salman Rushdie's *The Satanic Verses*, where prostitutes maximize their appeal by acting the part of Khadijah, Zaynab etc.), touches a very emotional nerve and provokes an emotional reaction. Questioning the legitimacy of Mohammed's self-image as God's spokesman, by contrast, may rather tend to provoke doubt and intellectual reflection.

I am all for the unfettered right of cartoonists to lampoon religious authorities and divine characters. In this instance, they have played a useful role in awakening us all to certain troubling realities. But if we want to make headway in the "dialogue" that everyone is now calling for, it might be advisable to move from the emotive issues to more fundamental matters of doctrine. No insult to the Prophet, just some careful scrutiny. Surely Mr. Ergün Top cannot find that "morally unacceptable".

11.3. Banning the Quran?

[Published in the *Brussels Journal*, 17-2-2006.]

The controversy over the Danish cartoons depicting the Prophet Mohammed has generated plenty of hypocritical commentary by politicians and other public figures who try to give an impression of moderation and neutrality. In most cases, they do so by picking up the quarrel in the middle and condemning both the "insensitivity" of the cartoonists and the "overreaction" of the Muslim world, both instances of "extremism". They expect us to believe that there is a moral equivalence between the exercising of a fundamental right, viz. freedom of expression, and the attempt to abolish this right.

Many also took the snobbish position that the cartoons shouldn't have been published because they were "substandard". Ooh, those gourmet cartoon connoisseurs, they will settle for nothing but the best. Other tricks of evasiveness include the imputation of ulterior motives, e.g. that both on the Danish and on the Muslim side, the "real" object of the controversy is Denmark's restrictive immigration policy rather than the cartoons. This goes against all the testimonies of Muslim government spokesmen and demonstrators interviewed in their and our media, but nonetheless I saw Ms. Miet Smet, Flemish MP, assert it on TV. Another diversionary tactic was tried by Rik van Cauwelaert, editor of the leading Flemish weekly *Knack*, who wrote that "the real issue" was unemployment of young Muslims in Europe, as if that had been a concern of the violent demonstrators in faraway Beirut or Peshawar.

I don't know if hypocrisy is better or worse than the second-most-common position in those circles, viz. openly siding with Islamic fanaticism and fully putting the blame on the cartoonists and their editors, as was done by Bill Clinton, Kofi Annan and the Foreign Affairs spokesmen of the Bush and Blair governments. In the latest issue of *Knack*, deputy editor Karl Van den Broeck launched the innovative conspiracy theory that the Neoconservative cabal, with its tentacles stretching from Washington DC and Tel Aviv to Aarhus and Brussels (i.e. the *Brussels Journal*), had planned the whole cartoon riot incident as the trigger for the Clash of

Civilizations and the invasion of Syria and Iran, no less. Well, not all that innovative: a similar explanation has been given by Ayatollah Khamenei.

Our Flemish novelist Kristien Hemmerechts, feminist and cultural relativist (hence her apologetics for female circumcision), simply stated that since the Muslims are so sensitive to these cartoons, we shouldn't have made or published them. Yes, if that's what they want, what else can we do than to obey them? I wonder why she doesn't notice how childishly selfish the Muslim position is. For centuries and till today, Islam has ordered the destruction of everything that is sacred to other religions, starting with the 360 idols in the Kaaba (including a Jesus and a Mary) smashed to pieces by Mohammed himself, down to the Bamian Buddhas destroyed by the Taliban in 2001, the Hindu temples vandalized in Bangladesh week after week, or the Christian churches that have been destroyed in Iraq in the last couple of months. And in many cases, not only the places of worship but the worshippers too have been levelled. What an effrontery for Muslims, with their heritage of iconoclastic insensitivity, to put up this show of indignation for a handful of harmless cartoons. And now we should feel pity for those poor touch-me-nots?

In Muslim circles, meanwhile, only a few independent intellectuals have come out unequivocally on the side of freedom of expression, most bravely the Jordanian journalists who confronted their readers with the poser: "Which is worse for Islam, these cartoons or the TV images of Iraqi *mujahedin* beheading their hostages?" They were arrested. So were several Algerian journalists for republishing the cartoons, and their paper was banned from further publication. Likewise a leftist Syrian journalist was arrested under the law against "insulting religious feelings" for having proposed a dialogue about the cartoon controversy on the plea that violent protests could only hurt the image of Islam. And in Konya, Turkey, a woman journalist was stoned to death for not wearing a headscarf while reporting on a demonstration held under the motto "loyalty to the Prophet".

By contrast, many Europe-based Muslim intellectuals who joined the debate, esp. those who opened their interventions with a plea against violent protest by way of *captatio benevolentiae* (then followed by "but..."), only did so as the non-violent first line of attack in the broader Islamist offensive against freedom of expression and of the press. They are at any rate the ones who stand to gain most from this type of crisis: with every Islamist bomb attack by the violent wing, the non-violent vanguard's stock with Western governments and media goes up. They become ever more needed as "dialogue partners" to keep the violent option at a distance. But objectively, they are working for the same goal as the armed Islamists: to curb democratic freedoms as a crucial step in the imposition of an Islamic order on the West.

A good example is the Flemish-Moroccan lobby group KifKif. Seven of its board members, including the well-known public intellectuals Tarik Fraihi and Sami Zemni, have published a plea for "limits on freedom of speech" ("Er zijn grenzen aan de vrijheid van meningsuiting", *De Morgen*, 14-2-2006). They argue that "an absolute freedom of expression can only play into the hand of antidemocratic extremists". This position is evidently the opposite of the truth. Unfettered freedom of expression is a fundamental precondition for a democracy, because a democratically sovereign citizenry needs to inform itself about the existing spectrum of opinions on the matters that come up for decision-making. In a democracy, there are no two unequal categories of citizens, with one of them allowed to select what the other is allowed to hear and read. By contrast, conditional freedom of expression is typical of dictatorships. Hitler and Stalin didn't oppose the freedom to express opinions that were in line with their own policies, and likewise, KifKif doesn't advocate limits on the expression of opinions in line with its own.

But since its job is to put a democratic face on this attack on the foundations of our democracy, it cleverly uses the language of human rights: "The self-declared defenders of absolute freedom of expression forget (deliberately?) the second part of the much-discussed article 10 of the European Convention on Human Rights, not coincidentally the part in which the limits of freedom of expression are defined." This is bluff aimed at fooling lazy readers, for those who take the trouble of reading the ECHR article in question, which guarantees freedom of expression, will find that the limits mentioned there are conceived in terms of national interests and morality, not of prohibiting criticism of religious doctrines and leaders. The only straw at which the KifKif authors can clutch, is this: "An important limit according to the ECHR is the 'protection of the rights of others'", which they take to include "the right to respect (art. 8) and the right to freedom of religion (art. 9)".

That is another attempt to fool unsuspecting readers, for the rights guaranteed in articles 8 and 9 are in no way thwarted by any possible form of self-expression. The "respect" dealt with in art. 8 is not the right to freedom from criticism which Islam is now demanding, but the very tangible right of freedom from encroachment on one's correspondence, home and family life. The freedom of religion guaranteed in art. 9 is likewise left wholly untouched by anyone's expression of an opinion. The religious freedom of Christians has not been violated at all by the various forms of criticism of which it has been the target since the 18th century (but it *has* been violated by various forms of prohibition, repression and pogroms in Communist and Islamic countries).

The KifKif authors continue: "Freedom of expression is limited in this sense that exhortation to hate or racism are forms of verbal violence and therefore punishable offences." That's not in the ECHR, but let us allow that this idea does at least underlie the anti-racist legislation in some European countries. The Newspeak notion of "verbal violence" is an attempt to vitiate the debate by pretending that strong rhetoric amounts to, and is somehow equivalent with, violence. This is again entirely typical of dictatorships, where dissenters are routinely criminalized as "trouble-makers irresponsibly sowing conflict in society" and their silencing and incarceration justified as "necessary for the people's well-being and social peace". In fact, it is precisely the so-called "violent" speech that is protected by the principle of freedom of expression. Sweet-talk isn't controversial and is not sought to be curbed, the opinions that need to be protected from censorship are precisely the opinions that hurt. As George Orwell has said: if freedom of speech means anything at all, it is the freedom to say things that people do not want to hear. That is, those things that the people targeted will resent as "verbal violence".

The reference to anti-racist restrictions is yet another attempt to distort the debate, for criticism of religion (which is the basis of *any* criticism, according to Karl Marx) has nothing to do with race. There are many Muslim-born critics of Islam, racially identical with the Islamists they criticize, people like Ibn Warraq or Ayaan Hirsi Ali. Conversely, there are quite a few European-born converts to Islam, often with a convert's militant zeal. I have been on debating panels with several of them, and a few have even made headlines by joining the armed struggle in Afghanistan or Iraq against Western forces, mostly white like themselves. If the KifKif advocates of Islam's right to veto criticism have to take umbrage behind the misplaced rhetoric of anti-racism, diverting attention from the religious basis of the controversy, they may well be betraying an apprehension that their core argumentation is weak.

And it is. Suppose we take them at their word when they argue: "Freedom of the press and of expression cannot and must not become a licence or alibi for gratuitous, mendacious and disrespectful messages." The first two adjectives are bluff, again. There was nothing "gratuitous" about raising the issue of whether artists are afraid to depict the Prophet. A Danish author of children's books had discovered this to be the case, which was the reason for *Jyllands-Posten*'s invitation to the cartoonists. Neither was it gratuitous when two of the cartoonists connected the person of Mohammed with the contemporary theme of terrorism. It so happens that hundreds of terrorists in the past several years have justified their actions with reference to the words and actions of their Prophet. It is not gratuitous or frivolous for a newspaper to address politically relevant facts.

Secondly, there was nothing "mendacious" about depicting Mohammed in a way that associates him with terrorism. KifKif has no monopoly on access to the orthodox Islamic sources about the life and works of the Prophet of Islam. We can check for ourselves that the *Hadīth* (traditions concerning the Prophet's words and deeds) and *Sīra* (biography) literature describe Mohammed as engaging in armed raids, plunder, hostage-taking, rape, assassination of critics and mass-murder of prisoners. Instances of this conduct are also confirmed and justified in the Quran itself. In a democracy, it is perfectly permitted to point this out, whether laboriously in a scholarly paper or more caustically in a cartoon.

As to the third point, we may agree that from a certain angle, the cartoons can indeed be considered as "disrespectful". But in that case, we must likewise judge "disrespectful" the sources on which the message they convey is based. As we have just pointed out, the notion that Mohammed was a kind of terrorist is not an invention of some 21st-century "Islamophobe" or "racist", it is based on Arabic sources compiled by orthodox Muslims and enshrined as the basis of Islamic doctrine and law. If cartoons critical of the Prophet have to be banned, what does KifKif propose to do with the Hadith collections and the Quran: ban those books *in toto* or merely excise the parts that testify to Mohammed's acting in contravention of the ECHR?

Lest I be misquoted on this, let me affirm unambiguously that I, for one, am not in favour of any curtailment of the freedom to buy and sell and read and discuss the Quran, on the contrary. Everybody should read it, for that is the best immunization against silly sop-stories about Islam being "the religion of peace" or Mohammed being "the first feminist". I am merely pointing that that *if* there should be restrictions on publications casting the Prophet in a negative light, as KifKif demands, *then* such restrictions would logically affect the basic texts of Islam. If logic had any force of law, the KifKif board members would be well advised to ponder the wisdom in the old proverb: "Be careful with what you wish for:— you might get it."

The question of how the Islamic texts would fare under a KifKif regime becomes all the more pressing when we consider another assertion of the board members: "Kif Kif is of the opinion that there are limits to freedom of expression. It is at least necessary that those limits are the same for everybody. (...) We wish to live in a tightly coherent society with equal rights and duties for everyone. A society without racism, whether it is Islamophobia or anti-Semitism."

This seems to mean that disrespect for any religion should receive the same treatment as disrespect for Islam. So, if insults to Islam or the Muslim community must be prohibited, then so must insults to other religions and their adherents. (In the new nomenclature, this might be called *Kafirophobia*, aversion to *Kafir*-s or "unbelievers"; if the KifKif authors mean what they say about equality, they should henceforth twin every mention of "Islamophobia" with "Kafirophobia".) How would the Quran fare in such a system?

It is well-known that the Quran contains dozens of verses preaching hostility to Pagans (polytheists, Zoroastrian "fire-worshippers" and atheists), Jews and Christians. It denounces their teachings as false and evil and a sure passport to hell. Which is fine with me, for whoever he was, the author of the

Quran too is entitled to his freedom of opinion on religions. But by KifKif standards, these insulting comments on other people's religions are not so innocent and ought to be curtailed, especially in a multicultural society. (And indeed, according to the orthodox sources, it was Mohammed's lifetime achievement to have transformed Arabia's multicultural society into a monolithic Islamic one.)

The Quran also expressly forbids conversion from Islam to other religions, while of course allowing and encouraging the reverse conversion. This ought to be problematic for the KifKif authors with their plea for equality and reciprocity. It is also in contravention of the ECHR's article 9, to which they pay lip service, for this article defines "freedom of religion" as including "the right to change one's religion".

The Quran further rejects the principle of "equal rights and duties for everyone", which KifKif now invokes. Leave aside the candidly affirmed inequality in rights and duties between the sexes (which admittedly exists in all religions), it explicitly ordains inequality between the different religious communities. To the non-monotheists, Mohammed denied freedom of religion completely, and as for Jews and Christians, the Quran only allows them to retain their faith if they accept a third-class status including the payment of a toleration tax.. When the Prophet's Islamic state developed into an empire under his successors, the "rightly-guided Caliphs", this principle was elaborated into a whole system of legal inequality between Muslims and non-Muslims. This inequality pervades the *Shari'a* (Islamic law) and even now it already makes itself felt in our society quite frequently, esp. in the immense and sometimes violent pressure of Muslim communities against affairs or marriages of their daughters with non-Muslims.

The matter gets really grim when we find that dozens of Quran verses go further than mere doctrinal disputation and actually enjoin the Muslims to go out and *fight* the "infidels". The core text of Islam is not merely disrespectful of other religions, it extols killing and glorifies dying in the war against the non-Muslims. In case the text of the Quran is not clear enough, we should remember that it is a companion volume to Mohammed's actual career as a religious leader and military conqueror. Thus, if doubts arise on the meaning of *jihād*, literally "effort" but in practice "war against the infidels", we merely have to put the verses concerned in their real-life context. We then find that Mohammed understood and used the term unambiguously in the sense of "war", not some ethereal or metaphorical "struggle against the evil in ourselves" but an actual war involving horses, weapons, stratagems and blood. The Quran explicitly teaches hatred, hostility and the use of force against other religions and their adherents. By KifKif's own standards, it clearly falls outside the "limits of freedom of expression".

Fortunately, most Muslims don't take the Quran literally. Their common sense as well as human inertia and immediate self-interest make them focus on their own life's business rather than on the struggle against the infidels. When pressed for a Quranic justification of this Islamically lax conduct, they may invent some conveniently soft and non-literal interpretation of the more militant verses, or even (before ignorant Westerners) deny their existence altogether. And so they get on with their lives much like their non-Muslim neighbours do.

Yet, this doesn't mean the Quranic injunctions against the infidels are all that innocent. Of the hundreds of dedicated Muslims who committed acts of terror in the last couple of years, a handful may have been temperamentally violent and predisposed to committing such acts regardless of their religion. They may be the "evil people" whom President George W. Bush blamed for the 9/11 attacks in his bid not to implicate Islam. But many others have been pushed over the threshold of terrorism by the teaching of the Quran and the example set by the Prophet. After all, they understand the Quran as nothing less than God's own revelation. Unlike the ephemeral cartoons, which have not motivated a single act of violence against Muslims in the months since their publication, the Quranic injunctions are meant to be taken seriously.

So, when people plead for restrictions on free speech on the grounds that it may cause offence and even inspire hatred and active hostility to certain communities, they ought to realize that they are in effect demanding limitations on our freedom to read and recite the Quran. Is that what the KifKif board members want? If not, they should altogether withdraw their plea for limits on the freedom to express criticism of religions and religious figures including the Prophet Mohammed.

PS: please note that in the present column and in other publications, I have practised a reasonable degree of respect for the founder of Islam. Of course I haven't used any sycophantic or reverential appositions every time I mentioned his name, such as "Peace Be Upon Him". But at least I have repeatedly referred to him as the "Prophet", and capitalized, no less. As a non-believer, I would have been entitled to describe him on every one of those occasions as "the so-called prophet". Since I am not in the business of annoying people with such pedantries, I have refrained from exercising that right. It's just a question of sensitivity, you know.

11.4. Whirlwind Ayaan

[This article was first published in *Brussels Journal*, 8-6-2006. Ayaan Hirsi Ali, née Magan in 1969 in a Somali Muslim family, obtained asylum in the Netherlands in 1992, where she was to gain fame as a campaigner for freedom and against Islam. Fresh from graduating in Political Science at Leiden University, she worked for the Labour Party, then defected to the less Islam-appeasing People's Party for Freedom and Democracy and got elected as an MP. After scripting the film about Islam's treatment of women,

Submission, directed by Theo van Gogh, she received death threats, including one pinned onto Van Gogh's body when he was murdered by Mohammed Bouyeri. She had to go underground or rely on bodyguards. Her brief but eventful career in Dutch politics was cut short in 2006 when immigration minister Rita Verdonk made an issue of her "discovery", actually a public secret explained in detail years before by Ayaan herself, that she had applied for asylum on false pretexts. After some controversy, with extremely strange coalitions on both sides of the argument, her Dutch citizenship was restored to her, but she resigned from Parliament and accepted a job offer at a think-tank in Washington DC.]

There are two sides to the expulsion of Ayaan Hirsi Magan (a.k.a. Ayaan Hirsi Ali) from the Dutch nation and her resignation from the Second Chamber of the States-General, the Dutch Parliament.

Yes, she was a gain to Dutch society and politics. And yes, there was something thoroughly dishonourable about the action against her. Her well-to-do neighbours wanted to get rid of her bodyguard-encumbered presence because it brought the scary realities of multiculturalism a bit too close to home for comfort. Politician Hans Wiegel, a leading member of Ayaan's own party, the People's Party for Freedom and Democracy (VVD), and an establishment elitist who had earlier sabotaged the enactment of a bill instituting the right to citizen-initiated referendums, smugly commented: "We will not be hearing much from Ayaan anymore, and we will not miss her."

Politician Hilbrand Nawijn, elected as a coattail to the late Pim Fortuyn, joined forces with the Red and Green defenders of Islam to destroy Hirsi Ali, the activist who survived the murders of Fortuyn and of her friend Theo van Gogh. Nawijn cried victory when his demand to annull her Dutch citizenship was implemented. The Calvinist Right never forgave her her liberal advocacy of a secular school system, which is a legitimate viewpoint but no grounds for wanting someone expelled. To me, the coalition of undeniable diversity that brought her down was itself reason enough to support her.

She was all the more irritating to the enemies of freedom because her skin colour made it difficult to dismiss her as a racist. Indeed, her race is an anti-racist statement in itself. The Somali people are a mix between what old race theorists would have called the "Semitic" and "Hamitic" races. The old school frowned upon race-mixing and taught that it never yielded stable mix-races and that the mixed-race individuals were an ugly and unhappy lot, yet the Somali are on average among the most beautiful human phenotypes on earth. Ayaan Hirsi Ali also gave the lie to claims about low intelligence among Africans, for within a few years she acquired a mastery of the Dutch language that put many native speakers to shame.

Nevertheless the fact remains that she played and lost. The initial lie with which she gained asylum – and subsequently a successful future in Dutch society – caught up with her. I have known asylum seekers whom I personally liked and whom I considered an asset to our society, but who were nonetheless guilty of spicing up their stories to get accepted as legitimate refugees. They were lucky, but if their endeavour had failed it could not have been called unjust. Those were people whom I considered an asset to our society on specific grounds (as distinct from the silly dogma that any newcomer constitutes an "enrichment"), they were well integrated and fundamentally grateful to our country, but more importantly, they were individual cases.

Sympathy for individuals loyally struggling to find a place among us should not make us abandon our powers of discernment. A society can absorb individuals, not the teeming masses who would like to enter. The dramatic cases of individuals who have integrated but are legally required to leave the country should be avoided in the future by a firmer asylum policy which deals quickly with asylum requests and swiftly implements the decision whether to give or withhold the right to stay. This is not a harsh toughening of asylum policy but simply a matter of common sense. That is also why it was supported by Ayaan Hirsi Ali, who has consistently spoken out in favour of the restoration of integrity to the asylum process and a policy of selectivity in the admittance of labour immigrants, guided by the national interest. In other countries, too, it would seem that native politicians avoid the topic for fear of being called racists, but there is nothing particularly racist about upholding the rule of law.

When Ayaan Hirsi Ali was faced with the allegation that according to a strict interpretation of the law she was an illegal immigrant, she did not ask for special favours. Dissenting from the common opinion among her sympathizers, she did not say: "I am among the good guys and so I have the privilege of overstaying my legal welcome." Among other considerations, she knew that an exception for her would be used by asylum lawyers to argue for an extension of her exception to all illegal immigrants. And this is exactly what happened: when Minister Verdonk announced that she would rethink her decision of expelling the pasionaria of the struggle against Islamic oppression: hundreds of illegal aliens in the Netherlands seized the opportunity to file requests for a similar exception. Not that they had comparable merits to their credit, but the law is blind to such distinctions.

So Ayaan Hirsi Ali did the right thing by resigning and packing up. And since she had a job waiting for her in the USA, she could leave in style and show the petty Dutchmen that she does not need them. Whether they need her remains to be seen. Who will stand up and carry the torch of freedom and of resistance to Islamist intolerance and aggression?

11.5. A Former Jihadist Dies: Anwar Shaikh, 1928-2006

[Published in *Brussels Journal*, 30-11-2006.]

On 25 November 2006 the British Muslim apostate Anwar Shaikh died in his home in Cardiff. I would like to pay him homage by reproducing my review of one of his last books, *Islam and Terrorism*.

Anwar Shaikh was born in 1928 in Gujrat, now in Pakistan, in a Muslim family that vaguely remembered its pre-conversion Hindu origin as Kashmiri Pandits. In an age of mounting religious tensions, however, he grew up to be a committed Muslim. Come 1947 and the Partition of India, he was living in Lahore, a Hindu/Sikh-majority city expected to remain with India yet allotted to Pakistan because it was the metropolis of Muslim-majority West Panjab. Consequently, the city became the flashpoint of the worst interreligious violence, ending in its complete cleansing of non-Muslims. The young Anwar Shaikh took part in the Partition violence against Sikhs and Hindus, killing three Sikhs with his own hands. Terrorizing the non-Muslims seemed like the right and natural thing to do for a Pakistani

In 1956 he quit his job as a schoolteacher, migrated to Britain and established himself as a successful businessman. In his new environment, he developed second thoughts about his native religion. He married a Welsh lady and made it a point to integrate fully in British society and culture. From 1973 onwards, he went public with his criticism of Islam. He started publishing a periodical for critical discussion of Islam, *Liberty*, in both English and Urdu, and a series of books on the relation between Islam and topics such as nationalism, violence and sexuality.

His demythologizing observations about the Prophet and the Quran caused considerable anguish among Britain-based Muslims, especially when the clerics they consulted failed to come up with a reassuring refutation. In the 1990s, he had the honour of being targeted by a number of Pakistani clerics with dire fatwas, finding him guilty of apostasy and of insulting the Prophet but mercifully confining the implied death sentence to the jurisdiction of properly constituted Islamic states. He ought to be safe as long as he doesn't travel to an Islamic state. Nonetheless, his home is equipped with a number of security precautions.

In his book *Islam and Terrorism* (2004, Principality Publishers, Cardiff PO Box 918, Penarth Road, Cardiff, UK), Anwar Shaikh sets out to discover and reveal the scriptural and historical roots of Islam's current involvement with terrorism. The question has been occupying the minds of some Indian scholars for decades, but after recent Islamic terror attacks on Western interests, it seems that it is at last being taken seriously by Western audiences, politicians and scholars. Many of them are no longer prepared to swallow the easy answer that terrorism is un-Islamic and that it is only advertised as an Islamic Holy War by misguided individuals unrepresentative of true Islam.

All those people who say that acts of terror such as those on 11 September 2001 are un-Islamic, should tell us on what grounds an Islamic court could sentence an Osama bin Laden. The basis of Islamic law is the Quran along with the Prophet's sayings and conduct (which has the value of precedent). So, can an Islamic terrorist cite the authority of the Quran and the Prophet in his justification, or can these sources be invoked to the opposite effect?

The answer, Mr. Shaikh argues, is quite straightforward. He says that Mohammed himself was a terrorist, the most authoritative precedent for contemporary Islamic terrorists. To prove his point, he presents long lists of quotations from the Quran, the better-known Hadith (tradition of the Prophet) and also some lesser-known Hadith collections. In this respect, his book is a treasure-trove of first-hand data on the foundations of Islam and its doctrine of Holy War (*Jihād*).

Numerous canonical statements affirm that the *Mujahid* or Holy Warrior undoubtedly counts as the best among Muslims, e.g.: "Acting as Allah's soldier for one night in a battlefield is superior to saying prayers at home for 2,000 years." (from *Ibn-e-Majah*, vol.2, p.162) Or: "Leaving for Jihad in the way of Allah in the morning or evening will merit a reward better than the world and all that is in it." (from *Muslim*, 4639) Jihad, while not a duty for every individual

Muslim, is a duty on the Muslim community as a whole until the whole world has become part of the Islamic empire.

The cult of martyrdom is an intrinsic part of the doctrine of jihad: the martyr "will desire to return to this world and be killed ten times for the sake of the great honour that has been bestowed upon him." (Muslim 4635) And from Allah's own mouth: "Count not those who were slain in God's way as dead, but rather living with their Lord, by Him provided, rejoicing in the bounty that God has given them." (Quran 3:163) Contrary to a recent tongue-in-cheek theory which reduces the heavenly reward for the fallen *Mujahid* from 72 maidens to mere grapes on the basis of some Arabic-Aramaic homonymy, a number of Prophetic sayings, in varied wordings mostly not susceptible to this cute Aramaic interpretation, confirm as Islamic belief that "the martyr is dressed in radiant robes of faith, he is married to houris (the paradisiac virgins)" etc. (Ibn-e-Majah, vol.2, p.174) This confirms that the suicide terrorists were not acting against Islamic tenets, as some soft-brained would-be experts in the media have claimed. On the contrary, to sacrifice one's life in a jihadic operation against the unbelievers is the most glorious thing a Muslim can do.

In Jihad, it is perfectly permitted to deceive the unbelievers and subject them to terror. Anwar Sheikh provides all the scriptural references plus many precedents from history, which we cannot reproduce here. Suffice it to say there is ample evidence that Islam permits, and that by his personal example or by that of the men under his command, Mohammed has given permission for abduction, extortion, rape of hostages, mass-murder of prisoners, assassinations of enemies and dissidents, breaking of the conventions of civilized warfare, breaking of treaties, and suicide missions. From Osama bin Laden to the murderers of children in Beslan, North Ossetia, the Islamic terrorists are faithful followers of the Prophet.

For all his grim discoveries about the religion of the Muslims, Shaikh is not anti-Muslim: "I was not only born and bred as a Muslim but also fought grimly for the glory of Islam. Even today, my loved ones are Muslim. There is no way I can be anti-Muslim." (p.306) Being a European outsider to Islam, I always get nasty replies when I say that "the problem is not Muslims, the problem is Islam"; but here you have it from the horse's mouth. It is perfectly possible to retain warm feelings for Muslims yet leave Islam and even criticize Islam.

He continues with some practical advice to Muslims. Setting an example in his own life, he is showing them the way to integration in non-Muslim societies: "I am a citizen of Great Britain, therefore I have a legal and moral obligation to live like other Britons and raise my children as British citizens, who are free to practise any religion they like." (p.306) This is admittedly a difficult thing to do for the believing Muslim, for the practical core of Islam is not some theological doctrine but the observance of Islamic law, preferably under an Islamic polity but otherwise even in a non-Islamic society. The idea of allowing their children the freedom to choose their own religion, i.e. to choose against Islam and for an allegedly false religion, is abhorrent to most believers. Yet, it is what they have to do if they want to integrate into Western (c.q. Hindu) society.

Unfortunately, Shaikh finds that the number of Muslims ignoring this common-sense rule has crossed a critical threshold to a point where it negatively affects not only Muslim-non-Muslim coexistence, but even the non-Muslim host society itself: "The Muslims in this country have not fully appreciated the hospitality that they have received. (...) It is no crime to be a Muslim in this country but it is a crime to be a terrorist because terrorism has demolished many of those civil liberties for which the West has worked for a long time and given tremendous sacrifices to gain them. Now, they have created such conditions that safety is becoming impossible without identity cards, emergency laws which authorise imprisonment without a trial", etc. (p.307)

Remember the good old days when the bobbies, Britain's police constables, did their rounds without carrying guns? It cannot honestly be denied that the behaviour of an ever-increasing number of young Pakistanis has contributed decisively to the sad discarding of this glorious tradition. Every non-brainwashed European can confirm that an influx of entire Muslim communities (as opposed to individuals or single families, who tend to blend in like most isolated immigrants do) has created a new set of problems for his society. The larger these Islamic islands in Western society become, the less willingness they show to adapt, and the more they insist on maintaining or restoring Islamic mores and laws within their communities and ultimately in society as a whole.

The one silver lining to the dark cloud of Islamic terrorism is that it alerts non-Muslim societies to the specificity of the problems which Islam poses. Westerners often feel guilty of xenophobia, "fear of what is strange or foreign", when they criticize Islam. But the problem of Islam is not one of strangeness or foreign origin, as will readily become clear when you compare it with Buddhism. In Western culture, Buddhism is even stranger than Islam, which shares certain common roots with Christianity, yet people find Tibetans in their native dress colourful rather than threatening. There are no Buddhist gangs attacking peaceful citizens, nor are there Buddhist associations making separatist political demands such as the right to observe a separate law system. Buddhism may be strange, but informed people will agree that it is an enrichment to our society. Islam is less strange, yet its enriching contributions are unclear while its nuisance value is all too palpable. The stark reality of Islamic terrorism blows away the fog of doubt and timidity hitherto surrounding the painful question of how to evaluate Islam.

12. The case of M.F. Husain

[This piece was written in February 2007 based on notes from June 2006.]

The first half of 2006 saw a number of incidents concerning the nude paintings of Hindu deities by veteran Muslim painter Maqbul Fida Husain. At least six court cases were filed against him and more than 150 demonstrations took place near Husain exhibitions, auctions, award ceremonies and litigation venues in places as far apart as New York, Washington DC, London, Mumbai, Delhi, Bhopal and provincial towns like Satara. In this article I have no intention of giving a full account of all this commotion, merely to develop my view on the basic question: are these nude depictions of deities justifiable under modern principles of artistic freedom?

12.1. Protests

Hindu organizations in Great Britain, most actively the Hindu Human Rights group, have organized protests against an exhibition of paintings by the Indian Muslim artist M.F. Hussein. The *Times of India* (24 May 2006) carried a story of the exhibition held in Asia House in London of two nude portrayals of Hindu goddesses drawn by M.F. Hussein. The exhibition was inaugurated by Kamlesh Sharma, India's High Commissioner. Mr. Ramesh Kallidai, the secretary-general of the Hindu Forum of Britain, an umbrella group that claims 270 Hindu organizations as members, told the *Times of India*: "When it came to the Prophet's cartoons, Prime Minister

Manmohan Singh personally condemned them. India was one of the first to ban Rushdie's book, *The Satanic Verses.* Why should artistic freedom only be enjoyed by those who hurt and insult Hindus?"

Hindus protested against the Asia House gallery because they objected to its decision to exhibit paintings of Hindu goddesses engaged in what looked like acts of bestiality. While the Hindu groups had agreed to meet the organizers for discussion, they were beaten to it by unknown individuals who entered the exhibition hall and destroyed some of the offending paintings. No further talks took place, and the exhibition was closed. Anti-Hindu commentators lost no time in amalgamating the dignified Hindu protests with the act of vandalism. The British Hindus set the record straight:

"These people also fail to acknowledge the right of the Hindu community to hold peaceful protests when our religion and culture are abused and defamed. The right to peaceful protest is integral to the functioning in any healthy democratic society. Following this logic, the thousands of anti-war protesters must also be bigots and fundamentalists. (...) The wider problem is that this is not the first case of defamation against Hindus and Hinduism and it is something that the Hindu community has been concerned about for a long time and it is this defamation that leads to persecution of Hindus elsewhere in the world. It also creates the atmosphere in the West where the media and public becomes apathetic, ignorant and indifferent to the persecution and discrimination of Hindus and Hinduism across the world."

When Lord Meghnad Desai, a prominent Nehruvian secularist, heard of the affair, he issued a comment putting forth three arguments. Firstly, the exhibition is being attacked because M.F. Husain is a Muslim. Secondly, Hindu Right groups have attempted to undermine artistic freedom. Thirdly, Hindu goddesses can be seen in a variety of poses which many may find erotic in the temples of Khajuraho, Tirupati and others. Let's look into these claims.

12.2. "It's normal for goddesses to be naked"

Like Lord Desai, M.F. Husain himself has claimed that his paintings were part of an existing Hindu tradition of depicting goddesses in non-Victorian poses: "'We Indians are proud to create a civilization of art and culture, enshrined in the sanctity of Ajanta and Ellora caves and temples for the last 5,000 years. There the images of Gods and Goddesses are pure and uncovered." (Sify.com, 13 March 2006)

However, it is simply untrue that goddesses are ever depicted while satisfying themselves with the help of a tiger's tail, the way Husain depicts Durga. As for the more modest nudes, even these are far from the rule in Hindu iconography.

In the Hindu worldview, *kāma* or eroticism has a place among the finalities of human life. This may well be the idea behind the depiction of some sexual scenes on the outside walls of the Khajuraho temples. However, it is not because the Khajuraho buildings are temples that they depict sex between deities. These sculptures are only on the outside, not inside the abode of the deity, and they depict scenes from all aspects of human life. They send the message that one should always have the deity as the central point in one's life even though one is engaged in worldly activities. About one tenth of them are of a sexual nature, and none of these involves characters recognizable as Saraswati, Lakshmi or other deities. Inside the Khajuraho temples, the idols of Shiva, Nandi, Durga, the incarnations of Vishnu and Lakshmi etc. are clothed normally. All over India, deities have been shown in temples as described in the scriptures and normally no idols of deities are shown nude or in sexual positions.

There are arguable exceptions. One is the Tantric deity-couples, frequent in Tibet but rare in India, who may be shown in a dignified copulation posture, not doggie-style or lying down missionary-style as pornographers would prefer, but the god sitting in lotus posture with the goddess sitting on his lap embracing him. I am the happy owner of a statue of Ganesha in copulation with a female partner, which incidentally gives the lie to Paul Courtright's thesis of Ganesha as a symbol of phallic limpness. None of Husain's contested paintings even dimly resembles these icons.

The second exception is the icons of naked saints, not gods, who observed a vow of nudity as part of their ascetic discipline. This chiefly concerns Mahavira Jina and some of his followers. But obviously there cannot be a trace of sensuality, let alone Husain's perversity, in those depictions of celibate saints.

In an open letter to Lord Desai, Hindu Human Rights also explained that Hindus were "offended at his depiction of Draupadi as naked, as in Hindu tradition it is Lord Krishna who saves her modesty in the Mahabharata". Effectively, in a central episode of the most influential text of Hinduism, the Mahabharata, Draupadi is threatened with nudity as an act of humiliation, and the deified hero Krishna is credited with saving her from this shame. Husain identifies with the Kaurava rascals by taking her clothes off after all. The very least that the epic story teaches is that ancient Hindus were not so carefree about nudity after all.

At this point I have to correct a position I had taken in an internet discussion after a naked depiction of goddess Saraswati by Husain had caused some commotion. I had pointed out that Saraswati had been introduced in Japan by the Buddhists under the name *Benzai-ten*, and that this goddess does get depicted naked. Indeed, a naked sculpture of Benzai-ten is shown in many books of Buddhist or Japanese art history (e.g. Louis Frédéric: *Les Dieux du Bouddhisme*, Flammarion, Paris 1992, p.223 ff.). However, that sculpture is not a functioning idol in a temple but is located in a museum. In a temple, such a naked sculpture is clothed every morning, and worshippers only see her clothed. This practice of clothing a sculpture is not uncommon in Hindu-Buddhist devotionalism, e.g. even the giant Bamian Buddhas in Afghanistan used to be clothed. The Japanese are less prudish than the Indians, but even they worship their deities in clothed form. Likewise, even the impudent Greeks depicted only Aphrodite, the goddess of erotic love, in the nude; but Artemis, Athena, Demeter and other goddesses are always shown covered.

12.3. "Nudity is normal in modern art"

In a letter published in *The Guardian*, 2 June 2006, the HHR, in line with its other progressive statements regarding full integration of Dalits, action against female infanticide etc., refutes the allegation that it represents an anti-art obscurantism: "We protested against the Asia House gallery because we object to its decision to exhibit paintings of Hindu goddesses engaged in acts of bestiality (Letters, May 26 and 30). Meghnad Desai seems to think such images can be found in Hindu temples, but, as we have written to him, we dispute this and challenge him to produce evidence. (...) All our statements show we have always maintained we are not anti-art. After all, where else can we find the range of expression we find in Hindu literature, poetry, paintings, dance, music, sculpture, drama, spiritual epics, architecture, costumes and jewellery. But when we see Hindu imagery and symbolism adorning toilet seats, bikinis, magazine covers etc., it becomes easier to see why so many people in the media and politics are ignorant and apathetic when it comes to highlighting the plight of Hindus in countries such as Pakistan, Bangladesh, [etc.]."

There is a certain pluralism and fluidity in contemporary standards about what is acceptable and what is not. Some standards are nonetheless still standing firm, and they can be ascertained approximately with the comparative method: replace the question of nudity in different contexts and see what is accepted there. For a precise instance: "Those supporting the nude paintings of Hindu goddesses by Husain should answer in the affirmative the following question: will they accept an exhibition of a nude painting of their beloved ones?"

Hindus may not realize that some artsy people in the West would indeed not mind having their loved ones or themselves depicted naked. But this is unlikely to be true of Lord Desai, much less of M.F. Husain. And for this, we have the testimony of Husain's own paintings.

"Nudity is a form of innocence", says Husain (Sify.com, 13 May 2006), who describes himself as "a humble and ardent contributor in creating a great Indian 'Composite' culture". Yet, the pattern emerging from a survey of his paintings suggests nudity isn't all that innocent to his own mind. Husain shows the Prophet's daughter Fatima fully clothed; his own mother fully clothed; Mother Teresa fully clothed; Muslim poets Faiz and Ghalib fully clothed; an unnamed Muslim lady fully clothed; but goddess Durga naked and in compromising position; goddess Lakshmi naked on Ganesha's head; goddess Saraswati naked; Draupadi naked; Hanuman naked with Sita sitting on Ravana's thigh; Bharat Mata naked, with names of India's provinces written on her flesh. Even more telling is a painting showing a fully clad Muslim king with a naked Brahmin, and one showing four 20th-century leaders, among them Gandhi decapitated and Hitler naked.

So, it is hard to find fault with the Hindu group's conclusion: "M.F. Husain depicts the deity or person he hates as naked. He shows Prophet's Mother, his own mother, daughter, all the Muslim personalities fully clothed, but at the same time Hindus and Hindu deities along with Hitler are shown naked. This proves his hatred for the Hindus." The HHR suggests to Husain's patrons: "It will be very much appreciated if these art traders dare to make nude paintings of their beloved ones, and what to say of Mohammed the Prophet, and exhibit [these] in the name of art."

Some secular modern painters might in good faith depict Hindu deities in the nude and mean it when they deny that this has any disparaging intention. But M.F. Husain is not one of those. He is a Muslim fanatic who gives a new expression to the old Islamic contempt for Hinduism. Muslim rulers in the past expressed their contempt by placing Hindu deity sculptures in roads for treading them underfoot, or in lavatories. Husain seeks the same effect by depicting the deities in poses that he and many onlookers find contemptible. As for the secular art collectors who now support him in the name of artistic freedom, he takes them for a ride by using the visual language of modernism and the liberal rhetoric of artistic freedom to package the age-old Islamic message of hatred.

12.4. "Husain is a Muslim"

The same Hindu bodies who have joined the sensitivity bandwagon are usually also those which avoid polemic with Islam. When given an opportunity, they will rather join hands with Muslims to prove how nice they are. Many Hindu organizations, such as the Hindu American Forum, have passed resolutions condemning the Danish Mohammed cartoons. In the State Assembly of Andhra Pradesh, the Hindu nationalist BJP supported a resolution to the same effect, which was passed unanimously, also and especially with the support of the so-called secularists. These Hindus were naïve to expect any signs of gratitude in return, whether from Muslims or secularists. Indeed, now that Hindus themselves allege blasphemy, no one comes out in solidarity with them.

Unlike in France or Germany, where prominent media came out in support of the Danish cartoonists by republishing the cartoons, the British and American media downplayed the affair as much as possible and refrained from showing the cartoons, possibly in a concern not to make matters worse for their occupation troops in Iraq. At any rate, they went out of their way not to offend Muslim sensibilities. An earlier HHR statement observes: "We understand that the media in the UK did not publish the Mohammed cartoons as a deliberate decision. And we also understand that no academics (or people like Lord Meghnad Desai) protested about the decision. In fact, it is possible that they would be all applauding the decision of the media."

Yet, when it comes to Hindu sensibilities, different standards apply. Here, Desai stands up for a Muslim painter's "artistic freedom to take Hindu gods and goddesses as his theme". In its letter to *The Guardian*, HHR explains: "More seriously, he accuses us of raising this issue because of M.F. Husain's religion. This is completely baseless; we are proud of our interfaith work and have spoken on radio with Muslim leaders to support their efforts to end attempts to demonize their community."

Another activist group, the Mumbai-based Hindu Janajagruti Samiti (Committee for Hindu Popular Awakening) claims in reply that it "has handled many similar campaigns against deliberate insults of Hindús and Hinduism by Hindu painters, for example Shri. Subhash Avchat, Dnyanesh Sonar, Mahendra Pandit amongst others." There are at any rate plenty of Hindu-born anti-Hindu secularists, and those among them with an artistic vocation might feel inclined to insulting Hinduism through paintings too, just as the scholars among them do with anti-Hindu theses. Reacting against one's own Hindu origins is one reason for hating and insulting Hinduism, but it is not the only one; a commitment to Islam is another.

The case of M.F. Husain is probably one of mixed motives. The encouragement by secularists to insult Hinduism certainly played a role, but the more fundamental reason may well be his own ingrained Muslim hatred of "idolatry".

In the debate about the Danish Mohammed cartoons, Muslims eagerly quote the words of UN Secretary-General Kofi Annan at the Organization of the Islamic Conference in Istanbul on 13th April 2006, where he affirmed the importance of basic freedoms as well as the need for sensitivity towards other cultures: "We must stress that rights carry with them an inherent responsibility, and should not be used to degrade, humiliate or insult any group or individual." But these Muslims have not matured enough to take this maxim to heart in their own treatment of non-Muslim cultures.

12.5. My view

In contrast with the Hindu Human Rights group, which has fully integrated the modern outlook, many Hindu advocacy groups have reacted to the Husain paintings in a humourless, unimaginative, crude and repression-centred manner. For example, the Hindu Janajagruti Samiti put forward the following demands: "1. That M.F. Husain be arrested and put behind the bars immediately. 2. Immediate removal of all objectionable paintings of Husain from the Kashmir Mission Auction. 3. That M.F. Husain be socially ostracized so that no one dares to commit such a mistake in future." And again: "Arrest of Mr. Chetan Bhatt [*a London-based political science professor who came out in Husain's support*] and other evil intellectuals for promoting hatred. Socially ostracise M.F. Husain, Lord Desai and others supporting M.F. Husain. Remove Husain's paintings from offices and galleries."

It can't be a good advertisement for Hinduism that its activists have not advanced beyond this stage of purely reactive, emotionalist and repressive thinking. The people who came out in support of M.F. Husain's insulting paintings can safely be suspected of an anti-Hindu animus, but that, after all, is their privilege. Neither in the ancient Hindu tradition of open debate nor in the modern Western framework of freedom of expression can their opinion be a valid reason for arresting or otherwise harassing them.

Within that framework, it is nonetheless legitimate to try and persuade people into abandoning insulting practices.

Companies depicting Hindu deities on shoes or underwear have indeed agreed to withdraw these products after friendly negotiations with Hindu protesters. The people concerned are usually outsiders to Hindu culture and South-Asian politics, and precisely because there is a silly innocence about their improper gimmicks, they don't insist on their "right to artistic expression" when properly informed.

The matter may be different with hate-driven secularists and Muslims. As demonstrated in the M.F. Husain affair, Hindu opposition only makes them more arrogant and more eager to rub it in. Even there, I believe Hindus should muster the self-control to maintain respect for ancient Hindu and modern international norms regarding freedom of expression. This is a very precious good and benefits everyone in the long run.

One reason why many Hindus don't value their right to free expression, is that they never use it, at least not in matters where it would provoke controversy. Kofi Annan's admonition cited above, which Muslims use to bully their critics into silence, is being sincerely observed by most Hindus. Without being asked or pressured, they try not to offend Muslims or Christians. It is commendable that Hindus have the good taste not to put images of Jesus or Mohammed on underwear or toilet seats. But it is regrettable that they also silence their own critical faculty and refrain from taking a frank look at the doctrines of their declared enemies. If they tried to do that once in a while, they would soon come to value the need for a legally guaranteed freedom of expression.

13. A Hindutva reader

[This book review was written in February 2007.]

13.1. Presumed prehistory of the book

According to the cover of his new book, *Hindu Nationalism, a Reader* (Permanent Black, Delhi 2007), Christophe Jaffrelot is "among the world's most eminent and respected scholars of South-Asian politics and society". He certainly has the ear of the French government in setting its India-related policies. Moreover, reliable sources inform me that he was instrumental in getting Hindu-sympathizing journalist François Gautier ousted from some of his French media avenues. So, he's an establishment man and has a record as an enforcer of *la pensée unique* ("single permitted opinion"), i.e. the "secularist" position vis-à-vis Hindu concerns.

Unmentioned in the introductory sections of this book is why it came about. However, the reason is easy to deduce, at least if you know about Jaffrelot's earlier publication, his book *The Sangh Parivar, a Reader* (OUP 2005). A "reader" normally means a collection of excerpts from the main primary texts in a given field. Thus, a "reader in Greek philosophy" would contain texts by Plato and Aristotle, Diogenes and Zeno, not commentaries on the same by modern philosophers. In spite of its title, Jaffrelot's book didn't contain any primary texts of the Sangh Parivar, but only secondary texts about and against it. This outrageous mistake was in fact entirely characteristic of the actual state of affairs: supposed experts on Hindu nationalism do little but copy the Indian anti-Hindutva crusaders and one another.

It seems, then, that somebody pointed out this abnormality of the *Sangh Parivar Reader* to Jaffrelot. Subsequently, his publisher must have seen the commercial opportunity in doing for real what the title had falsely promised, viz. make available a genuine collection of primary Hindutva texts. Thus the idea for the *Hindu Nationalism Reader* was born.

13.2. "Hindu nationalism"

How does Christophe Jaffrelot define Hindu nationalism? He sees it as contrasting with Mahatma Gandhi's "universalist definition of the Indian nation", actually launched by Gandhi's guru and Congress pioneer G.K. Gokhale: "For the founders of Congress, the Indian nation was to be defined according to the territorial criterion, not on the basis of cultural features: it encompassed all those who happened to live within the borders of British India. Therefore, it was not perceived as being within Congress's purview to deal with religious issues which, in fact, were often social issues – such as child marriage and widow remarriage – all such issues being those that came under the personal law of the different denominations." (p.4)

Actually, Gandhi dissented somewhat from this purely secular definition: "In contrast with the founders of Congress, Gandhi acknowledged religious identities in the public sphere, even as he viewed the nation as an amalgamation of many different communities." (p.5) Yes, Gandhi was a communalist. By contrast, the Nehrus "advocated a liberal nation-building process based on individuals, not groups".

Like many nationalisms, Hindu nationalism took the majority culture to be the national culture: "Hindu nationalism, like Muslim separatism (a movement which in India was formed around the same time), rejected both versions of the universalist view of nationalism articulated by Congress. This ideology assumed that India's national identity was summarized by Hinduism (...) For Congressmen like Nehru this ideology – like that of the Muslim League or of Sikh separatists – had nothing to do with nationalism. They branded it with the derogatory term 'communalism'. But in fact the doctrine that was to become known by the name 'Hindutva' fulfilled the criteria of ethnic nationalism. Its motto 'Hindu Hindi Hindustan' echoed many other European nationalisms based on religious identity, a common language, or even racial feeling." (p.5)

In the West, few critics of Hindutva will deny it the label "nationalism", because the term has acquired negative, illiberal connotations. In India, by contrast, it is often decried as "majoritarianism" (which it actually has in common with most nationalisms) because "nationalism" has a positive aura coloured by the struggle for freedom. But this helps to clinch the issue in favour of Hindutva: while the Muslim League and Sikh or Dravidian separatism were patronized by the British in their anti-nationalist strategy, Hindu nationalism was always part of the freedom movement. So yes, "Hindu nationalism" is a genuine nationalism.

The problematic part in the term "Hindu nationalism" is not the second word but the first. Hinduism is a conglomeration of sects, each with its teachers' lineage or holy book, and Hindu nationalism developed despite these divisions. To be sure, this historical dividedness need not preclude a newfound unity in the modern age. But modernity introduces a new problem into our understanding of the term "Hindu": the Hinduism of the nationalists was always an idealized Hinduism, removed from the really existing Hinduism.

As Jaffrelot acknowledges (p.8), Brahmo Samaj founder Ram Mohan Roy already said that "original" Hinduism was egalitarian. Ever since, the Arya Samaj and other reform movements including the RSS have always said that caste and other inequalities are aberrations from "real" Hinduism. They try to make the most of the fact that the Self (Atman) is common to all sentient beings and hence a foundation for their equality. Yet, for thousands of years, Hindu philosophers have never seen a contradiction between this transcendental sameness in the Self and the day-to-day inequalities in society. The Self also animates the child, or the monkey, or the donkey, but that doesn't mean you should give them voting rights. So, the Hindu doctrine of the Self does not by itself imply notions of social equality.

In other respects too, such as Hinduism being "tolerant" or "non-violent", purely modern values have crept into the modern Hindus' self-understanding and distorted their relation with the traditional Hindu values which regulated the lives of their families. So, what many scholars have termed "Hindu revivalism" has always been a reinvention or redefinition of Hinduism rather than a genuine return to the roots. Hindu nationalism is part of the modernization process of Hindu society.

13.3. What's still missing

We need have no quarrel with Jaffrelot's selection of texts. Among Arya Samajis, it features not only Swami Dayananda Saraswati but also Lal Chand, Lala Lajpat Rai, and most importantly Swami Shraddhananda, whose booklet *Hindu Sangathan, Saviour of the Dying Race* truly encapsulates the Hindu concerns from which the Hindu nationalist movement was born. The only Arya Samaj pioneer sorely missing here (maybe because he didn't write in English?) is Pandit Lekhram Arya, an articulate critic of Islam who, like Shraddhananda in 1926, was murdered by a Muslim in 1897. From the Jana Sangh (1952-77), we get texts from Balraj Madhok, K.R. Malkani and Deendayal Upadhyaya, of whom Jaffrelot readily accepts the unofficial account that he was "murdered". Apart from myself, Jaffrelot must be the first foreign Hindutva watcher who gives Deendayal his due as the ideologue of "integral humanism" (*etâtmatâ mânavavâd*), still the official party doctrine of the BJP.

The collection also pays sufficient attention to the struggle over Jammu & Kashmir and the expulsion of the Pandits from there. It has been most irritating to find that for all the years since this event (1990), the standard secularist account of Hindu nationalism leaves it unmentioned, even when every Hindu militant whom I questioned about his motivation mentioned the plight of the Pandits as the most immediate proof of the deplorable Hindu condition in "secular" India. From the Jana Sangh days, the language issue is also highlighted, when Hindu nationalists had not yet given up on *shuddh* Hindi as the national language. Attention is also given to the conversion issue and the reconversion movement (with reference to Raj Eshwar's Hindi booklet *Parâvartan*, "return"), caste-based reservations and social justice, education policy, defence policy, and the vexing question of secularism.

On p.289, we even learn that to L.K. Advani, 6 December 1992 (demolition of the Babri Masjid) was "one of the most depressing days of my life",— in flagrant refutation of the secularist "consensus" about Advani's cunning mastermind role in the incident. Jaffrelot acknowledges the division within the Hindu nationalist movement between time-serving politicians and passionate activists: "Paradoxically, its success in UP, where the BJP was able to form the state government, did not enable it to solve the Ayodhya issue. Hindu nationalist militants put an end to this deadlock by demolishing the mosque on 6 December 1992." (p.21) The BJP's rise to national power has only made matters worse, because "the rules of the coalition game had diluted the agenda. As a result, Hindutva forces are today deeply divided." (p.23)

This assessment is entirely factual, yet it is a somewhat dissident position. Most secularists and especially their parrots abroad prefer to depict Hindu nationalism as not only evil but also as increasingly powerful, not just a monster but a threat that requires remedial action. Even after the BJP's defeat in 2004, popular accounts in the Western media just kept on repeating their worn-out warnings against "the *rising* threat of Hindu nationalism".

So, to my pleasant surprise, Jaffrelot's selection and comments are essentially fair and accurate. Perhaps he has concluded that the heyday of Hindu nationalism is over, so that there is no longer reason for the bloodhound attitude that has characterized secularist writing about it until very recently. Or maybe he has decided that at this stage in his career, he doesn't have to prove his political correctness anymore and is finally in a position to practise simple honest scholarship.

The only important editorial choice open to criticism is his decision to keep out authors not belonging to *organized* Hindu nationalism. It is on this ground that he justifies omitting Swami Vivekananda ("Say with pride: we are Hindus!") and Sri Aurobindo, whose *Uttarpara Speech* is one of the founding doctrinal texts of nationalism as an instrument of the revival of Hindu Dharma. Given the already respectable size of the present book, the need of the hour is not redoing it with the additional inclusion of such individualistic contributors, but yet another *Reader* collecting specifically the important statements by authors outside of the Hindu nationalist organizations.

That will yield another sizable volume, for after Vivekananda and Aurobindo (and before them Bankim Chandra Chatterji), there have been quite a few who are either unknown themselves or whose occasional or systematic allegiance to Hindu nationalism is insufficiently realized. Thus, some texts by Bipin Chandra Pal, Bal Gangadhar Tilak and even (as was frequently alleged back then by Muslim League spokesmen) by Mahatma Gandhi can be characterized as "Hindu nationalist". Others are articulately pro-Hindu and express all the concerns seen in Hindutva texts, but would not fit the "nationalist" label. This is the case with the two most important post-Independence Hindu thinkers, Ram Swarup and Sita Ram Goel. Attention should also be given to the Hindu activist critiques of organized Hindu nationalism, particularly of the Sangh

Parivar, e.g. those by Siva Prasad Ray, Abhas Chatterjee, Shreerang Godbole or Shrikant Talageri. Finally, there is the leadership role of independent Hindu gurus on particular parts of the Hindu agenda, such as the current anti-conversion campaign by Swami Dayananda Saraswati of Coimbatore.

In recent years, this non-Sangh Hindu activism, often born from disillusionment with sterile and confused Sangh policies, has locally led to the creation of independent Hindu groups, especially in the diaspora, such as the Hindu Human Rights group in London. The signs are that this represents the wave of the future in India too, where modern Hindus feel alienated from the quaint ways of the past-oriented Sangh Parivar. So, there is quite a world of Hindu awakening and mobilization outside the Sangh, and even after Jaffrelot's otherwise fruitful research, it has remained largely uncharted.